50¢

D0771041

the EDIBLE GARDEN

VEGETABLES

&

GREENS

Rosalind Creasy

Special Edition for the National Home Gardening Club ®

THE EDIBLE GARDEN
Vegetables & Greens
Special Edition for the
National Home Gardening Club ®

First published in 1999 by
PERIPLUS EDITIONS (HK) LTD.,
with editorial offices at 153 Milk Street,
Boston, Massachusetts 02109 and
5 Little Road #08-01
Singapore 536983.

Photographs and text copyright © 1999 Rosalind Creasy
All photos credit to Rosalind Creasy except those that appear courtesy of:
W. Atlee Burpee Company: page 37 *(below right)*
David Cavagnaro: page 43 *(below)*
Seminis Seeds: page 62
Illustrations by Marcy Hawthorne

Library of Congress Cataloging-in-Publication Data
Creasy, Rosalind.
     The edible salad garden / by Rosalind Creasy.—1st ed.
          p. cm.
     Includes bibliographical references (p.   )
     ISBN 962-593-290-9 (paper)
     1. Salad greens. 2. Salad vegetables. 3. Salads. I. Title.
SB351.S25C74 1999
635--dc21   98-38197
                                             CIP

Creasy, Rosalind.
     The edible salad garden / by Rosalind Creasy.—1st ed.
          p. cm.
     Includes bibliographical references (p.   ).
     ISBN 962-593-290-9 (paper)
     1. Salad greens. 2. Salad vegetables. 3. Salads. I. Title.
SB351.S25C74 1999
635—dc21   98-38174
                                             CIP

First edition
05 04 03 02 01 00 99
10 9 8 7 6 5 4 3 2 1

Design by Kathryn Sky-Peck

PRINTED IN USA

Foreword

A mere ten years ago I would bring a basket of blue potatoes, or green radishes, or blue corn to my lectures, and the audiences would gasp in disbelief. "Certainly they are not real." They'd say. I even had people come up to me after my presentation and ask why I used Easter egg dye to color my vegetables. Americans had clearly been blind-sided. We thought we ate from one of the largest vegetable palettes on earth, yet here were these colorful vegetables most of us had never seen before. It seemed like, out of nowhere, there were orange and purple bell peppers; yellow and orange watermelons; purple asparagus and radishes; white, red, and yellow carrots; and chard in nearly every color of the rainbow. Where had all these vegetables been all these years? Nowadays, a salad seems to be a nest of baby red and green lettuces garnished with a host of cheeses or roasted red bell peppers. The whole definition of a salad has changed right before our eyes. The other day a chef I knew offered on his salad menu: marinated roasted beets and carrots served with orange sections, and a coleslaw made with Chinese cabbage, pac choi, cilantro, peanuts and grated ginger. Why not? It seems nothing is sacred any more, even those traditional icons of the American table, the red tomato and green string bean, have been replaced by multi-hued pink and golden heirloom tomatoes, and yellow, even purple, string beans. It's clear, today, instead of dining in black and white, we now feast in full living color.

Of course, our vegetable gardens now reflect, and in some cases, force these dramatic culinary changes. I know few gardeners now who grow only red tomatoes. Instead, we also grow yellow and orange varieties, and maybe even a white or purple one. And the pepper row, my goodness how that has changed. Remember when we all grew only green bell peppers? I didn't even know that green peppers left on the plant turn red, or that bell peppers could also be yellow, gold and deep orange; much less lavender, purple or even brown. Then there are all the blazing hot peppers that come in all different shapes, colors, and intensity.

Rows of multi-colored tomatoes, peppers, and a planting of bush beans that bears yellow, green, and purple string beans-a la Renee's Garden-or a small patch of mesclun salad greens that provides a crop of baby greens for weeks at a time-this is the new American vegetable garden. Join me and discover this new Technicolor world. Explore the new red sweet corn, purple artichokes and broccoli; even try the new yellow peas. Life is too short to only grow and cook with green vegetables or to only dine on iceberg lettuce.

-Rosalind Creasy

contents

Part I: Rainbow Vegetable Gardens

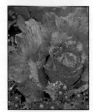

Part II: Gardens for Greens and Salads

Edible Art of Salad Gardens *page* 91

Encyclopedia of Salad Greens *page 113*

Favorite Salad Recipes *page* 146

Appendixes *page* 182

edible rainbow gardens

I LOVE BRIGHT COLORS! My dresses are red, bright blue, even deep purple. My house is decorated with primary colors, and sometimes you practically need sunglasses to look at my garden. I dream in Technicolor. While I thrill to Ansel Adams's black-and-white photographs, I photograph in color only. Intellectually I realize that not everyone feels the way I do about color. I tell myself there are people who love beige and others who decorate solely with black and white, but in my heart I'm not sure these people really exist.

Given my predilection for colors, it's not surprising that I'm enamored with colorful vegetables. Why grow only standard green kale or broccoli when I can have purple ones too?—providing, of course, that they taste good. Why

limit myself to green bell peppers when I can have yellow, orange, and violet varieties as well? It's not the colors alone that I glory in; it's the infinite variety that nature offers. Just as I delight in seeing exotic birds and insects and growing unfamiliar species of flowers, so I enjoy growing and cooking with vegetables of unusual colors. I love putting my hands on

them and sharing them with others. When a neighbor's child helps me harvest blue potatoes, we take pleasure in the color together. I get a kick out of serving pink scallions or thinly sliced raw purple artichokes to a visiting gardener. All in all, color is a whole dimension of my edible garden to experiment with and enjoy.

I can trace my fascination with colorful vegetables back twenty years to my discovery of orange tomatoes and purple string beans. These vegetables were so much fun I started looking for other varieties in unusual colors. At first, my collection built slowly. In those "monochromatic days," most people thought it quite odd to grow or eat vegetables in colors they had not grown up with. And few colorful varieties were offered. Before long I met Jan Blüm, fellow color enthusiast and owner of Seeds Blüm, and we started playing that great gardening game, "Have I Got Something for You!" I'd

Why plant only the standard colors of vegetables? Why not plant a harvest of unusual vegetables *(opposite)* that includes 'Yellow Doll' watermelon, 'Plum Purple' radishes, 'Cherokee Purple' tomato, 'Lemon' cucumbers, 'Asian Bride' eggplant, and 'French White' zucchini.

show her lavender eggplants and she'd tell me about yellow peas and red celery. I'd describe chartreuse broccoli and she'd present me with red orach and green radishes. I always felt on the cutting edge with my vegetables, but I was constantly outclassed! Jan had an advantage. She worked with people who sought and saved heirloom vegetables—many of which were very colorful. These heirloom gardeners were dedicated to preserving an eroding gene pool, which was a much more serious reason to be passionate about unusual varieties.

Given the extra energy from dedicated heirloom gardeners and the awakening interest among savvy chefs who saw the culinary potential, colorful vegetables couldn't stay under wraps forever. By the mid-1980s,

organic growers in California like Doug Gosling, then garden manager of the Farrallones Institute in Occidental, and Michael Maltus, manager of the garden at Fetzer Vineyard in Hopland, were growing tomatoes, eggplants, and peppers in a rainbow of colors. Meanwhile, the Seed Savers organization in Decorah, Iowa was collecting hundreds of colorful varieties including watermelons with yellow or orange flesh and purple tomatoes and sweet potatoes and reintroducing them to the public.

At about the same time, I visited the New York Botanical Garden and mentioned my color experiments to Debra Lerer, then director of children's gardening. Immediately inspired, Debra felt the desire to grow a rainbow garden in the children's section of the

Farmer's markets are a great place to seek out colorful vegetable varieties and find out which grow best in your climate. Craig and Toku Beccio *(above)*, owners of Happy Boy Farms of San Juan Bautista, California, offer many different colors of organically grown tomatoes, peppers, and potatoes.

botanical garden the next summer. Why hadn't I thought of that? Of course! Children and colorful vegetables were a natural combination and yet another reason to grow these vegetables. Visiting Debra later, I saw that the plot of rainbow vegetables was clearly a big hit. The children thought it much more fun to grow yellow zucchini than green. The purple potatoes were great because the young gardeners could show their parents vegetables they had never seen before. And the youngsters dubbed the purple beans "magic beans" because they turned green when cooked.

In the 1990s the movement toward colorful vegetables was well under way. Heirloom vegetables were going mainstream. Organic farmers, ever on the look out for an edge over the grocery store, found that colorful heirloom vegetables sold well. Seed company owners like Renee Shepherd of Renee's Garden and Rose Marie Nichols of Nichols Garden Nursery offered many colorful varieties. And garden books and magazine articles routinely recommended them.

In recent years, yet another reason to grow rainbow vegetables has emerged. Nutritionists and plant breeders now know that vivid color often goes hand-in-hand with additional health benefits. Colorful varieties often yield more vitamins A and C and have more disease-fighting chemicals than some of their drab cousins. In the new millennium gardeners will find more and more vegetables like the red carrot and the orange tomato with extra beta carotene as many vegetable breeders select for these beneficial traits.

Saving a gene pool, making children's gardening more fun, and growing super nutritious vegetables are all excellent reasons to become a rainbow vegetable maven. And then there are the reasons that hooked me in the first place—growing rainbow vegetables is really great fun and harvesting a rainbow garden is an aesthetic experience in itself. Picture yourself taking a large basket into the garden to harvest your rainbow of vegetables and flowers. Place the red chard and pungent red nasturtiums into the basket. Move on to the golden beets and sunny calendulas. Your succulent yellow tomatoes and the yellow zucchini might be next. Add green, sweet, and ripe tomatoes and green radishes if you have some; these will make you chuckle. Dig up a few blue potatoes and finish the rainbow array with a luminescent 'Rosa Bianco' eggplant and purple string beans. No matter how many times I gather my vibrant rainbow vegetables, harvesting still makes me smile.

'Bright Lights' chard *(below)* comes in a mix of colors. Here, bright orange and yellow chard plants shine in a flower/vegetable border.

how to grow a rainbow garden

With a few exceptions, most unusually colored vegetables grow much like standard vegetables. For detailed information, consult "The Rainbow Vegetable Encyclopedia." For the nuts and bolts of soil preparation, fertilizing, watering, composting, mulching, and garden maintenance, see Appendix A.

Starting with Seeds

A small number of rainbow varieties are a little challenging to grow; for example, yellow beets are somewhat harder to germinate than the red varieties. Also, the all-red and the all-blue potato varieties usually yield half as much as most modern hybrids, so you must plant more than the regular amount.

Quite a few rainbow vegetables, however, are downright advantageous. For example, purple beans, blue-podded peas, and golden zucchinis are easier for gardeners to find on the vines than the usual varieties. As unpicked peas and beans make the vines less productive, with colorful vegetables you need not wonder why the beans and peas have stopped producing or what to do with a three-foot zucchini that has grown unnoticed for a week or two. 'Hopi Blue' corn needs less water than the average corn crop. And purple and yellow string bean varieties can be started in much cooler soil than standard string beans. Purple and orange cauliflower varieties need no garden blanching to be tender and sweet. The only real problem with growing a rainbow garden is locating the seeds of

Renee's Garden Seeds sprays the seeds of their colorful vegetable mixes with dyes *(above)*. The color-coded seeds help gardeners know which color vegetable the plants will produce. Colorful herbs and vegetables *(right)* can sparkle in a mixed border. 'Red Rubin' basil has been planted among lemon basil and species orange zinnias at the Kendall Jackson winery display gardens in Santa Rosa, California.

Growing more than one color of snap beans makes the harvest more appealing. Pictured above are three varieties of bush beans in one bed: yellow 'Roc d'Or,' 'Purple Queen,' and green 'Slenderette.' All are available in one package from Renee's Garden.

Rainbow flowers and vegetables make a Technicolor presentation. In the basket *(opposite)* are 'Burpee's Golden' beet, 'Gypsy' peppers, 'Ruby Red' chard, 'Mandarin Cross' tomato, 'Gold Rush' zucchini, and 'Albina Verduna' white beets.

some varieties. While the market is changing, many unique varieties are not readily available from local nurseries. The seed companies listed in the Sources section are good places to start.

Color Planning before Planting

The color range of your harvest will be a major planning consideration. You'll need to pay particular attention to the number of plants to grow, and to selecting and coordinating particular varieties. For example, the special effect of some colorful vegetables depends on lots of different colored varieties being served together. Envision three colors, not one, of tomatoes or peppers arranged on a tray. To achieve that effect, you'll want to grow two plants of three or four

varieties where possible instead of three or four plants of one or two varieties. For a mix of color with root vegetables and lettuces, forgo planting one row of each color. Instead, mix the seeds of many colors of beets, carrots, or radishes and sprinkle them together in the planting bed. In most cases you'll be able to tell the colors apart when you harvest because beets have distinct foliage and most shoulders of these vegetables show above the soil. (See the interview with Renee Shepherd for more information on mixing colorful vegetables in the same bed. Her seed company, Renee's Garden, offers packages of mixed colors of vegetables and the seeds are color-coded so you can see which colors you are planting.)

designing a rainbow garden

Cheryl Chang *(above)* helps to harvest the glorious bounty from the Hidden Villa rainbow garden. Meanwhile, the Hawthorne family, including Noah, Marcy, and baby Sierra *(opposite),* visit and enjoy the Hidden Villa garden under the watchful eye of "The Rainbow Lady" scarecrow.

When I first planted colorful vegetables, I primarily focused on their use in the kitchen. Finding many rainbow varieties more lovely in the garden than their monochromatic cousins, I soon started planning gardens that featured their bright colors. About the same time I became fascinated with colorful vegetables, I developed an interest in edible flowers. Again, their enticing colors drew me to them. Soon my passion for edible flowers and colorful vegetables dovetailed and I often grew them together. My favorite combinations became purple and pink violas and tulips with burgundy lettuces; orange and yellow nasturtiums and calendulas among the red and orange chards and beets; red onions and scallions with red dianthus; and 'Lemon Gem' marigolds interplanted with orange and yellow peppers.

With each garden I've grown, the rainbow effect gets stronger and the palette of plants expands. My first rainbow garden looked mostly green. Even though the radish roots were red and the corn kernels blue, their green foliage gave little hint of the unique vegetables. To enhance the impression of a rainbow garden, I've learned to include flowering plants in primary colors such as zinnias, salvias, violas, statice, calendulas, and marigolds. At first, I randomly interspersed the flowers. Now, for my favorite rainbow gardens, I arrange separate beds for the red, orange, yellow, green plants. Using poetic license, I combine the purple, indigo, and blue plants in the fifth bed.

Checking the Site

When planning a rainbow garden, I use the same techniques as when designing landscapes for my clients. My first step is to make sure the light exposure is correct. Most all edible plants need at least six hours of midday sun to survive; eight hours is better. I check for good rich soil and great drainage. (Appendix A includes information on soil preparation.) Then I compile a list of the vegetables to grow, noting each plant's height and spread, and which varieties grow best in my climate.

Drawing to Scale

My next step is to draw the garden area to scale, one-quarter inch equaling one foot. Graph paper or an architect's vellum with a grid for one-quarter-inch scale drawings is helpful. The vellum is available from drafting supply stores and can be purchased by the sheet. With my scale drawing and vegetable list ready, I design the garden.

I start by noting the garden's southernmost point on the scale drawing. This is important because I want the tallest plants situated on the garden's south side so they don't shade the shorter plants. I also plan paths or locate stepping stones for easy access to weed and harvest.

Creating the Rainbow

Next I plan the beds according to the order of the colors in the rainbow— red, orange, yellow, green, and a combination of the blue and purple tones. It's fun to select red vegetables for the

cutting flowers and vegetables and a few edible flowers, and my own winter Wizard of Oz garden filled with unusual colored vegetables and lots of edible flowers.

[note]

Make sure the flowers you are going to eat are edible and are not sprayed with commercial pesticides unfit for human consumption. The most versatile species in the kitchen and in a rainbow vegetable garden are: borage (blue), broccoli (yellow), calendulas (yellow and orange), chives (lavender), dianthus (red), species marigolds 'Lemon Gem' and 'Tangerine Gem' (yellow and orange), mustards (yellow), nasturtiums (orange, yellow, and red), dwarf runner beans 'Scarlet Bees' (red), tulips (orange, yellow, lavender, red), violas, pansies, and Johnny-jump-ups (lavender, blue, purple, yellow, and orange).

red beds, orange varieties for the orange beds, and so on. I flesh out the unusual colors with the more common varieties by adding, say, orange carrots to the orange bed and red beets to the red bed. Using the height and spread data from my plant list, I arrange the red row from back to front, choosing the tallest plants for the back, south side. For example, the twelve-foot-tall 'Bloody Butcher' corn would be in the back row, the six-foot-tall red tomatoes situated in front of the corn, and the two-and-one-half-foot-tall red peppers and maybe some red chard in front of the tomatoes. Then I plan the orange-, yellow-, green-, and blue-tone beds in the same manner, from back to front.

After selecting the vegetables, I choose ornamental or edible and ornamental flowers in bright primary colors to give an all-over rainbow effect. I intersperse bright, clear red flowers in the red rows, placing the tall varieties in the back and the shorter ones in the front. I place clear orange flowers in the orange row and so on.

Through the years I have designed many rainbow gardens including a preplanned rainbow garden kit for W. Atlee Burpee & Co. I never tire of the process and the fabulous gardens that result. The following pages include specific examples of a few of my rainbow gardens. They include a summer garden at Hidden Villa in Los Alto Hills, California, filled with colorful

The Hidden Villa Rainbow Garden

Hidden Villa is a magical place, an oasis of untamed nature in the midst of suburbia. It is the dream of Josephine and Frank Duveneck who envisioned preserving hundreds of wild acres for future generations to enjoy. Thousands of city children visit during the school year. In the summer, Hidden Villa becomes a children's camp filled with the smell of bay leaves underfoot, and the culinary delights from a very large vegetable garden.

A number of years ago—completely immersed in colorful veggies and knowing children loved them too—I was looking for a place to plant my fantasy of a huge rainbow vegetable garden. As I live not far from Hidden Villa, it seemed a perfect place for my culinary rainbow.

Once the Hidden Villa trustees gave approval, I turned to the local junior college horticulture department for help with this ambitious project. The professor recommended Gudi Riter, which led to a fortuitous pairing as Gudi is a talented cook as well as gardener. You will enjoy trying many of the recipes she helped me develop.

Because Gudi and I were planting so many unusual colors of vegetables, and to some extent flowers, we planned our garden early in the year (January) to have a good selection of colorful varieties. We needed plenty of time to order seeds and get the peppers, eggplants, and tomatoes sown in late February. In late March, we started more flats of flowers and vegetables including chard, scallions, parsley, and basil, and the

flowering zinnias, statice, salvia, verbena, safflower, species marigolds, kochia, and 'Bells of Ireland.' Before we planted in late April, the folks at Hidden Villa plowed the area, which was about twenty feet deep and a hundred feet long, and divided the plot into five twenty-foot-square sections approximately five rows deep. They also mixed in lots of manure.

Gudi finished the soil preparation by laying out and digging the beds and paths. With the help of her son and daughter, soon we were able to plant much of the garden. We placed our transplants then seeded the beans, corn, amaranth, beets, carrots, potatoes, and sunflowers in place. The area was so very large; we'd underestimated the number of plants to fill the rows. So we purchased dwarf marigolds, lobelia, verbena transplants from a nursery.

The garden got off to a great start with the exception of most of the blue potatoes that rotted. A few gophers gave us problems until they were trapped. By late June the garden was filling in very well.

By then, the area's grasses and brush had dried up. In California, we get no rain from May through September. Consequently, the deer moved out of the woods and down the hillside into our rainbow garden. In a flurry of creativity we decided to outline the different beds with a kaleidoscope of yarns. Besides initially foiling the deer, the bright strands gave more of a rainbow feeling to the garden. When the camp children arrived, the garden had yet to bloom but the colorful yarn outlines gave a hint of the fun

to follow. Although the yarn seemed to confuse the deer for a few weeks, soon they were back.

We then tried a scarecrow—a lady built from stockings and straw and dressed in one of my dresses straight from the 1970s, my quasi-hippie stage. This only kept the deer at bay for a few more weeks.

We finally resorted to black plastic bird netting placed here and there and resigned ourselves to some damage.

Despite the hungry intruders, by the end of July we started harvesting lots of vegetables and flowers. The camp cooks used some; we fed our families; and we even started bringing neighbors and friends to help. Let me tell you, two thousand square feet of vegetables is a lot of vegetables. We all seemed most to enjoy assembling large harvests of vegetables and flowers and arranging them by colors to really experience the rainbow effect.

The Hidden Villa rainbow garden came to a close in October and we deemed it a great success. It introduced hundreds of visiting schoolchildren to unusual colors and varieties of vegetables. The garden looked really "cool" and attracted the local TV station to come do a story. Most of all, we shared an exciting summer full of surprises in our special place. I'm sure the Duvenecks are smiling.

Clockwise from top left: Gudi Riter, her son Andy, and daughter Tina plan out the marigolds for the orange row in the Hidden Villa rainbow garden; Sandra Chang sorts her rainbow treasures in the Hidden Villa garden; Gudi sorts the vegetables from the Hidden Villa garden by color.

Red Row

4- to 6-foot plants for back row
'Burgundy' amaranth, grain type
'Illumination' amaranth, leaf type
'Bloody Butcher' corn
'Red' okra
'Red Currant' tomato

2- to 3-foot plants
'Big Red' zinnia
Hibiscus sabdariffa— annual
    hibiscus
'Early Red' bell pepper
'Serrano' chile pepper
'Anaheim' chile pepper
'Ruby' chard

1- to 2-foot plants
'Detroit Dark Red' beets
'Flare' salvia
'Red Beard' scallions

Plants under one foot
'Peter Pan' scarlet dwarf zinnia
'Romance' red verbena

Orange Row

4- to 6-foot plants for back row
'Large Flowered Mix' ornamental
    sunflowers
Orange tithonia
'Golden Jubilee' tomato
'Mandarin Cross' tomato

2- to 3-foot plants
'X-20' marigold
Safflower
Apricot statice

1- to 2-foot plants
'Golden Belle' pepper
'Tequila Sunrise' chile pepper
'Habañero' peppers

Plants under one foot
'Orange Gem' marigolds
'Gold Nugget' marigolds

Yellow Row

**4- to 6-foot plants
    for back rows**
'Giganteus' sunflower
'Teddy Bear' sunflower
'Taxi' tomato
'Yellow Pear' tomato
'Yellow Currant' tomato
'X-15' marigold

2- to 3-foot plants
'Sunburst' summer
    squash
'Gold Rush' zucchini

1- to 2-foot plants
'Pencil Pod Wax' snap
    beans
'Gypsy' bell pepper
'Burpee's Golden' beet

Plants under one foot
'Lemon Gem' marigold
'Yellow Sophia' marigo
Golden sage

Green Row

4- to 6-foot plants
'Italian White' sunflowers
'Bells of Ireland'

2- to 3-foot plants
Kochia
'Envy' green zinnia
'Burpee Hybrid' zucchini
'California Wonder' bell pepper
'Jalapeno' chile pepper

1- to 2-foot plants
'Burpee's Tender Pod' bush snap
    beans

Plants under one foot
'Spicy Globe' dwarf basil
French thyme
'Extra-curled Dwarf' parsley
Chamomile

Violet, Blue, and Indigo Row

4- to 6-feet plants
'Hopi Blue' corn
'Purple Striped-leaf' ornamental
    corn
'Sicilian Purple' artichoke

2- to 3-foot plants
Purple zinnia
Deep blue statice
'Royalty Purple Pod' bush snap
    beans
'Rosa Bianco' eggplant
'Dusky' eggplant

1- to 2-foot plants
'Victoria' blue salvia
'Opal' purple basil

Plants under one foot
'Buddy' dwarf purple gomphrena
'Crystal Palace' blue lobelia
'Blue Mink' ageratum

The Rainbow
Oz Garden

Many, many years ago I removed the front lawn and planted a vegetable garden in my sunny front yard. I had become weary of trying to grow sun-loving plants in a shady area. As a landscape designer I knew I could make my garden lovely enough for a formal suburban neighborhood; judging from everyone's reaction I succeeded. A fallout from front yard gardening I had not anticipated was that neighborhood children would come to visit and want to be involved. After a few years we were having lots of fun together and I found myself moving away from formal vegetable gardens and leaning more toward what "my kids" wanted. One year, that meant lots of flowers for drying; another summer we planted huge pumpkins. From one year to another I found myself growing more of their favorite rainbow-colored vegetables. Eventually I decided that while I had already grown a rainbow garden at Hidden Villa, it had been a summer garden. This time I would fill my rainbow garden with cool-season vegetables and grow them during the winter. Thanks to "my kids," my garden style really loosened up. I thought, "Why not plan the garden with a Wizard of Oz theme and design it around a yellow brick road?" Well, that idea met with enthusiastic hoorays. All the kids on the street from ages three to ninety deemed it a spectacular idea.

I designed a graceful, curving path through my front garden; my crew installed a brick path and painted it a bright, bright yellow. Getting in the spirit of the project my daughter-in-law Julie Creasy and assistant Gudi Riter started sewing costumes. Dorothy and the Scarecrow were stuffed with straw and dressed delightfully. My friend and the artist who drew the line drawings in this book, Marcy Hawthorne, painted Dorothy's face. Barbara Burkhart assembled the Tin Man from five-gallon nursery containers, hand trowels, a hose nozzle, and a plastic watering can; she sprayed him with chrome paint.

By the time the brick path was complete it was really too late to put in a cool-season garden. Instead, for a summer garden we planted the Oz garden with corn and lots of zinnias. It sure was a lot of fun but by early September we were ready for the main event—the Oz Rainbow vegetable garden. Out came the corn and zinnias and in went the cool-season vegetables. I designed color-matched beds on both sides of the yellow brick road and placed the shortest plants next to the road and the tallest the furthest away. Unlike the plot at Hidden Villa, no plants were very tall so planting them at the garden's northern end was not an issue. I chose edible flowers of clear, bright, solid colors to fill in the beds; they also gave the garden and my salads a festive look.

Both the summer and winter Oz gardens became a neighborhood institution—a part of Sunday family strolls. More than once I saw some of the kids skip down the path on their way to school. Delivery people said it was the favorite address on their route; joggers and walkers told me they found them-

selves drawn to the street. The most fun, though, was picking baskets of those colorful vegetables and flowers and laying them out in their glory for all of us to admire.

The Scarecrow sits between the yellow and orange rows of the Creasy Oz rainbow vegetable garden. His harvest includes the many colors of 'Bright Lights' Swiss chard, 'Burpee's Golden' beets, 'Detroit dark Red' beets, 'Stockton' red onions, garlic, 'Easter Egg' radishes, and 'Danver's Half Long' carrots. Behind him a broccoli plant flowers, attracting beneficial insects to keep the pests under control.

Plant List: ~ The Oz Rainbow Garden

Red Rows

2- to 3-foot plants
'Ruby' chard
'Detroit Dark Red' beets
'Stockton Red' onions
'General Eisenhower' red tulips

Plants under one foot
'Juliet' red lettuce
'Telstar Crimson' dianthus
'Red Empress' nasturtiums

Orange Rows

2- to 3-foot plants
'Bright Lights' orange chard
'Danvers Half Long' orange
    carrots
'Royal Chantenay' orange carrots
'Orange Sun' orange tulips
'Pacific Beauty' orange
    calendulas

Plants under one foot
'Orange Crystal Bowl' violas

Yellow Rows

2- to 3-foot plants
'Bright Lights' yellow chard
'Burpee's Golden' beets
'Pacific Giant' yellow calendulas
'Garant' yellow tulips
'Yellow Sweet Spanish' onions

Plants under one foot
Golden sage
Golden lemon thyme
'Yellow Crystal Bowl' violas

Green Rows

2- to 3-foot plants
'Premium Crop' broccoli
'De Cicco' broccoli
'Romy' fennel

Plants under one foot
'Nevada' crisp-head lettuce
'Nordic II' spinach
'Tres Fine Maraichere' endive
'Triple Curled' parsley

Purple/Blue Rows

2- to 3-foot plants
'Osaka Purple' Japanese mustard
'All Blue' potatoes
'Tokyo Mix' ornamental cabbages
'Attila' purple tulips
'Purplette' scallions

Plants under one foot
'Easter Egg' radishes
Johnny-jump-ups
'Blue Princess' violas
'King Henry' purple violas

Renee Shepherd

Renee Shepherd and I have been friends and colleagues for years. Both of us are fascinated with colorful vegetables. Researching this book gave me the excuse to ask her to share her views. "Before I even get them in the kitchen I enjoy these vivid vegetables," Renee began. "Picking a basket filled with many colors is beautiful. Food in vibrant colors is more exciting. I enjoy simple cooking. And simple dishes made with diverse colors seem more complex. For example, if I cook up green snap beans and sprinkle them with crumbled feta cheese, it's interesting. However, if I cook both yellow and green snap beans together, the recipe becomes exciting."

"Then there is the satisfaction of growing all these special exotics from seeds," Renee continued. "Growing three varieties of a vegetable instead of one extends my interest in the crop. It's like taking a theme and adding a variation. I find it hard to imagine why someone wouldn't want to grow vegetables in many colors."

Renee is the owner of a new seed company, Renee's Garden. Her seed packets are perfect for the rainbow gardener. For instance, she offers a trio of cayenne peppers in one package: a purple variety, a red pepper, and a yellow one. The beets come in three colors as do the tomatoes, zucchini, snap beans, bell peppers, lettuces, etc. So the gardener doesn't need to buy three different seed packages of the same vegetable to get the rainbow effect. Further, the gardener needn't research whether the vegetables will ripen at the same time. Renee has done all the work for you.

"I was flying cross-country when the idea

came to me," Renee explained. "Then I puzzled over how to color-code the seeds so gardeners could tell which color they were growing. No rainbow gardener wants to start seeds from a multi-color package and end up with four red bell pepper seedlings, one yellow variety, and no orange. There had to be a way to mark the seeds. Easter egg dyes came to mind because they are nontoxic and readily available. As soon as I got home, I tried spritzing the seeds with different colors. Sure enough, the dye dried quickly and left just enough stain so you could tell the different colors apart."

Renee Shepherd, seeds woman extraordinaire, has long been enamored with colorful vegetables. Her latest seed company, Renee's Garden, offers a rainbow in a package. For instance, she sells red, yellow, and orange bell pepper seeds all in one package. The gardener can tell the colors of the pepper varieties apart because Renee has dyed the seeds.

yellow, dark-green, and light-green summer squash and carrots in the chicken broth (see recipe, page 78). She also likes to make a confetti of dry red and yellow cayenne flakes to sprinkle over pizza. Asked how she serves tomatoes of many colors, Renee said, "I love the different colored cherry tomatoes—I call them garden candy. They're so sweet and jewel-like. I stir fry them lightly until they start to burst, then add herbs and gar-lic and serve them as a warm salad. Sometimes I arrange large colorful tomatoes slices over a tart or I hollow out tomatoes and stuff them with an orzo pasta stuffing. Another of my favorite ways to feature their colors is to make two sauces, one of red and the other of orange tomatoes, and create a pool of color and flavor on the plate for roasted vegetables."

Renee's colorful menus are famous. I remember the time she roasted bell peppers of many colors and drizzled them with olive oil, balsamic vinegar, and melted anchovies (see recipe, page 76). Then there's her exotic salad made with multicolored 'Easter Egg' radishes combined with the sweetness of fennel and apples (see recipe, page 71). Renee adapted her Aunt Alice's braised summer squash recipe with dill. Rather than using only one color of summer squash like her aunt, Renee combines

Renee has done a great deal to expand the home gardeners' seed choices by offering her seeds in many retail nurseries and homestores. Rainbow gardeners no longer have to mail away for colorful varieties. I, for one, am very grateful.

the rainbow vegetable encyclopedia

The vegetable varieties I have chosen for this encyclopedia are those that are the most colorful, whether it be in the garden, in the kitchen, or both.

For me, vegetable gardens are beautiful and the addition of especially colorful varieties often makes them even more lovely. Further, given their beauty, many of these plants are suitable for edible landscapes—in a flower border say, or in containers on the patio.

Growing colorful vegetables is a rather new phenomenon, and unlike their more common relatives, some "rainbow" vegetable varieties are hard to obtain, available only from one or two seed sources, say. I have noted sources for many of the unusual varieties.

In the average kitchen there are already many colorful vegetable vari-

'Fire Dance' cabbage (opposite) is one of many varieties of red cabbage that can brighten a garden corner.

eties—red beets and orange carrots come to mind. In this encyclopedia, however, I have ignored the familiar ones, my emphasis instead is with vegetables that by today's standards are considered eccentric or to be unusually colored. (As an aside, food color biases change from culture to culture and with the times, so for example, 200 years ago in Europe instead of red tomatoes and beets, people preferred yellow varieties and instead of white cauliflower they favored purple.)

The colors in vegetables are the result of different pigments. The presence of particular carotenoids, for instance, will cause a carrot to be orange and certain anthocyanins are responsible for a cabbage being red. Some of these pigments are stable, others are destroyed by heat or are water soluble, and in the latter cases the vivid color disappears. Further, some vegetables turn brown when cut and exposed to the air. As the emphasis in this book is to feature vivid colors on the table, where possible, I have included this type of information.

The color of a vegetable often correlates to its nutrition content and I have included some of this information as well. For an overview of how pigments and the color of vegetables respond to cooking, see the section on Cooking with Colors on page 64, and for more information on the nutrients in vegetables, see page 62.

For the basic information on soil preparation, mulching, composting, irrigation, and organic controls for pests and diseases see Appendicies A and B on pages 182 and 192.

'Illumination' amaranth

AMARANTH

Amaranthus hypochondriacus,
A. cruentus, A gangeticus,
A. tricolor

AMARANTH IS BEAUTIFUL IN THE garden and nutritious in the kitchen. The leaves and seed heads can be red, purple, green, cream, or a combination. Use the tall varieties in the back of vegetable and flower beds and the shorter ones in the middle of the border.

How to grow: Amaranth glories in warm weather. Start seedlings after any danger of frost has passed. Plant seeds $1/8$ inch deep, 4 inches apart, in full sun, in rich, well-drained soil. Plant the large-grain amaranths in blocks with the rows 1 foot apart to prevent lodging. Thin the plants to 1 foot apart and keep the plants fairly moist. Generally, amaranth grows with great enthusiasm. The leaf-types grow to 2 feet, some of the grain varieties to 6 feet. Cucumber beetles are occasionally a problem.

Harvest the leaf-types when they are young. Harvest the grains after the first frost in the North; in mild-winter areas wait until seeds begin to drop. Lay harvested tops on a tarp in the sun to dry for about a week; protect against rain and heavy dew. Thresh the grains by laying the heads on sheets—then step on them, to knock the seeds free (or rub the seed heads with on a screen; wear gloves to prevent your hands from being stained when processing the red varieties). Use an electric fan to separate the seeds from the lighter chaff as you pour them into a container.

Varieties

The leaves and seeds of all varieties can be eaten, but the leaf-types have the tastiest leaves and the grain-types have more seeds.

Grain Amaranths

'All Red': 5 feet tall; extremely deep red leaves with red plumes; does not readily fall over

'Golden Giant': 110 days; 6 feet tall with beautiful golden stems and flower heads; grown for its white grain and edible young leaves; high yielding

'Hopi Red Dye' ('Komo'): 120 days; to 6 feet tall; reddish-purple

'Purple Amaranth': 110 days; 6 feet tall; green-red variegated foliage; reddish-purple and green seed heads

Leaf Amaranths

'Illumination': spectacular magenta, pink, to crimson leaves born upper third of plant, grows to 5 feet; often used as a garnish

'Joseph's Coat' (tricolor): 70 days; a spectacular tricolor variety from India with red, cream, and green leaves

'Merah': 75–80 days; leaf-type with crinkled green and red leaves

How to prepare: In theory, because the red pigments in amaranths are betacyanin like red beets, the color should be stable when cooked, but I find the red amaranth leaves I've cooked often turn pale and grayish. Obviously there is more to learn about amaranth colors. To enjoy red amaranth leaves I select young, tender leaves from the leaf-types and use them raw in salads or as a spectacular garnish. I cook the green varieties as I would spinach. The leaves are very nutritious and high in calcium and iron.

Amaranth grain has a mild and nutty flavor, is high in protein, and contains essential amino acids. It can be cooked and eaten alone or mixed with other ingredients. It contains no gluten so must be combined with wheat flour to make risen breads. The seed can be popped like popcorn; stir ½ cup of seeds in a hot frying pan for about 30 seconds or until popped. Mix with honey to create a traditional confection from Mexico.

ARTICHOKES, PURPLE
Cynara scolymus

THE ARTICHOKE IS A GIANT thistle whose flower buds, when cooked, are deliciously edible. The plant is fountain shaped and grows to about 4 feet tall and almost as wide. The flower buds are usually green, but some varieties have purple buds.

How to grow: Artichokes prefer cool, moist summers and mild winters but tolerate summer heat if the soil is kept moist. Give them full sun in mild areas and partial shade in hot-summer climates. Below 28°F they need winter protection, for example an overturned basket filled with leaves placed above the roots. In coldest-winter areas bring the roots inside during winter and keep them moist and cool. In hot, early summers the artichoke buds open too soon and are tough.

Green varieties of artichokes are started when bare root from plants are

'Violetto' artichokes

'Violetto' artichoke buds

How to prepare: In French kitchens, immature purple artichokes are traditionally served raw: the slightly bitter bud is cut into quarters, the stem end is dipped in salt, and the dish is accompanied by bread and sweet butter. In Italy, pieces of young, tender raw artichokes are dipped in olive oil as part of an antipasto, or the heart is thinly sliced and served drizzled with lemon juice, olive oil, and salt.

Young fresh buds can be eaten without removing the choke (fuzzy, inedible center). Most mature artichokes must have the choke removed, but homegrown ones, if harvested while still young, do not.

To prepare a mature artichoke bud, cut off the top inch or so of the leaves. Then, with your hand, peel back the outside layer of leaves to where they break readily. If there is a fuzzy choke at the bottom, scrape it out with a sharp spoon. Immediately soak them in acidulated water until you are ready to cook them.

Whole artichokes can be stuffed and baked, steamed, or boiled in water with the juice of two lemons. Cook them until a knife inserted in the bottom of the choke is tender and present them whole. To eat a whole artichoke, pull off the outside leaves and use your teeth to scrape out the flesh. The remaining heart, or bottom, is cut into bite-size pieces and relished.

Artichokes may also be incorporated into many cooked dishes. Trim tender small bulbs lightly and use whole or use the hearts of larger bulbs cut in pieces in salads or casseroles.

offered in spring. (Bare-root plants are dug up while dormant and sold with their roots wrapped in plastic.) In contrast, the purple variety of artichoke is usually started from seeds. In cold climates, sow seeds indoors eight weeks before your last spring frost date, about 1/4 inch deep and 1/4 inch apart. In mild climates, fall plantings work well too. When sowing, soil temperature should be between 70°F to 80°F. Transplant seedlings to 4-inch pots. Grow at cooler temperatures (70°F during the day, 60°F at night). Transplant to the garden when 8 weeks old. (Spring plantings need at least 250 hours of temperatures under 50°F to induce budding.) Protect from frost.

Artichokes require rich, moist, well-drained soil with plenty of organic matter. They respond well to deep mulches and manure. Extra nitrogen should be added halfway through the growing season and after harvest. Dig up and thin plants every three years.

Aphids, earwigs, and snails are sometimes a problem.

When harvesting, cut off young artichoke buds, about 4 inches below the bud, well before they start to open. The younger the bud, the more tender it is and the more of it that is edible.

Varieties

The Cook's Garden, Redwood City Seed Company, and The Gourmet Gardener carry seeds of purple artichokes.

'Purple Sicilian': produces bronzy-purple buds

'Violetto': Italian variety; produces medium-sized, purple buds

How to prepare: The anthocyanins in purple artichokes lose their color when cooked, so serve them raw to emphasize the color. Raw artichokes once cut and thus exposed to the air, quickly turn brown. So to use them raw, keep them in water with added lemon juice to prevent discoloring.

ASPARAGUS, PURPLE
Asparagus officinalis

ASPARAGUS IS AN HERBACEOUS perennial that goes dormant in winter; its edible spears appear in spring. Asparagus shoots, whether they are green or purple, not cut for eating develop into airy, ferny foliage plants 5 feet high that can line a walkway or serve as a billowy background in a flower bed.

How to grow: Asparagus grows in all but the most hot and cold climates. The green varieties, and one purple variety are available as one-year-old rooted crows (the base of the plant plus roots). A family of four will need thirty to forty plants. Because asparagus plants remain in one place for many years and are heavy feeders, the soil must be prepared very well. Asparagus needs a deep organic soil, with a pH of 6.5. Excellent drainage is critical. Asparagus plants also need full sun.

In the early spring, prepare the soil and remove any perennial weeds. For thirty to forty plants, spade up the area as follows: dig two trenches 6 inches deep (a foot in coldest areas), 12 inches wide, about 20 feet long, and 3 feet apart. Amend the soil in the trenches with compost or aged manure and 4 pounds of bone meal worked 8 inches into the soil. Then place the crowns in the bottom, 15 inches apart with their roots well spread out. Cover with 2 inches of soil. As the shoots emerge,

continue to fill the trench with soil. Once the trenches are full, mulch with 4 inches of an organic mulch.

On normal soil, annual applications of compost or modest amounts of chicken manure is all that is needed for fertilizer. After the first season, only moderate amounts of water are needed during the growing season. In the arid Southwest, to encourage dormancy do not irrigate in winter.

Asparagus beetles are generally the most serious pest. Diligent hand picking of the beetles in early spring as soon as they appear helps reduce the population. If the beetles are taking over, knock them off into a bucket of soapy water or use a Bt (*Bacillus thuringiensis*) developed for their control and apply it according to directions. Further, fall cleanup removes some of the breeding adults. If the bed is free of beetles from planting time on, use floating row covers to keep them out.

A fungus disease called asparagus rust can be a problem in damp weather. Cercospora leaf spot can be a serious problem in the Southeast. Where gophers are numerous they can destroy the whole bed. Plant the crowns in wire baskets to protect them. Perennial weeds can quickly take over and crowd out a bed of asparagus, so remove all weeds and keep the bed mulched.

Harvest the spears by snapping them off an inch above soil level. No harvest is recommended the first year. In the second year limit the harvest to three weeks. In subsequent years, harvest for six to eight weeks, and until the spears begin to thin to a pencil thickness.

'Purple Sweet' asparagus

Fertilize with fish meal after the harvest. In mild climates, cut down plants when they turn brown; in cold climates wait until early spring as the stalks help maintain a snow cover.

Varieties
'Purple Sweet' ('Sweet Purple'): old variety; large, tender, deep burgundy spears; sweet flavor; Park Seed Company and R. H. Shumway's carry this variety as rooted crowns

How to prepare: The purple pigments in asparagus are anthocyanins and they fade quickly when cooked. Young shoots are delicious raw in salads or served with flavorful dips. If you cook the purple asparagus, simmer it in an inch of water with $1/4$ cup of lemon juice to help maintain some of the color, the longer you cook it the more color it loses, so whenever possible serve them al dente.

25

BASIL
Ocimum basilicum

WHILE THERE ARE MANY TYPES of basil, the ones we are interested here have purple foliage.

How to grow: Basils are annual herbs that glory in hot weather and wither with frost. Plant it in full sun in fertile, well-drained soil with much organic matter. Start basil seeds inside a month before the weather warms up in spring, or use transplants from the nursery. Place plants about 1 foot apart and keep them moist during the grow-ing season. Fertilize with a balanced organic fertilizer every six weeks and after a large harvest.

Occasional pests are slugs and snails, and cucumber and Japanese beetles. When harvesting, leaves are picked by hand or cut. Keep the flower-heads continually cut back or the plant will go to seed and give few leaves.

Varieties

'Osmin Purple': purple leaves and stems; glossy, slightly ruffled leaves; fragrant; lavender flowers

'Red Rubin': purple leaves; fragrant; pink flowers; similar to the old standby 'Dark Opal' but more uniform

'Purple Ruffles': dark purple, ruffled leaves; fragrant; lavender flowers; seedlings are variable, select most colorful plants as you thin

How to prepare: The purple basils are high in anthocyanins. To best enjoy the color, use these basils raw in salads, sandwiches, and as a garnish. They will lend some of their pink color to vinegars and apple jelly. If you cook, puree, or mince purple basils though, they turn a disappointing brown.

'Red Rubin' basil and Lemon Basil

'Royalty Purple Pod'

'Dragon's Tongue'

'Wax Romano'

BEANS

PURPLE AND YELLOW SNAP BEANS

Phaseolus vulgaris

PURPLE AND YELLOW SNAP BEANS are more popular with children than their green cousins.

How to grow: Beans are adaptable annuals and are planted after all danger of frost is past. Purple and wax varieties can tolerate colder soil than most green snap beans. They need full sun and a good, loose garden loam with plenty of added humus. Sow seeds of bush beans 1 inch deep in rows 18 inches apart; thin to 6 inches. Pole beans need a strong trellis to climb on. Plant the seeds 1 inch deep; thin to 8 inches apart. If the plants look pale midseason fertilize with fish emulsion. Beans are best watered deeply and infrequently.

Beans have their share of pests, including bean beetles, beanloopers, whiteflies, aphids, mites, and cucumber beetles. Anthracnose and leaf spots diseases are most prevalent in humid climates.

Harvest snap beans when the seeds inside are still very small and the pods are tender. Make sure to keep all beans harvested or the plants stop producing.

Varieties

Renee's Garden offers a combination package of green, purple, and yellow beans in retail stores.

Purple Snap Beans

'Hopi Purple String Beans': purple bean with black crescent-moon-shaped stripes; can be grown with little or no irrigation; available from Native Seeds/SEARCH

'Purple Queen': 55 days; bush; purple pods and flowers; sweet flavor; common bean mosaic-virus tolerant

'Royal Burgundy': 51 days; bush; dark purple pods; vigorous

'Royalty Purple Pod' ('Royalty'): bush; deep-purple pods and flowers; vigorous; some resistance to Mexican bean beetles

'Trionfo' ('Trionfo Violetto'): 65 days; pole; deep purple pods and lavender flowers; vigorous

Yellow Snap Beans

'Cherokee': 55 days; bush; sweet, wax bean; early; high yielding; widely adapted; rust and common bean mosaic-virus resistant

'Dragon's Tongue' ('Dragon Langerie'): 65 days; bush; unusual creamy yellow wax bean with pur-

'Pencil Pod Wax'

Renee's rainbow collection beans: green slenderette, 'Roc D'or,' and 'Purple Queen'

ple stripes; available from Bountiful Gardens

'Pencil Pod Black Wax ('Pencil Pod'): 53 days; bush; tender yellow pods with black seeds; early

'Roc D'or': 57 days; bush; slender yellow pods; productive; resistant to common bean mosaic virus and anthracnose

'Wax Romano': 58 days; bush; light yellow pods with meaty texture; vigorous

Yellow Anellino ('Gancetto Burro'): 80 days; pole; small, crescent-shaped pods; rich bean flavor

How to prepare: Yellow wax beans keep their color when cooked and are used as you would any snap bean, boiled or steamed until just tender, though cooking times are short as the beans turn to mush quickly. Try them in a three-bean salad garnished with raw purple beans. The purple beans get their color from anthocyanins and loose the purple color and turn a vivid green when boiled for two minutes—like magic—kids love to watch. (No guess work to know if your purple beans are properly blanched for freezing, when the color changes from purple to green they are perfect.) Even marinating them in vinegar or lemon juice will eventually turn them green. In my experience, making them into a pureed soup creates a decidedly unappetizing gray soup.

To preserve the deep purple color, serve the young beans raw in salads or on a festive dip platter mixed with other colorful vegetables.

Three colors of beets from Renee's Garden

BEETS
Beta vulgaris

THE ANCIENT GREEKS AND Romans appreciated both red and white beets; and yellow beets were popular in Europe for centuries.

How to grow: Sow beet seeds directly in rich, well-drained soil, in early spring or fall, in full sun. They can take some frost. Plant the seeds ¼ inch deep in wide rows or broadcast over a 3-foot-wide bed. I like to mix colors of beet varieties in the same bed so I can combine them in a recipe. Plant extra seeds of the golden beets as they germinate poorly. Beet seeds are actually a cluster of seeds; therefore,

they must be thinned to 3 inches apart for full size beets—2 inches for babies. Fertilize midseason with a balanced organic fertilizer and water evenly.

Occasionally, leaf miners tunnel through the leaves. A fungus disease cercospora flourishes in humid conditions and makes orange spots on the foliage. A rust fungus can also be a problem.

Harvest when the beets are 3 inches across or less.

Varieties
Renee's Garden carries three colors of beets in the same package.
'Albina Verduna' ('Snow White'): 65 days; pure white; large and sweet
'Bull's Blood': 60 days, a beet grown

for its deep red leaves as well as the roots; some resistance to leaf miner; the "greens" retain most of their color when cooked; available from Garden City Seeds
'Chioggia': 50 days; red on outside, red and white peppermint-striped rings inside; sweet
'Burpee's Golden Beet': 60 days; delicious, sweet yellow beets; leaf midribs are golden; low germination rates

How to prepare: The red pigments in beets are betacyanins; the yellow, betaxanthins. These pigments are fairly stable, though they do fade and change if food is overcooked. (If I boil my borscht too long it turns from a

29

'Chioggia,' 'Burpee's Golden,' and 'Cylindra' *(above left);* 'Albino Verduna' and 'Detroit Dark Red' *(above right);* Doug Gosling and beet harvest *(below)*

CABBAGES AND THEIR KIN

BROCCOLI
Brassica oleracea var. italica and B. oleracea. var. botrytis

BRUSSELS SPROUTS
B. oleracea var. gemmifera

CABBAGE
B. oleracea var. capitata and B. oleracea var. bulata

CAULIFLOWER
B. oleracea var. botrytis

KALE
B. oleracea var. acephala

KOHLRABI
B. oleracea var. gongylodes

MOST OF THIS FAMILY OF vegetables has green leaves and buds, but it is the purple or pink varieties we are most interested in here.

rich red to a dull reddish-brown.) Use beets raw or cooked in salads, cooked in soups and stews, or simply boiled or steamed and served with butter. The yellow, white, and the striped 'Chioggia' beets will not bleed and discolor the other ingredients in a cooked dish as do the red varieties and are great roasted in the oven with a little olive oil and garlic. To highlight yellow beets, serve them julienned with red ones or as baby beets. Note: pureed yellow beets sometimes oxidize, turning yellow-brown.

'Bull's Blood' greens are deep red and are one of the few "red" greens to retain their color and are a meltingly rich vegetable if steamed briefly. When the leaves are very young they are beautiful when added raw to a mixed salad.

How to grow: These vegetables are grown as cool-season annuals. They can bolt and become bitter-tasting in extremely hot weather. All need full sun, or light shade in hot climates.

Start most seeds indoors eight weeks before your last average frost date. Transplant them into rich soil filled with organic matter about two weeks before the last average frost date. (Start cauliflower a little earlier,

as it grows more slowly; start Brussels sprouts four weeks before the last frost date and transplant them in a month.) Most can also be planted in midsummer for a fall crop. Sow cabbage, broccoli, Brussels sprouts, and cauliflower seeds 3 inches apart, $1/2$ inch deep; thin or transplant small cabbages 12 inches apart and the larger cabbages, broccoli, Brussels sprouts, and cauliflower 24 inches apart. As they all tend to be top-heavy, when transplanting, place them lower in the soil than you would most vegetables—up to their first set of true leaves (the first leaves after the seed leaves). Plant kale seeds $1/2$ inch deep, 1 inch apart, and thin to about 1 foot. Unlike most cole crops, kohlrabi is best seeded in place, rather than started indoors. In early spring or late sum-

mer, sow kohlrabi seeds $1/4$ inch deep, 1 inch apart, thin to 4 inches for baby kohlrabi and 6 inches for full size. Work compost and one cup of a balanced organic fertilizer into the soil around each plant at planting time. A month after planting, side dress an organic nitrogen fertilizer scratched into the soil around the plants. Mulching helps retain moisture.

Most cabbage-family plants are susceptible to the same pests and diseases. (Kale tends to have far fewer problems than most.) Flea beetles, imported cabbageworm, cabbage root fly, and cutworms are potential problems. Use floating row covers to prevent these pests. You can also prevent the cabbage root fly from laying her eggs by placing black plastic directly over the roots

Chinese elogated cabbage, green drum-head, and red 'Ruby Perfection' cabbages *(above)*; 'Red Peacock' kale among lettuces *(below)*.

31

Purple sprouting broccoli *(above)*; 'Romanesco' broccoli *(below)*

'Red Russian' kale *(above)*; 'Lacinato' kale *(below)*

open; once the primary head is harvested, smaller heads may form. Cauliflower heads are traditionally protected from the sun to keep the curds white and tender. In contrast, the orange and purple varieties we are interested in need direct sunlight to develop their colors. Harvest cauliflower heads at the base when they are full but before the curds begin to separate. Harvest a few very young kale leaves as they are needed and use them raw for salads. Use the more mature kale leaves for cooked dishes. Many varieties of kale winter over in most climates. Start harvesting kohlrabi bulbs once they are an inch across. The young small bulbs are best for eating raw.

Harvest Brussels sprouts in the fall or winter. Cold weather causes the purple color to be more vibrant and the flavors to mature. If the plants are kept well mulched with straw, sprouts often develop and mature well into the winter. Brussels sprouts mature up the stem, from the bottom to the top, so harvest in that direction when they are no larger than one inch in diameter.

Varieties

Broccoli

'Purple Spouting' ('Early Purple Sprouting'): 120 days; purple-green leaves and purple flower buds; to 3 feet high; very hardy

'Romanesco': 85 days; heads are an attractive, chartreuse, conical whorl of mild, sweet florets; large plant; extremely variable in form

'Violet Queen': 60 days: purple buds; early; uniform

of the plant. Rotate members of the cabbage family with other vegetable families to prevent diseases.

Harvest cabbages anytime after they have started to form a ball, but before they split. If a hard freeze is expected, harvest all cabbages and store them in a cool place. Harvest broccoli when the buds begin to swell but before they

Brussels Sprouts

'Rubine' ('Rubine Red'): clusters of red sprouts; red foliage; large; late; hardy; popular in Europe, carried by Bountiful Gardens

Cauliflower

Purple and orange cauliflowers are easier to grow than white varieties as

mended; available from Johnny's Selected Seeds

'Purple Cape': rich purple heads with excellent flavor; hardy; carried by Bountiful Gardens

'Sicilian Purple': 85 days; deep purple, large heads; turns bright emerald green when cooked; available from Nichols Garden Nursery

Kale

Cold weather intensifies the colors of these kales.

'Lacinto': 70 days; blue-green strap leaves, tender; available from Shepherd's

'Nagoya Garnish Red': 60 days; ornamental kale; frilly leaves with red centers and green edges; available from Johnny's Selected Seeds and Harris

'Red Russian': 55 days; tender, frilly gray-green leaves with red veins; withstands summer heat

'Red Peacock': 60 days mature; ornamental kale; red center; feathery leaves; excellent for baby salad greens; 'White Peacock' is a white version; both available from Johnny's Selected Seeds

Kohlrabi

'Kolibri': 55 days; hybrid, purple-skinned kohlrabi, crunchy, sweet flesh; heat tolerant

'Purple Vienna': purple bulbs; old favorite; available from Landreth

Red Cabbage and Flowering Cabbage

'Lasso': 75 days; open pollinated; firm, bright red-purple, good tasting

'White Peacock' kale *(above);* 'Miniature Flowering' cabbage and 'White Peacock' kale *(below)*

they do not require garden blanching (covering the leaves to prevent the sun from reaching them and making them tough).

'Orange Bouquet': 58 days; pastel orange heads; the orange color is from carotene; sunlight intensifies the color, so blanching is not recom-

'Purple Vienna' kohlrabi *(above);* 'Red Fire Dance' cabbage *(below)*

heads; early; available from Garden City Seeds and Pinetree Garden Seeds

Miniature Flowering Cabbage, Tokyo Series: showy 12-inch heads; pink, white, and red, with green edges; cold resistant; available from Nichols Garden Nursery

'Red Drumhead': red Savoy-type cabbage; sweet crinkled leaves; hardy, widely adaptable; available from Seeds of Change and Bountiful Gardens

'Rougette': 80 days; red French variety; 3 pound heads; available from The Gourmet Gardener

'Ruby Perfection': 80 days; purple cabbage with great taste; available from The Cook's Garden

How to prepare: The purple pigments in the cabbage family are anthocyanins and in many cases are not stable when cooked. In particular, the purple in broccoli, cauliflower and kale turns green. However, if not cooked too long, red cabbage and Brussels sprouts can be colorful, especially if vinegar, lemon juice, or as is popular in much of Europe, red wine are added. With the addition of an acid they go from purple to a lovely bright magenta (see the discussion on acids and anthocyanins in "The Chemistry of Cooking" on page 60, and the recipe for Braised Red Cabbage on page 76). If cooked too long, however, both red cabbage and Brussels sprouts turn a dull red-gray.

To keep its color best, use the young leaves of kale raw in salads or as a garnish. Mature leaves are best cooked but lose purple coloring.

The purple pigments in broccoli, cauliflower, and kohlrabis turn green when cooked. To preserve their color, use them raw in salads and with dips. Romanesco broccoli keeps its lovely chartreuse color and the light orange cauliflower varieties stay colorful as well, as long as neither is overcooked.

CARROTS
Daucus carota var. sativus

ANCIENT CARROTS CAME FROM Afghanistan and the roots were mainly purplish or red. Our familiar orange-colored carrots are relative newcomers having been bred in Holland in the 1600s.

How to grow: Plant carrots in early spring as soon as your soil has warmed, or plant late summer for a fall crop. Cultivate and loosen the soil 1 foot deep to make room for the roots. Sow seeds $1/2$ inch apart in rows or wide beds and keep the seed bed evenly moist. Thin to 2 inches. In most parts of the country, once sprouted, carrots are easy to grow. When the plants are about 3 inches tall, fertilize with fish emulsion.

Once the seedlings are up, protect plants from slugs. In the upper Midwest, the carrot rust fly maggot tunnels its way through carrots. Floating row covers and crop rotation help. Alternaria blight and cercospora blight can also be a problem.

'Nutri-Red,' 'Danvers Long,' 'Sweet Sunshine,' and 'Belgium White' *(above);* 'Long Orange' and 'Red Surrey' *(below)*

Most carrot varieties are ready for harvesting when they are at least $1/2$ inch across and starting to color (except in the case of white carrots). The optimal time to harvest carrots is within a month after they mature, less in warm weather. Harvest when the soil is moist to reduce breaking off the roots in the ground.

Varieties
'Belgium White' ('White Belgium'): 75 days; white roots with green shoulders; 10 inches long; productive; in cool weather these carrots have a sweet "carrotty" flavor; in hot weather the flavor becomes too strong and "soapy"; best when eaten cooked

'Dragon': 75 days; red-to-purplish exterior, yellow to orange interior; sweet, spicy flavor; the purplish exterior is high in anthocyanin; available from Garden City Seeds

'Lubina': 70 days; bright yellow-gold with green shoulders; hearty, sweet flavor; vigorous grower; available from Garden City Seeds

'Nutri-Red': 118 days; deep-red carrot; high in lycopene, a precursor to beta-carotene; tastes best cooked

'Sweet Sunshine': 72 days; striking true yellow; tender, extra-sweet, 7 inch carrots; available from Burpee

How to prepare: The yellow and orange colors of carrots are carotenoids and are quite stable when cooked. In contrast, the purple pigments in purple carrots, because they are anthocyanins turn an unappetizing gray. To take advantage of the color and the extra nutrients in these purplish carrots, enjoy them raw. Serve baby purple carrots whole or cut mature ones into carrot sticks—combining them with the orange and yellow carrots makes a striking plate.

Cook the white, yellow, and red-orange carrots as you would the familiar orange varieties. To accent their colors, combine the different colors julienned on a plate, sprinkled over a salad, on a dip platter, or as baby cooked carrots with a vinaigrette or herb butter. Carrots, if peeled or grated and thus exposed to the air, eventually turn brown; sprinkle with lemon juice or vinegar to prevent discoloring or add your vinaigrette immediately to stop the oxidation.

CELERY
Apium graveolens var. dulce

RED CELERY HAS BEEN GROWN for many years and is fairly popular in England. Golden celerys are enjoyed in Asia.

How to grow: Celery is a cool-season vegetable that grows best in the spring or fall, or as a winter crop in warm-winter areas. Celery needs full sun (or partial shade in hot areas) and a highly organic soil that drains quickly. Start celery indoors 10 weeks before planting outdoors. Germination takes up to 20 days. After the weather has warmed to the upper 50s (Fahrenheit), move seedlings into the garden and place them 1 foot apart in all directions. Celery requires applications of fish fertilizer every four weeks and a continually moist soil—an organic mulch is helpful. Celery takes 3 to 4 months to mature.

Parsleyworms (the caterpillar of the eastern black swallowtail butterfly), carrot rust fly maggots, and carrot weevil larvae feed on celery. If they are a problem, protect plants with floating row covers. Celery may be afflicted with early blight fungus a disease that grows and spreads in cool, damp weather. Yellows, another disease, is spread by leafhoppers. Practice crop rotation, and rid the garden of all diseased plant residue over the winter.

Some gardeners elect to garden-blanch their red celery. When you blanch celery it becomes less stringy but much lighter in color and contains

fewer nutrients. To blanch: after the plants start to mature, exclude light by wrapping the stalks with burlap or straw, surround the bundles with black plastic, and then tie them with string.

Celery is harvested as soon as the stalks are large enough to pull off.

35

New stalks will continue to form from the plant's center, and thus harvesting can be continuous. Or harvest the whole head by cutting the plant off at the ground with a sharp knife.

Varieties

'Chinese Golden': 60 days, small leaves, tender narrow stalks; available from Evergreen Y. H. Enterprises

'Golden Self-Blanching': 115 days; a popular, open-pollinated, early, dwarf variety with pale gold color; available from Seeds Blüm and Bountiful Gardens

'Red': has bronzy-colored green stalks until the frost brings out the dark red color; a splendid variety with very solid heads; cold tolerant; stays fairly red when cooked

How to prepare: The red pigments in red celery are anthocyanins. To preserve the color, use it raw on a crudities platter, for dips, and for stuffing with flavored soft cheeses. Red celeries often need to have the strings removed before serving them. Gold celery keeps its color and can be used raw or cooked.

Pink chard

CHARD
(Swiss chard, leaf chard)
Beta vulgaris var. flavescens

THE NEW STAINED-GLASS COLORS of chard promise to add real pizzazz to the garden and lots of color to the table.

How to grow: Chard can be grown in a vegetable garden but it is equally at home in a flower border. When planting the color mix start the seeds in flats and choose the color of plants you want by waiting until the seedlings are a few inches tall and show their colors.

Swiss chard tolerates a lot more heat than most greens and is moderately hardy. Start in early spring or late summer for mild-winter areas. Plant chard seeds $1/2$ inch deep, 6 inches apart, and thin to one foot. Plant in full sun and neutral soil with lots of added organic matter. For tender succulent leaves, keep plants well watered. Mulch with a few inches of organic matter. When

plants are about six weeks old, fertilize with $1/2$ cup of balanced organic fertilizer for every 5 feet of row.

A few pests and diseases bother chard, mainly slugs and snails (especially when the plants are young), and leaf miner, a fly larvae.

To harvest chard, remove the outside leaves at the base; tender new leaves keep coming throughout the season.

Varieties

'Bright Lights': 55 days; a mix of vividly colorful plants with stems and midribs of red, gold, orange, purple, white, pink—and tender leaves from green to bronze; mild flavor

'Ruby Red' ('Rhubarb'): 60 days; solid red (sometimes dark pink) stems and midribs, and dark green leaves

How to prepare: The pigments in chards are the same as in their close cousin beets—namely betacyanins for the red, and betaxanthins for the gold colors. These pigments are fairly stable if not cooked very long. One caveat:

cut raw chard stems oxidize and soon turn brown if not treated with an acid solution such as a vinaigrette or citrus juice.

For the brightest colors use the chard stems raw. For example, just before serving, julienne the stems of different colored chards into matchsticks and sprinkle them over a winter salad in place of the usual red cabbage. Or pickle the stems and serve them as a relish with roasted meats or mushrooms (recipes, page 66). You can also use the colorful leaves to garnish platters and large salad bowls. Young chard stems can be stuffed with cheese mixtures as you would celery.

Colorful chards can also be added to traditional chard tarts (recipe, page 87) and the leaves can be stuffed with a risotto stuffing and steamed.

Stalks of 'Bright Lights' chard *(top);* 'Ruby' chard *(above left);* closeup of the leaf of ruby red chard *(above, right)*

CORN (MAIZE, INDIAN CORN)

DENT CORN
Zea mays var. indentata

POPCORN
Z. m. var. everta

SOFT CORN (FLOUR CORN)
Z. m. var. amylacea

SWEET CORN
Z. m. var. saccharata

CORN HAS MANY DIMENSIONS. In simple terms, sweet corn is the one that bears those luscious ears we smother with butter; dent and soft corns are used primarily for grinding into corn meal or corn flour; dent varieties are also used as roasting ears; and popcorn for popping.

How to grow: Corn requires summer heat and full sun and is best sown directly in the garden. Corn pollen is transferred by the wind, from the male flower (the tassel) onto the pistil of the female flower (the silk). If corn is planted in long single rows, the silks won't be well pollinated. Instead plant corn in a block of shorter multiple rows, at least four rows deep. Plant seeds in rich soil, 1 inch deep, 4 inches apart; thin to 1 foot apart.

Fertilize sweet corn with organic nitrogen fertilizer at planting time and when plants tassel (when the flower stalks produce pollen). Grinding corns are lighter feeders and more drought tolerant than the sweet corns. With all corn, however, extra water is needed at tasseling time, to guard against poorly filled out ears.

'Hopi Blue' corn

Birds steal seeds out of the ground so cover newly planted seeds with floating row covers until 1 foot tall. The most common insect pests are corn earworms. Other insect pests include corn borers; southern corn rootworms; corn flea beetles, and seed corn maggots. The most common corn diseases are Stewart's bacterial wilt, root rot, corn smut, and southern corn leaf blight.

Sweet corn is ready to eat when the silks are dry and brown and the ears are well filled out. Test for ripeness by tasting a few kernels. Grinding corns and popcorn should be left on the plant until the kernels are dry. If the weather is very wet, cut the stalks after the husks begin to turn brown; store them in a dry place. When the corn is completely dry—which can take weeks—husk the ears and store them in a dry place, or remove the kernels and store them in sealed jars.

Varieties

Some colored varieties of dry corn will be white in the milk stage and only color up when ripe.

Sweet Corn

'Ruby Queen': 75 days; deep red, 8-inch-long ears; sweet, tender kernels; available from Burpee

Grinding Corns

'Bloody Butcher': 100 days; dent corn, large ears of red kernels; makes pink cornmeal; plants grow to 12 feet; available from Fox Hollow Seeds and Seeds Blüm

'Hopi Blue' ("Sakwa-pu"): 90 days; flour corn with blue kernels; ground use for blue cornbread;

drought tolerant; available from Redwood City Seed Company, Native Seed/SEARCH

Popcorn

'Strawberry': 80–110 days; small, deep red ears, to 3 inches long and strawberry-shaped; plants 5 feet tall; resistant to corn earworm; available from Fox Hollow Seeds and The Cook's Garden

How to prepare: The red color in 'Ruby Queen' is from anthocyanin and the color fades and changes unless you microwave it. Serve it as you would any sweet corn or after microwaving it, cut it off the cob and sprinkle the kernels over tacos (recipe, page 84), salads, and chowders. Use 'Strawberry' popcorn as you would regular popcorns (it pops up white). Anthocyanins are also the pigments in blue corn. Use the grinding corns for corn meal as you would in most recipes (See the recipes on pages 88–89). Have some fun experimenting. 'Bloody Butcher' makes a very flavorful red-flecked cornbread. You can use 'Hopi Blue' for bread that retains its bluish-purple color when baked in blue cornbread and blue tortillas (though it usually gets a greenish-hue from the baking powder). Combining 'Hopi Blue' cornmeal with white flour makes a bluish-gray pie crust with a nutty crunch.

If you have only small amounts of corn, grind dry corn in a hand-powered grain mill. For larger amounts of corn, it's possible to purchase grain-grinding attachments to fit popular models of stand mixers.

CUCUMBERS
Cucumis sativus

CUCUMBERS ARE AN ANCIENT vegetable that originated in India.

How to grow: Cucumbers are warm-season annuals and tolerate no frost. Plant the seeds when the soil and weather are warm, about 1 inch deep, 6 inches apart in rows. Thin to 2 feet apart. Cucumbers grow on vines and are grown on trellises put in place at the time of planting.

Cucumbers need rich, humus-filled soil and ample water during the growing season. Work bone meal and blood meal into the soil before planting. If plants are pale, apply fish emulsion.

Young cucumber plants are susceptible to cutworms and snails, and striped and spotted cucumber beetles can destroy young vines as well as carry serious diseases. Powdery mildew is a common problem, particularly late in the season. More serious diseases are mosaic virus, scab, and anthracnose; pull up affected plants as there is no cure for any of these conditions.

Harvest cucumbers when they are

young and firm but filled out. For best eating, pick lemon cucumbers when about the size of a lime and don't let them get too yellow. Pick white cucumbers when about 5 inches long and ivory white. Harvest regularly and pick off all overripe or damaged fruits or when plants stop production.

Varieties

'Lemon': 65 days; round, yellow fruits; mild flavor; drought- and rust-resistant plants

'White': 60 days; crisp, slicing cucumber with white skin and flesh; skin eventually turns yellow-orange; available from Landis Valley and Seed Savers Exchange

How to prepare: Use cucumber slices raw as you would green cucumbers. To emphasize the colors try alternating green, white, and yellow cucumbers on the top of a salad or buffet plate.

EGGPLANTS
Solanum melongena var.

Many variations of eggplant colors

esulentum, S. integrifolium

EGGPLANTS ARE GENERALLY purple but there are pink, white, green, and red varieties as well.

How to grow: Eggplants are tender perennials grown as annuals. They tolerate no cold. Start seeds indoors 6 weeks before the average date of your last frost. The seeds germinate best at 80°F. Plant the seeds ¼ inch deep, in flats. When all danger of frost is past and the soil has warmed, transplant into the garden 24 inches apart and water well. Grow eggplants in full sun, in rich well-drained garden loam that has added nitrogen. To increase yield and to keep the plants healthy, feed them about three times during the growing season with fish emulsion. If you are growing eggplants in a cool climate, cover the soil with black plastic to retain heat. Eggplants need moder-

'White' cucumber

'Snowy White' eggplant

ate watering.

Flea beetles, spider mites, and whiteflies can be a problem. Flea beetles often appear early in the season, right after transplanting. Spider mites can be a nuisance in warm, dry weather. Nematodes are sometimes a problem in the South. Verticillium wilt and phomopsis blight are common disease problems in humid climates.

Eggplant is ready to harvest when the skin is full-colored but has not yet begun to lose any of its sheen. Press down on the eggplant with your finger, if the flesh presses in and bounces back, it is ripe.

Varieties

'Asian Bride': 70 days; white skin streaked with lavender; to 6 inches long, 1 ½ inches diameter; creamy flesh; productive, lavender flowers; available from Shepherd's

'Rosa Bianca': 75 days; large, rose-lavender and white fruit with creamy flavor; one of the most beautiful eggplants, productive; available from Shepherd's

'Snowy White': 70 days; pure white color and great eating quality; 5 inches long, 2 ½ inches diameter; early; available from Shepherd's

'Turkish Italian Orange': small orange-red fruits; 4 feet tall, spineless plants; high yielding; available from Southern Exposure

'Violette De Firenze': 80 days; spectacular, Italian; large oblong lavender fruits, often with wide white stripes; available from The Cook's Garden

How to prepare: The color of these eggplants will be enjoyed most in the garden, because in preparation the skin is either peeled off or discolors when cooked. Even though the skin changes color, eggplants are wonderful grilled on a barbecue along with other colorful vegetables. Use these colorful eggplants as you would the purple ones in stews, stir-fried, grilled in sandwiches, and pureed with garlic for a dip.

HUÀUZONTLI
Chenopodium nuttaliae

THE BUSHY SPEARS OF THIS TALL plant's seed heads are edible and used in Mexico as a pot herb.

How to grow: Huauzontli is an annual plant that is started from seed in spring and grows to 3 feet in height. Keep the plant fairly moist during the growing season. In autumn its leaves turn red.

How to prepare: The mild-tasting shoots are eaten like spinach. Traditionally, shoots covered with seed heads are blanched in boiling water; then small bunches are put together with cheese, dipped in egg batter, and fried. According to Craig Dremman of Redwood City Seed Company, it looses little of its fall red color if cooked briefly.

'Aztec' red spinach—Huàuzantli

'Lollo Rossa' and 'Cerise' red lettuces

'Rouge d'Hiver' red romaine *(above)*; Red and Green Oak leaf lettuces *(below)*

LETTUCE

Lactuca sativa

RED LETTUCES ARE ESPECIALLY showy in the garden and can be interplanted among flowers.

How to grow: Lettuce is a cool-season annual crop. Most will go to seed or become bitter rapidly once hot weather arrives. In warm weather, lettuce grows better with afternoon shade. In mild-winter areas, lettuce will grow through the winter.

Lettuce prefers soil high in organic matter, needs regular moisture, and profits from light feedings of fish fertilizer every few weeks. Sow seeds ⅛ inch deep outdoors, start seeds indoors in flats, or buy transplants. You can start lettuce outside as soon as you can work the soil in spring. Plant seeds 2 inches apart and ⅛ inch deep. Keep seed beds uniformly moist until seedlings appear. Thin seedlings to between 6 and 12 inches apart, depend-

ing on the variety. Failure to thin seedlings can result in disease problems.

Protect seedlings from birds, slugs, snails, and aphids with floating row covers and by hand picking pests. Botrytis, a gray mold fungus disease, can cause the plants to rot off at the base. Downy mildew, another fungus, will cause older leaves to get whitish patches that eventually die.

You can harvest lettuce at any stage. Leaf lettuces can be harvested one leaf at a time or in their entirety. Heading lettuces are generally harvested by cutting off the head at the soil line.

Varieties

Most of the following red varieties are carried by The Cook's Garden, Johnny's Selected Seeds, and The Gourmet Gardener.

'Brunia': 62 days; a beautiful red oakleaf; leaves dark green with red-brown; large frilly heads

'Cerise': 30 days baby, 48 days full size; deep red color; good for

baby lettuces; matures to an iceberg type

'Impuls': 55 days; intensely red 'Lollo Rossa' type; 6- to 8-inch circular mound of frilled leaves

'Mighty Red Oak': 50 days; bronzy-red oakleaf; to 16 inches across; productive; slow to bolt; available from Burpee

'Red Sails': 52 days: burgundy-red fringed and ruffled leaves: fast growing; heat tolerant; deepens in color as it matures

'Red Salad Bowl' ('Red Oak Leaf'): 50 days; pale red color increases to deep red with maturity; withstands heat well

'Rouge d'Hiver': 60 days; deep red romaine; sow in early fall; if you plant earlier it may bolt prematurely

How to prepare: Red lettuces are higher than their green cousins in anthocyanins. Red lettuces are spectacular when used to line a platter and filled with any type of filling imaginable. They are lovely by themselves with a simple vinaigrette or combined with raspberries or sliced pears. All of these colorful lettuces enhance a mixed salad with their color.

'Red Giant Mustard'

MUSTARD, JAPANESE RED
Brassica juncea var. rugosa

JAPANESE RED MUSTARDS ARE tangy, handsome plants with crinkled, wine-red leaves that are enjoyable as baby greens or when fully mature.

How to grow: Mustards are cool-season crops. Plant seeds ¼ inch deep, 2 inches apart in early spring or fall in full sun and rich loam. Thin to 1 foot apart if growing to maturity. Or broadcast the seed in a wide bed and grow for cut-and-come-again baby greens. Water regularly or leaves become too hot to eat. Mulch with an organic mulch. Mustards are occasionally plagued by the pests that bother cabbages (see the "Cabbages" entry). Harvest a few leaves at a time as needed. The younger the mustard leaf, the less bite it has.

Varieties

'Osaka Purple': 40 days; 3-foot plants; purple leaves with white veins; mild; great for baby greens

'Red Giant Mustard' ('Giant Red'): 45 days; purple-red, savoyed leaves; tangy; 4 feet tall; great for baby greens

How to prepare: The pigments in mustards are anthocyanins that fade when cooked. Use the leaves raw in sandwiches and salads—they add zing! Baby mustards are fairly mild; they add texture, color, and a slight tang to mes-clun salads. Use mustard leaves sparingly in light salads or pair them with other strong-flavored greens in a hearty fall or winter salad with a rich dressing. Though they'll lose most of their color, enjoy the leaves in omelets or stir-fries.

OKRA, RED

Abelmoschus esculentus
(Hibiscus esculentus)

WITH ITS RED PODS AND STEMS
and yellow blossoms, red okra is a
showy plant.

How to grow: Okra must have hot
weather and full sun. Plant seeds 6
inches apart in warm, organic-filled,
well-drained soil; thin plants to 2 feet.
Apply fish fertilizer after the pods
begin to set and once again midway
through the season. Okra requires
about 1 inch of water a week. In cool-
summer areas, mulch plants with
black plastic for extra warmth.

Okra is susceptible to a few pests,
namely, Japanese beetles, caterpillars,
and stinkbugs. Nematodes, verticillium wilt, and fusarium wilt are occasional problems.

Okra pods are usually best harvested before they are 3 inches long or they
become woody and the plants stop producing. Use clippers to cut a pod off at
its base.

Varieties

'Burgundy': 49 days; stems, leaf veins,
and pods are deep red-maroon;
plants average 4 feet; pods stay tender until nearly 8 inches; not very
disease resistant; carried by
Southern Exposure Seed Exchange
and Bountiful Gardens

'Red': 55–65 days; tender, tasty red
pods; 5 feet tall, yellow-and-red
flowers; carried by Abundant Life
Seed Foundation

'Red Velvet': 60–70 days; scarlet pods,
stems, and leaf veins; 5 feet tall; carried by Seeds of Change

How to prepare: Red okra pods
turn greenish-brown when cooked but
keep their color when pickled. Use red
okra pickled and with marinades.

ONIONS, RED

Allium cepa

PINK SCALLIONS

A. cepa

RED ONIONS AND SCALLIONS ARE
usually milder than most yellow and
white versions.

How to grow: Onions prefer cool
weather, particularly in their juvenile
stage. They grow best in a neutral, well-
drained soil rich in organic matter and
phosphorous. They like even watering.

Onions and scallions are generally
grown from seeds or sets. For full-size
onions, select the right variety for your
climate and time of year because bulbs
are formed according to day length.
Short-day onions bulb when they get 10
to 12 hours of light per day, best for
spring planting in southern latitudes.
Long-day onions require about 16
hours of sun to bulb and are best for
northern areas. Medium-day onions
require 12 to 14 hours of light a day and
do well in most parts of the country.

Start seeds inside in late winter or
sow them 1/4 inch deep outside in
spring (or fall in mild climates). Plant
them in rows or wide beds. Fertilize
onions with a balanced organic fertilizer when plants are about 6 inches tall
and are beginning to bulb. Large bul-
bing onions should be thinned to give
each plant adequate room for unham-
pered development. Use the red onion
thinnings as pink scallions.

I enjoy serving pink, pearl-type
onions in colorful dishes. Some vari-

are the onion maggot (a fly larvae) and thrips. Since scallions are harvested at a younger stage, they tend to have fewer problems with these pests.

Harvest scallions just as the bulbs begin to swell by pulling the entire plant out of the ground. Onions may be harvested anytime from the scallion stage to mature bulb formation.

Varieties

Red Onions

Onions may be hotter in one part of the country than in another or when grown in different soil.

'Italian Blood Red Bottle': 120 days; day-neutral; large, red, bottle-shaped onion; tangy; available from Nichols Garden Nursery

'Red Burgermaster': 102 days; long-day; reddish-purple skin; spicy; vigorous; stores well

'Red Torpedo': 75 days; medium-day; deep purple outside, white to pink interior; sweet; available from Pinetree Garden Seeds

eties are bred to produce these small onions. You can also produce small onions from large red varieties by forcing them as you would to make your own onion sets. To produce small onions (sets), plant seeds in poor soil and sow the seeds thickly. (I've had success sowing them in a shallow nursery flat.) The crowding and lack of nourishment force the plants to bulb up prematurely. 'Red Weathersfield' is a variety especially suitable for this process. (Don't be tempted to cook with the red onions sets available from the nursery; they have probably been doused with fungicides to prevent them from rotting when planted.)

The most common pests of onions

ORACH
Atriplex hortensis

'Purplette' pink scallions

THIS ATTRACTIVE PLANT HAS green and red cultivars. Unlike most greens, orach tolerates fairly warm weather.

How to grow: Plant orach seeds $1/4$ inch deep in good soil 6 to 8 weeks before the last expected spring frost date. Thin to 18 inches apart if growing to maturity. Or grow orach as a baby cut-and-come-again "green" by planting seeds in wide rows and thinning plants to only a few inches apart. Mulch to conserve moisture, as plants should be kept moist but not soggy. Orach has few pests and diseases.

Start to harvest leaves in about 6 weeks. If kept pinched back, plants will produce until the weather gets hot. They go to seed if not pruned.

Varieties
'Red Orach': 37 days; red leaves; to 6 feet; available from Garden City Seeds and Bountiful Gardens

How to prepare: Harvested leaves add a vibrant pink-purple to mixed salads. They have a mild flavor that's a good foil for strong-flavored greens. Orach is a delicious midsummer spinach substitute but it looses much of its color when cooked.

'Red Weathersfield': 105 days; for northern growing areas, a large, flat, purplish-red, pungent onion; best known for the production of onion sets; available from Lockhart

'Stockton Red': 188 days; medium-day; less sensitive to day length than most onions; available from The Cook's Garden and Lockhart

Pink Scallions
'Deep Purple': 60 days; very attractive; for spring or summer sowing; available from Johnny's Selected Seeds

'Purplette': 60 days; purple skin, pinkish flesh; if allowed to mature, it forms small pearl onions that turn pastel-pink when cooked or pickled; Johnny's Selected Seeds and Seeds Blüm

How to prepare: The onion's red color comes from anthocyanins that tend to fade when cooked, especially for any length of time. For the brightest colors, use red onions chopped or sliced over green salads and tomato salads, in sandwiches, and in omelets and frittatas. My favorite way to feature the pink onion color is with the small, round baby pearl onions that are pickled; pink, pearl onions (recipe, page 75); or cooked to just tender and served with other colorful vegetables in a vinaigrette. My friend Jesse Cool, chef and owner of Flea Street Café in Menlo Park, California, pickles these little onions in dry vermouth and uses them in martinis.

Enjoy pink scallions as you would any scallions. They are particularly nice served raw on colorful appetizer platters, with dips, and sliced and sprinkled over salads and cream soups.

PEAS, SHELLING

GARDEN PEAS, SOUP PEAS

Pisum sativum

PEAS, EDIBLE-PODDED

SUGAR SNAP PEAS, SNOW PEAS

P. sativum var. macrocarpon

MOST PEAS ARE GREEN, OF course, but there a few colorful podded ones that are fun to try.

'Golden Sweet' peas

'Capucijner's Purple Pod' peas

How to grow: Pea plants are either short bushes or long, climbing vines. Peas require well-drained, organic soil; full sun; high humidity; and cool weather. They tolerate some frost but do poorly in hot weather. Seeds should be planted 1 inch deep, 4 inches apart, in rows 1 foot apart. Most varieties need some form of support that's best placed at planting time. Peas need only a light fertilizing at midseason, but they benefit from regular and deep watering—1 inch per week is ideal.

Seedlings succumb to slugs, snails, and birds, so it's best to cover them until they are 6 inches high. Control pea weevils by lightly dusting wet foliage with lime.

Ideally, peas should be harvested daily during the mature-pod stage. Harvest snow peas when the pod becomes full size but before the seeds enlarge. Left past maturity, they lose sweetness and their production declines. For dry peas, allow pods to ripen and turn brown on the vine. If the weather is very wet or heavy frosts are predicted, bring the vines into a dry barn or porch to dry.

Varieties

'Golden Sugar': flat snow-pea type of pea with light golden pods; available from Seeds Blüm

'Golden Sweet': 70 days; beautiful, lemon-yellow edible pods; two-tone lavender flowers; harvest for pods or for soup peas; available from the Seed Savers Exchange

'Capucijner's Purple Pod' ('Blue Podded'): 80 days; vining; purple pods and lavender blossoms; best for soup peas; available from Abundant Life Seed Foundation and the Seed Savers Exchange

How to prepare: Use yellow snow pea pods sliced in salads or whole on a dip platter. They hold their color and make a delightful stir-fry with colorful peppers and carrots. The purple-podded pea is primarily a dry pea, tasty in a creamy winter soup.

PEPPERS

Capsicum spp.

PEPPERS IN THE GARDEN ARE A virtual rainbow unto themselves. There just may be more color variations in peppers than in any other vegetable.

How to grow: Peppers are a warm-weather crop. They cannot tolerate frost and won't set fruit unless the temperature is between 65°F and 80°F. Start seeds indoors in flats eight weeks before the average last frost date. When all danger of frost is past and the weather is warm, transplant seedlings into the garden. Transplant peppers 2 feet apart, in full sun (or partial shade in hot climates). They require deep, rich soil, and regular watering. Peppers are fairly heavy feeders so apply fish fertilizer midseason.

Young pepper plants can fall victim to snails, slugs, aphids, and cutworms. Peppers are occasionally prone to the same diseases and pests that afflict tomatoes, although peppers succumb less often.

When peppers are nearly full size, pick them at any color stage. Cut, rather than pull, peppers from the plant's stem.

"Golden Bell" Peppers

Burpee's Giant Golden

Pretty Purple Pepper

Varieties

Mail-order suppliers The Pepper Gal, Totally Tomatoes, and Tomato Growers Supply Company carry most of the listed varieties. A number of seed companies carry "rainbow" collections of peppers including W. Atlee Burpee & Co., Park Seed Company, Renee's Garden, and in retail stores.

Sweet Peppers

'Albino' ('White Bullnose'): 80 days; creamy-white a long time before going red-orange

'Chocolate Bell': 75 days; large, dark brownish-red fruits

'Golden Bell': many blocky, golden, thick-walled varieties at your local nursery or in catalogs may be generically labeled as simply 'Golden Bell'

'Golden CalWonder': 72 days; a golden bell type that is TMV resistant

'Gypsy': 60 days; from pale yellow to orange-red; tasty elongated fruits; early; productive; performs well in both hot and cold regions; TMV resistant

'Hungarian Sweet Banana' ('Sweet Banana,' 'Long Sweet Hungarian'): 52 days; yellow to flaming orange; 4 to 7 inches long; cylindrical shaped; dependable, high yields; very ornamental

'Mandarin': 74–78 days; green to red to deep red-orange; flavor is best at orange stage; high yields

'Lilac Bell': 70 days; ivory to lavender to crimson with extended lavender stage; blocky fruits with thick sweet flesh; vigorous plants; TMV resistant

'Purple Beauty': 70 days, green to deep purple to red blocky bell, productive, TMV resistant

'Romanian Rainbow': 60 days; ivory to orange then to red bells, often all three colors are on the plant at one time

'Valencia': 72 days; from green to deep tangerine-orange; large, blocky bell; productive; TMV-resistant

'Yellow Belle': 65–75 days; yellow to yellow-orange to crimson red; 'CalWonder' type; thick flesh; productive and reliable; in southern areas, fully ripe peppers may develop fungus in the seed cavity during hot weather

'Yellow Cheese Pimiento': 73 days; green to yellow to orange; large, squash-shaped fruits

Hot Peppers

'Bolivian Rainbow': 75 days; purple, yellow, and red fruits; purple leaves; tall plant, fruits early; productive; available from Seeds of Change

'Cayenne, Golden': 60 days; dark green to golden; from Renee's Garden

'Long Red Cayenne' ('Long Cayenne'): 75 days; slim, 5-inch-long peppers; very hot

'Purple Cayenne': slim, purple peppers to 5 inches; available from Renee's Garden

'Poinsettia': 90 days; 2-foot plants bear-

Orange peppers—both hot and sweet

POTATOES
Solanum tuberosum

POTATOES GENERALLY HAVE white flesh but there are lovely varieties with blue or red flesh as well.

How to grow: Potatoes prefer cool weather so plant them in the spring as soon as the soil has warmed. Potatoes are generally started by planting pieces of the tuber that contain at least one "eye." Set them out as soon as the ground can be worked in the spring. If hard frosts are expected, protect the young plants with floating row covers. Potatoes are best grown in well-drained, fertile, organic soil. For an easy and large harvest, plant potatoes in a trench 6 inches wide by 6 inches deep. Space tubers about 1 foot apart and cover with 4 inches of soil. As the potatoes begin to sprout, fill the trench with more soil until it is level with the existing bed or taller. For highest production, keep the plants moist. If planted with plenty of finished compost, potatoes generally require little fertilizer.

Colorado potato beetles, flea beetles, and aphids can attack potato foliage; wireworms and white grubs damage tubers. The tuber pests are best controlled by regular crop rotation. In highly alkaline soil potatoes may develop a disease called scab, so raise the soil pH to 6. If a plant shows signs of wilt or viral disease, remove and discard it. When potato foliage has died back, dig tubers from one plant to check the crop for tuber size. To avoid damaging underlying tubers, dig carefully and at some distance from the plant's crown.

ing 2-inch, upright, pointed fruits from green to purple to red; available from Fox Hollow Seeds and W. Atlee Burpee & Co.'s Heirloom Seed catalog

'Pretty Purple': 75–90 days; green to lavender to red fruits; foliage and flowers are purple; available Southern Exposure Seed Exchange

'Variegata': 65 days; green, purple, and red fruits; spectacular dwarf plants; leaves variegated green, white, and purple

How to prepare: Red and orange peppers have more vitamins A and C than the unripe green, ivory, and purple ones. The primary pigments in peppers are various carotenoids that are quite stable when cooked. The purple and lilac peppers, however, must derive their color from anthocyanins because they fade quickly when cooked. I feature the purple peppers by serving them raw in salads and presenting them on dip platters.

To accent the colors of the red, orange, yellow, and white bell peppers, prepare them as containers for dips on a buffet table, or stuff them with risotto or bread stuffings. Also cut them into rings or match sticks to decorate a salad or serving platter. All colors of peppers, raw or cooked, are tasty in combination on pizzas and in frittatas, pasta salad, peperonata, and tacos. They are delicious pickled, roasted, and marinated in olive oil, and are splashy and tasty garnishes.

Roast and puree the cooked red and orange peppers and use them in cream soups or sauces. These colorful peppers also can be dried and ground to make different colors of either hot or sweet "paprikas"; sprinkled on potato salads, cream soups, and stuffed baked potatoes; and blended into soft cheeses. For an unusual and healthy appetizer, mix the paprika with salt and dip slices of jicama or white baby turnips into the spicy mixture.

'All Blue' and 'All Red' Potatoes in a harvest with many types of white potatoes.

Varieties

Becker's Seed Potatoes and Ronniger's Seed & Potato Company are mail-order sources specializing in potatoes; they carry both varieties.

'All Blue' ('Purple Marker'): more than 80 days; purple-blue flesh; medium-sized potatoes good for mashing, steaming, and baking

'All Red': more than 80 days; brilliant red skin and pink flesh; medium tubers; good for steaming and boiling

How to prepare: While the pigments in these colorful potatoes are primarily anthocyanins, the deep blue potatoes particularly can be coaxed to keep much of their color. However, if you start with pale blue or very light pink potatoes, the finished dish will probably have little or no color—or in the worst case, turn an unappetizing gray. To retain as much color as possible, boil potatoes with a little vinegar or lemon juice in the water; or microwave them until they are just tender (over-cooking fades the color). To feature the blue and pink varieties in salads, use colorless vinaigrettes instead of creamy dressings. Adding acidic ingredients like vinegar or citrus juices changes the color. The blue potatoes become a bright, deep, magenta-purple; the pink ones turn more red. Combine these dramatic potato slices with yellow and green zucchini, red and orange bell peppers. Top with a spicy dressing—and Olé!—an instant fiesta dish.

While colorful potatoes are interchangeable with white potatoes in most recipes, potato salads (recipe, page 75), lavender or pink mashed potatoes, and vichyssoise (recipe, page 65) are among the most successful presentations.

Caution: Dispose of all portions of a tuber that show any green coloration; they are toxic.

RADISHES
Raphanus sativus

I'M INCLUDING TWO TYPES OF colorful radishes. The standard European types are usually red but they also come in purple, white, and pink. Asia is the home of a type of daikon called "beauty heart" radishes. Large with colorful pink or green flesh, "beauty hearts" are especially popular in northern China.

How to grow: Standard radishes grow easily and can be planted after the last frost in spring and again in early fall. The "beauty hearts" are a bit more difficult to grow. The resulting roots are quite variable; some have deep color and others remain pale. The Asian radishes are best planted in August in cold-winter areas and from September through December in mild-winter areas for fall and winter harvests.

Plant all radish seeds directly in the garden 1/2 inch deep. Thin the standard radishes to 2 inches and the beauty hearts to 8 inches. All radishes can be planted in rows or wide beds. The soil should be light and well-drained with a generous dose of compost. Radishes are light feeders so they need little fertilizer. Keep the young radishes constantly moist to avoid cracking and a "too-hot" taste.

In some areas of the country, radishes are bothered by root maggots, a pest best controlled by rotating crops. Flea beetles also can be a considerable problem.

Generally, standard radishes mature within 30 days. They're best harvested

'Easter Egg,' 'French Breakfast', and 'Sparkler' radishes

when about the size of cherries—3/4 inch in diameter—or 1 inch across for the long, narrow type, usually within 30 days. "Beauty hearts" take about 2 months to mature and are ready when they have reached full size. In cool weather, they can be left in the ground for weeks. Insulate radishes with straw if a hard freeze is expected. If left in the ground too long, short-season radishes have a tendency to get hot and fibrous.

Varieties

Short-Season European Radishes

'Easter Egg': 28 days; flavorful and crunchy; produces a mixture of purple, lavender, pink, and white radishes

'Plum Purple' ('Purple Plum'): quick growing; with deep purple skins and crisp, white flesh; heat tolerant; available from The Cook's Garden

Easter egg radishes

Long-Season Asian Radishes

'Chinese Misato Rose Flesh': 65 days; mild; 4-inch round roots; creamy outside and rosy pink inside; stores well; available from Park Seed Company

'**Green Meat**': usually ready about 60 days after sowing; 10-inch root with white skin and green flesh; available from Evergreen Y. H. Enterprise

'**Misato Green**': usually ready about 60 days after sowing; for autumn and winter crops; cylindrical Chinese radish with green flesh; juicy and sweet; easier to grow than the red beauty hearts; available from Nichol's Garden Nursery

'**Shinrimei**': The name translates to "beauty heart;" Chinese round radish with white skin, green shoulders, and red flesh; needs some late-summer heat to grow well; available from Evergreen Y. H. Enterprises

How to prepare: Serve standard radishes sliced raw in salads, as garnishes, on hors d'oeuvre platters, and with butter on bread or crackers (see the radish salad recipe, page 71). The pink color from anthocyanins fades when cooked. The "beauty heart" radishes are traditionally carved into flowers like water lilies, peonies, and chrysanthemums and are beautiful garnishes on buffet dishes. Crisp and succulent, they are often enjoyed raw—frequently julienned to show off their colors. Sometimes they are sprinkled lightly with sugar. They're also served Western style with a light herb dressing or cut into fancy shapes for a dip platter.

'Gold Rush and 'Sunny Delight' squash

SQUASH, SUMMER
Cucurbita pepo var. melopepo

SUMMER SQUASHES ARE COLORFUL additions to your garden and your table.

How to grow: Squashes are warm-season annuals. In short-summer areas, start seeds indoors. Transplant into hills about 3 feet across and 5 feet apart, placing 3 plants to a hill. Squash needs rich humus soil, full sun, and ample water during the growing season. They also benefit from regular applications of a balanced organic fertilizer that is not too high in nitrogen. Keep young plants well-weeded and don't let them dry out.

Squash may be afflicted with squash bugs as well as the spotted and the striped cucumber beetles. East of the Rockies, squash vine borers can be a problem. Mildew is the most common disease so expect it by season's end.

Pick summer squash when it's quite young and tender; or in its "adolescent" stage when the blossoms have just withered, indicating that the squash is still tender but has developed its flavor; or when it is more mature but still tender. Harvest the fruits regularly, or the plant drastically slows its production.

Varieties

'**French White**': 50 days; bush; white zucchini with mild flavor; firm meat with few seeds; available from Nichols Garden Nursery

'**Gold Rush**': 52 days; delicious golden zucchini on a vigorous plant

'**Golden Dawn II**': 45 days; golden zucchini; uniform fruits; productive plants; high in lutein; available from Garden City Seeds

Yellow and pale green pattypan squash

'Sunburst': 50 days; beautiful, bush-type plant with vivid golden, scalloped pattypan squashes; high in lutein, squashes are mild and tender; available from Nichols Garden Nursery

'Sunny Delight': an improved 'Sunburst'-type; golden, scalloped pattypan

How to prepare: The skins of most summer squash are high in lutein. For maximum nutrition, harvest summer squash while they're quite young so the skins don't need to be peeled. Slice them raw for salads or for dipping or serve them grilled with a tasty marinade or stuffed and baked. Mix the yellow and white varieties with the dark green varieties to feature the contrast of colors in cooked dishes (recipe, page 78). Grilled baby squash with their flowers intact are an exquisite treat when served with a marinade or sauce.

TOMATOES
Lycopersicon esculentum

CURRANT TOMATOES
L. pimpinellifolium

NO RAINBOW GARDEN WOULD be complete without tomatoes—red, orange, yellow, gold, white, and green.

How to grow: Tomatoes are heat-loving plants. Though perennials, tomatoes are grown as warm-weather annuals as they cannot tolerate frost. Extreme heat can sunburn the fruit, though, so it is necessary to protect them in extremely hot climates. Many varieties, especially the big heirloom, beefsteak types, do not set fruit well in temperatures higher than 96°F or lower than 50°F. Start plants from seed about six weeks before the last average frost date; sow seeds $1/4$ inch deep in good potting soil. Keep seedlings in a very sunny window or under grow lights. Transplant seedlings when they are about 6 inches tall and after there's any danger of frost. Place plants in full sun, about 4 feet apart in well-drained soil amended with a lot of organic matter. Place the transplants deep; the soil should reach the first set of new leaves. Stake or trellis plants to save space and keep the fruit from spoiling on the ground. After transplanting and again when the fruit begins to set, fertilize tomatoes with fish meal, chicken manure, or a premixed, organic fertilizer formulated for tomatoes. Be careful not to apply excess nitrogen fertilizer, as it favors leaf growth at the expense of the fruit. A form of calcium is often

'Big Rainbow,' 'Green Zebra,' 'Green Grape,' and 'Yellow Brandywine' tomatoes

needed to prevent blossom-end rot. If you have acidic soil, adding lime may be necessary every few years because tomatoes prefer a soil pH of about 6.5. Water mature plants infrequently but deeply. Mulch with compost after the soil has warmed thoroughly.

Major pests that afflict tomatoes include tomato hornworms, cutworms, tobacco budworms, nematodes, and whiteflies. A number of diseases are fairly common to tomatoes; they include fusarium wilt, verticillium wilt, alternaria blight, and tobacco mosaic virus. Control diseases by rotating crops, planting resistant varieties, and practicing good garden hygiene.

Harvest tomatoes as they ripen. A rich color and a slight give to the fruit indicate ripeness. Harvest with a slight twist of the wrist or with scissors or shears.

Varieties

Medium to Large Tomatoes

Most of the following recommended varieties are available from Tomato Growers Supply Company and Totally Tomatoes.

ps36912: a new variety that is very orange; bred to contain more lycopene and more beta-carotene than other varieties; look for it soon (with a fancy name) from the breeders, Seminis Seeds

'**Big Rainbow**': 90–100 days; indeterminate; bicolored, beefsteak-type fruit weighing 2 pounds or more; golden orange fruits with ruby red radiating from the blossom end; sweet and meaty; 'Pineapple, Georgia Streak,' and 'Striped German' are very similar varieties

'**Caro Rich**': 80 days; determinate; slightly flattened, 5- to 6-ounce, deep orange fruits have ten times the provitamin A as other tomatoes

'**Cherokee Purple**': 72 days; short vines; unusually colored purplish, red-brown tomato; full of flavor; available from Southern Exposure Seed Exchange

'**Green Zebra**': 75 days; indeterminate; 2-inch amber-green fruits with darker green stripes; light green flesh

'**Italian Gold**' VF: 70 days; determinate; a golden 'Roma' paste tomato, pear-shape; compact plants; prolific

'**Mandarin Cross**': 77 days; indeterminate; succulent 3-inch orange fruits; late to ripen; for gardeners with long growing seasons

'**Taxi**': 64 days; determinate; early; meaty, 3-inch lemon-yellow fruits; compact plants; available from Johnny's Selected Seeds

'**White Beauty**' ('**Snowball**'): 85 days; mild, meaty, creamy white fruits averaging 8 ounces

'**Yellow Brandywine**': 100 days; indeterminate; yellow fruit with creamy texture; extremes of temperature may cause the fruit shape to vary

'**Yellow Stuffer**': 76 days; indeterminate; a hollow, yellow tomato perfect for stuffing; tall, productive vines

Cherry Tomatoes

'**Green Grape**': 70 days; determinate; 1-inch, yellow-green, juicy fruits; short, compact plants

'**Sun Gold**': 57 days; indeterminate; 1-inch, bright orange fruits with delicious flavor; vigorous plants with long clusters of fruits

'**Sweet Gold F1**': 60 days; indeterminate; yellow-gold, 1/2-ounce fruits; vigorous and productive vines; available retail from Renee's Garden

'**Yellow Pear**': 78 days; bite-size, yellow tomatoes shaped like small pears; low in acid; vigorous vines; disease resistant

Currant Tomatoes

Currant tomatoes are huge plants that sprawl and reseed.

'**Yellow Currant**': 62 days; indeterminate; related to the wild, yellow currant tomato of South America; vines produce hundreds of 1/2-inch, sweet, tart fruit; thick-skinned, disease resistant, hardy; available from Harris

How to prepare: To fully enjoy the different colors of tomatoes, serve them raw. The pigments in tomatoes are carotenoids, however, and are fairly stable when cooked. The red pigment lycopene in tomatoes has been found to lower the risk of prostate cancer.

The large-fruited, gold, red, orange, yellow, purple, and green tomatoes are lovely sliced on the salad plate or on top of a fresh tart (recipe, page 77). They can be cut in wedges and arranged on a platter or around a dip plate or on a pizza. Use the rainbow of colorful cherry tomatoes in salads, with dips, as hors d'oeuvres. Sauté briefly in olive oil and garlic and arrange over cheese toasts (recipe, page 68), on a green salad, or in pasta. These colorful little tomatoes can also be dried; they keep much of the color. Try white tomatoes mixed with other colors on a salad plate. Or "mess" with people's minds and make a mystery marinara sauce for pasta (recipe, page 86), or pour a white Bloody Mary.

Top row, from left: 'Mandarin Cross'; 'Yellow Stuffer'; 'Striped Cavern.' *Middle row:* harvest of 'Taxi,' 'Yellow Pear,' and 'Caro Rich' tomatoes; 'White Beauty'; mix of cherry tomatoes. *Bottom row:* Harvest of orange tomatoes; tomato slices; 'Yellow Pear';'Sungold'

WATERMELON
Citrullus lanatus

WATERMELON FLESH CAN BE
red, orange, yellow, peach, even white.

How to grow: For general growing
information about watermelons, see the
"Cucumber" entry on page 40. Melons
are more sensitive to cool conditions
than cucumbers, so in cool-summer
areas use a black plastic mulch to raise
the soil temperature. Reduce watering
toward harvest time; too much water
then results in insipid fruits and split
melons.

Watermelon is ripe when the fruit's
surface skin is dull, tough, and difficult
to puncture with your fingernail; the
bottom of the melon has changed from
green to yellow; and the tendrils on the
stem near the fruit are brown.

Varieties

'Moon and Stars': 100 days; to 30
pounds, pinkish-red flesh, fine flavor; leaves and green rind are covered with golden splotches (moons)
and small gold speckles (stars)

'New Orchid': 80 days; 8 to 10 pounds,
bright orange flesh; available from
Johnny's Selected Seeds

'New Queen': 75 days; orange flesh; 6
pounds; spreads to 9 feet; a 1999 All
American selection; available from
Park Seed Company

'Yellow Doll': 68 days; crisp, sweet, yellow flesh; oval, 4 to 7 pounds

How to prepare: Lycopene is one of
the carotenoids that gives watermelon
its red color. The lovely yellow, orange,
and red flesh of watermelons lends

itself to endless colorful party dishes.
Create sunset salads with cubes of red,
orange, and yellow melons drizzled
with a sweet lime dressing. Make them
into margaritas—cubes stacked in a
goblet and sprinkled with a mixture of
lime, sugar, and tequila. Arrange colorful melon balls in a buffet fruit salad
or a rainbow of watermelon cubes
sprinkled with a spicy Thai mixture of
roasted peanuts, chilies, *nam pla* (a fish
sauce used like soy sauce), and cilantro.
Lay out different colors of watermelon
slices or strips on platters to create a
color shift from yellow to orange to red
or stand them up around the edges of a
crystal bowl filled with crab salad.

'New Queen' *(above)*, 'Yellow Doll' and 'Tiger
Baby' icebox watermelons *(below)*

cooking from the rainbow garden

I've been attracted to vegetables of unusual colors for as long as I can remember. As a gardener I enjoy both their novelty and beauty and as a cook I glory in their eye appeal. And why not? A plate of sliced red, orange, and yellow tomatoes becomes an artistic creation. Further, red, orange, and yellow bell peppers not only look more exciting than green peppers, they taste much better too. Then there's the fact that I'm a "show-off" cook. Through the years I found I could set guests a-twitter when serving pureed 'All Blue' potatoes or lavender vichyssoise or drizzling margaritas over a melange of red, orange, and yellow watermelon cubes!

My experiences with these colorful varieties were not always positive. Twenty years ago, when I was new to

Red, white, and blue potato salad, a tomato tart of many colors, and rings of bell peppers show the range of colorful dishes that utilize vegetables of many hues.

cooking them, most of the chefs and cookbook authors I knew had never even seen blue potatoes much less prepared them. Fumbling in the dark I would gnash my teeth when the lovely lavender vichyssoise I'd visualized turned into a dismal gray soup (through trial and error I learned to start with only the darkest blue potatoes and to add lemon juice to set the

pigments. See the recipe, page 65). I remember making and refrigerating a chiffonade of orange chard stems in the morning only to find them an unappetizing dull, orange-brown at dinner that night. Then there were all those puzzling results: Why did purple asparagus, beans, and cauliflower turn green when cooked but purple cabbage remained purple? Why did red okra lose its color when cooked but red beets and all the red and orange peppers and tomatoes keep their color?

At first, I gleaned a few answers from Jan Blüm and Renee Shepherd as well as a few chefs. Then, bless Harold McGee. In 1984 he wrote *On Food and Cooking,* a fabulous dissertation about the science of cooking including detailed information about pigments in vegetables. With McGee's information I could more reliably predict how a vegetables' color would hold up in the kitchen.

59

Basically, there are four major groups of pigments in plants. Each group has different functions in the plant and in the kitchen. The pigment groups are the chlorophylls, the anthocyanins, the carotenoids, and the betalains. Because vegetables often contain more than one pigment, the color of a vegetable can be deceptive. For example, while the orange carotenoids in carrots are obvious, the same orange pigments are masked in dark green leafy vegetables because of large amounts of chlorophyll.

The Chemistry of Cooking

Chlorophylls: We're most familiar with the chlorophylls and their life-giving ability to take the sun's energy and through photosynthesis convert water and carbon dioxide into sugars. Chlorophylls are the green pigments in leaves and vegetables, and they are marginally stable when cooked. While most green vegetables are not the focus of this book, it certainly is most pleasing to be able to cook them well and produce lovely bright green, not khaki-colored, asparagus and broccoli to combine with other colorful vegetables. It helps, therefore, to know that chlorophyll is affected adversely by heat, acids, different metals, and enzymes. For example, long cooking dulls the color because the cell walls

break down and the green pigments leak out. Green pigment also degrades when the cook covers the pan so acids from the vegetables deposit on the lid and drip back in the water. To keep the green pigments as bright as possible in green vegetables like beans, peas, and spinach, McGee recommends cooking them as quickly as possible in a large volume of boiling water, uncovered, and for a maximum of seven

minutes. Cut large vegetables in pieces so they cook in the allotted seven minutes. Drain them immediately.

Anthocyanins: Anthocyanins comprise a large family of pigments that give flowers, vegetables, and fruits a range of colors from purple and blue to shades of red. The amount in plants can vary from season to season; for instance, pale red kales and lettuces

The red varieties of basil are a great addition to herbal vinegar, turning it a lovely shade of pink.

usually turn a dark burgundy in cold weather. Anthocyanins are water-soluble and the majority fade badly when cooked. I find some anthocyanin pigments more stable than others, even from plant to plant, and I can't always predict their behavior when cooked. This is especially true when these pigments come in contact with acidic and alkaline substances, as anthocyanins are sensitive to pH. The anthocyanin family is so sensitive to pH that they can be used as a rough litmus test. To experience this effect I followed McGee's suggestion: I slivered red cabbage and put half of it in a bowl with a tablespoon of vinegar and the other half in a bowl with two teaspoons of baking soda dissolved in water. As predicted, the vinegar mixture turned bright pink and the baking soda mixture turned a lovely sky blue.

Anthocyanins are the colorful pigments in red cabbage, red mustard, red lettuce, red onions, blue corn, purple basil, purple asparagus, purple artichokes, purple potatoes, purple beans, purple carrots, eggplants, and radishes. (See the individual listings in "The Rainbow Vegetable Encyclopedia" for plant-by-plant details.)

To get the most benefit from the colors, whenever possible I use these vegetables raw. If they need to be cooked, I cook them for as short a time as possible. Some, like purple string beans and asparagus, lose all their purple color and turn green before the vegetable is tender. Others, such as red cabbage and blue potatoes, can be coaxed to keep much of their color, especially if you add lemon juice or

The pigment anthocyanin in red cabbages, basil, and blue potatoes is pH sensitive. They turn blue when put in a baking soda solution *(above)*, and they turn pink in vinegar water. When green vegetables are boiled too long they lose their bright green color. Pictured directly above are overcooked beans on the left and properly cooked beans on the right.

vinegar. The acid helps preserve the color though they turn from purple to magenta.

Carotenoids: Carotenoids consist of a large group of pigments that play an indirect role in photosynthesis. We see these red, yellow, and orange pigments in sweet potatoes, muskmelons, water-

melons, tomatoes, peppers, yellow squash, and carrots. These pigments are fat-soluble; when cooked, they keep most of their color. Carotenoids, however, fade if cooked for a very long time or change color at elevated temperatures. For example, red tomatoes turn yellow-orange when cooked in a pressure cooker. All things considered, the carotenoids are a joy for the color-maven cook. As Harold McGee says, "…compared to the green chlorophylls and multihued anthocyanins, the carotenoids are a model of steadfastness."

Betalains: This is another category of pigments found in only one order of plants, the *Chenopodiales*, a classification (order) of plants that includes the genera Beta and Atriplex. The betalains include the compounds betacyanin and betaxanthin. Betacyanin gives red beets, red chard, and red amaranths their color; betaxanthin gives golden beets and orange chard their bright sunset hues. Unlike the anthocyanins, these rosy pigments are fairly stable if cooked briefly. In my experience, pickling seems to make the colors even more stable. Long cooking gives the vegetables a brownish look. As a note, betalains are never found in combination with anthocyanins.

Super-healthy Vegetables

Pigments and vitamins are related chemicals in vegetables and usually there is a direct correlation between vivid color and their health-giving benefits. The red and orange carotenoids and the blue and red anthocyanins are categorized by scientists not only as pigments but also as phytochemicals (plant chemicals), a broad class of thousands of substances derived from plants that can have a beneficial effect on health. Dr. John

Many breeders, such as those at Seminis Seeds, are introducing vegetables with extra nutrition, such as this as-yet-unnamed red-orange carrot with extra beta carotene.

Navazio, a plant breeder with Alf Christianson Seed Company, prefers to call them phytonutrients, and explains, "Most phytonutrients are antioxidants, that is they collect and remove "free radicals" (highly reactive molecules that have the potential to

damage our DNA and arteries). These antioxidants also may also boost our immune systems; inhibit attacks from bacteria, fungi, and viruses; and help protect against cancer, premature aging, and age-related blindness." Research indicates that relatively high amounts of these chemicals are needed when compared to vitamins; that some work in combination with other phytochemicals and vitamins; and that while all vegetables and fruits contain phytochemicals, they do so in varying degrees. With the latter in mind, plant breeders like John are hard at work developing new varieties especially high in these phytochemicals. Look for new, especially colorful (and thus healthful) vegetable varieties to be introduced in the future. See the many available now that are listed in "The Rainbow Vegetable Encyclopedia."

When preparing these extra-nutritious vegetables, it helps to know that raw vegetables usually have the most color when we use them in recipes, but not necessarily the most nutrition. To quote Dr. Navazio, "While some nutrients are lost in cooking, some become more available. For example, light cooking actually increases beta-carotene availability in carrots and lycopene in tomatoes, probably by softening the tissue and making it more digestible." Further, valuable nutrients are lost when some vegetables are peeled. For instance, much of the lutein in squash is located in the skin; when beets are peeled before boiling, nutrients are lost to the water. Another aspect of rainbow cooking involves creating especially colorful meals. Consequently, a platter of vegetables for a rainbow party platter might include slices of pink radishes, yellow zucchini, purple broccoli florets, snap beans, and orange and red cherry tomatoes. What an array of both colors and nutrients! So you can

see, the most eye appeal, can also mean the most nutrition.

Since the 1970s, research about antioxidants as "chemopreventers" has highlighted carotenoids and anthocyanins with their ability to cut down on cardiovascular disease and certain forms of cancer. The latest information indicates that chlorophylls are antioxidants; betalains may be too, but the carotenoids and the anthocyanins are best documented at this time.

Carotenoids: There are dozens of carotenoids in foods, the most familiar being beta-carotene, one of the orange pigments. Its healthful benefits have been known for years as it is the primary source of provitamin A, which our bodies convert to vitamin A. Vitamin A is an essential nutrient required for a healthy immune system, for growth, for reproduction, and to prevent night blindness. More recently research shows beta-carotene also acts as an antioxidant and may lower the risk of several cancers. Evidence also shows beta-carotene works well only when consumed with other carotenoids, not when isolated in pill form. Further, most Americans consume only 1.5 mg a day, far less than the recommended 5 to 10 mg. Beta-carotene is in many vegetables; for instance, a single sweet potato contains 5 to 10 mg. Other vegetables that are great sources of beta-carotene include carrots, leafy greens including beet greens (generally the darker green the leaf the higher the carotenoid content), broccoli, cantaloupe, orange tomatoes, and red peppers. Another carotenoid,

lycopene, lends its red color to watermelon and tomatoes; evidence shows it may help protect against prostate cancer. Yet another carotenoid, lutein, helps prevent damage to the retina as we age; people who consume little lutein are more apt to suffer from macular degeneration. Lutein is a yellow pigment that gives bright color to summer and winter squashes where it is found primarily in the peel. Lutein is present but masked in spinach, beans, and green peppers.

Anthocyanins: The pigments that make many vegetables red, blue, or violet are in a group of cancer-fighting phytochemicals called flavonoids. Anthocyanins are in red cabbage, basil, and lettuce; purple carrots; blue potatoes and corn; eggplants; and radishes. The healthful effects of anthocyanins are less well known than the carotenoids but John Navazio says they also are considered antioxidants that neutralize free radicals that cause cell damage and protect against cardiovascular diseases and certain cancers.

cooking
with
colors

Now that you know the chemistry of cooking colorful vegetables, it's on to creating Technicolor layouts. First some of the basics.

To arrange colorful raw vegetables on a dip plate, try making combinations. Instead of using orange peppers or tomatoes alone, experiment by combining them with red, green, and yellow varieties too. Salads lend themselves to the multicolor approach. Use red orach, ornamental kale, lavender radishes, and any of the vegetables mentioned above. Arrange them on a plate to enhance their many colors or add them to a conventional tossed salad.

If you are serving the vegetables cooked, look for light, transparent dressings to feature the colors best. Dark or opaque sauces and dressings muddy the colors. For instance, roasting red onions with olive oil and balsamic vinegar features the rosy colors better than a cream sauce; blue and red potato salads look best with a vinaigrette instead of mayonnaise. For many more ideas enjoy Renee Shepherd's interview, the multitude of suggestions in "The Rainbow Vegetable Encyclopedia," and the recipes that follow.

These exotic vegetables should inspire your own creations as perhaps no other produce has. Here's a chance to treat your garden as an artist's palette. Make a multicolored quiche, bicolored paprika from orange and yellow peppers, or nestle a rainbow of red, yellow, and green cherry tomatoes among your spaghetti squash strands. I plan to serve a white Bloody Mary

with a swizzle stick of red celery. Someday I would like to bake tricolored cornbread from my red, blue, and yellow grinding corns; one section of the loaf will be pink, one light blue, and the other yellow. Maybe I'll even use one of those cake pans with compartments to separate the batters to make checkerboard cornbread. With a rainbow garden, the sky's the limit.

In a large saucepan, melt the butter and sauté the onions over medium heat till softened but not browned, about 7 minutes. Add the potatoes and 3 cups of water. Cover and simmer until potatoes are tender, 15 to 20 minutes.

Add the lemon juice, half-and-half, and seasonings and puree the soup in a food processor or blender. Chill and serve cold. Garnish by sprinkling the soup with the chives and the chive flowers, separated into florets.

Serves 4.

Golden Gazpacho

This classic Spanish recipe is usually made with red tomatoes and green peppers, but here I put a spin on the ball and make it with gold tomatoes and yellow bell peppers.

    7 to 10 medium ripe gold tomatoes
    1 large yellow pepper
    1 small onion, or 2 to 3 scallions
    2 garlic cloves, minced
    1/2 green Anaheim chile pepper
    1 small hot red chile pepper, or to
        taste
    1 large or 2 small cucumbers,
        peeled
    1 tablespoon extra virgin olive oil
    1/3 cup white wine vinegar
    1/2 cup dry white wine
    Salt and freshly ground black
        pepper
    3 or 4 sprigs fresh cilantro
    Garnish: cilantro sprigs, a slice of
        tomato, or diced avocado

Lavender-Tinted Vichyssoise

Vichyssoise is an elegant but easily made first course. Make it with blue potatoes and you'll really delight your guests. To get the lavender effect you need to use the very deep purple varieties. The medium or light blue potatoes carried by some seed companies will give you a sickly gray, not lavender, soup. Serve this lavender vichyssoise in white or clear glass bowls so the color is featured, garnished with chives and chive florets.

    2 tablespoons butter
    3 onions, diced (about 3 cups)
    3 to 4 deep-blue potatoes, peeled
        and cubed (about 3 cups)
    1 tablespoon fresh lemon juice
    1 cup half-and-half
    Salt and freshly ground black pepper
    Dash of nutmeg
    Garnish: fresh chive leaves and
        flowers

Immerse the tomatoes in boiling water for 30 seconds, or until the skins have loosened. Peel them and remove the seeds and cores. Remove the seeds and membranes from the yellow pepper. Chop the rest of the vegetables coarsely for processing in the food processor or blender (if you use a food processor the soup will have some crunch; using the blender will give a smoother texture).

Process all ingredients in batches, pouring them into a large nonreactive bowl to mix. Refrigerate the soup at least 3 hours before serving. If the gazpacho is too thick, thin it with a little cold vegetable or chicken stock before serving. Taste and adjust seasonings. Serve the soup in individual bowls and garnish each serving as desired.

Serves 4.

Two Rainbow Chard Relishes

These two chard relishes are both quite spicy and crunchy, yet have very different flavors. Offer them with poultry or mild fish and with egg dishes. Use them within two weeks.

Ruby Chard Relish with Spicy Beets

1 teaspoon whole peppercorns

1 teaspoon whole cloves

1 1/2 cups diced red chard stems
   (3–4 medium stems)

1/2 cup diced cooked red beets (1
   medium beet)

1 tablespoon diced red onion

1/2 teaspoon celery seeds

1/8 teaspoon salt

1 tablespoon honey

1 1/2 cups red wine vinegar

Select a sterilized pint jar that seals well. In the bottom put the peppercorns and cloves. In a small bowl, combine all ingredients except the vinegar and transfer them into the pint jar. Add vinegar until it covers all the ingredients. Screw the top in place and rotate the jar a few times to stir the ingredients. Refrigerate.

To blend the flavors, repeat the rotating process a few times over the next several days. When serving, leave the cloves and peppercorns in the bottom.

Makes about 1 pint.

Golden Chard Relish with Curry

8 pearl onions, peeled

1 cup diced yellow chard stems (2
   to 3 stems)

1 teaspoon yellow mustard seeds

1/2 teaspoon coriander seeds

1/2 cup white wine vinegar

1 tablespoon honey

1 tablespoon curry powder

1 garlic clove, crushed

Pinch of salt

In the bottom of a sterilized 1 1/2-pint jar with a tight fitting lid, put 4 of the onions. Cover the onions with half of the chard stems. Top the chard with the remaining onions and then fill the jar with the rest of the chard.

Combine the remaining ingredients in a small bowl and mix well. Pour them into the jar and rotate it to stir the ingredients. Refrigerate. Rotate the jar a few times a day for the first few days.

Makes 1 cup.

Pickled Golden Beets

When I was a child, my cousin and I got into big trouble by consuming almost the entire batch of my aunt's pickled beets that she had made for a potluck dinner. We started by sampling them but we just couldn't stop. She used red beets, but I like to use golden beets because they don't bleed all over my plate. I serve these beets as a condiment with a salad or to accompany a sandwich. The pickled beets will last a few weeks in the refrigerator.

    6 large or 9 medium Burpee's
        Golden Beets
    1 large sweet white onion, sliced
        thin
    1/3 cup sugar
    1 cup cider vinegar
    Beet juice
    1 teaspoon mixed pickling spices

Remove all but 1 inch of the greens from the beets. Wash the greens and put them in a large kettle. Barely cover the beets with water, and boil until just tender. (Depending on the size of the beets, this will take 1 hour to 1 hour and 20 minutes). Drain the beets and reserve the liquid. Set them aside to cool. Peel the beets and cut them into thin slices.

In two wide-mouth (pint-size) sterilized mason jars, layer the beets with the onion slices within a half inch of the top. In a saucepan put the sugar, vinegar, about a cup of the reserved beet juice, and the pickling spices and bring to a boil.

Pour the hot pickling mixture over the beets and onions until they are completely covered. (If you run out of pickling liquid, top the jars off with hot beet juice.) Close the jars. Cool them slightly and refrigerate until ready to serve.

Makes 2 pints.

[note]

Pickling spices are a combination of mustard seeds, cloves, cinnamon, peppercorns, hot peppers, celery seeds, and coriander seeds.

Toy Box Cherry Tomatoes with Warm Gruyère Cheese Toasts

Doug Gosling, of the Occidental Arts and Ecology Center in Occidental, California, sold a mix of different cherry tomatoes at farmer's markets for years and called them his Toy Box selection. Jesse Cool, executive chef and owner of Flea Street Café in Menlo Park, California, takes Gosling's colorful concept to the table in the following rustic appetizer.

For the marinated tomatoes:

2 tablespoons chopped chives

$1/4$ cup finely chopped parsley

1 tablespoon finely chopped rose-
	mary

1 tablespoon finely chopped basil

$1/3$ cup extra virgin olive oil

2 garlic cloves, minced

3 tablespoons balsamic vinegar

Salt and freshly ground black pepper

2 pounds (5 to 6 cups) cherry
	tomatoes of all colors: select
	from Green Grape, Red Cherry,
	Yellow Pear, Locerno's Ivory
	Pear, Sweet 100, Sun Gold, and
	many others

For the Gruyère cheese toasts:

2 tablespoons extra virgin olive oil

3 garlic cloves, finely chopped

4 large slices of thick rustic Italian
	bread

4 thin slices Gruyère cheese, $1/2$
	ounce each slice

To make the marinated tomatoes: In a large bowl, put the chives, parsley, rosemary, basil, olive oil, and vinegar and mix. Add salt and pepper and stir to combine. Add the tomatoes, cover, and marinate for a minimum of an hour.

To make the toasts: Preheat the broiler. Mix the olive oil with the garlic and let sit 10 minutes. Brush the mixture on one side of each slice of bread. Broil the brushed side until lightly browned. Put a piece of cheese on the raw side of each piece of bread and set the bread aside until the tomatoes are ready.

Just before serving, preheat broiler again if necessary. Lay bread on a rack or cookie sheet and toast under the broiler 2 or 3 minutes or until the cheese has melted.

To assemble, place a slice of still-warm toasted bread on a plate or in a shallow soup bowl. Spoon one quarter of the tomatoes and some of the marinade around each piece of toast.

Serves 4.

Romano Bean Salad with Grilled Tuna

This mid-summer treat is great with crusty bread, and just right for a light fancy lunch.

For the dressing:

1/2 cup extra virgin olive oil

3 to 4 tablespoons fresh lemon juice

Salt and freshly ground black pepper

For the salad:

1/2 small red onion, thinly sliced

1 teaspoon salt

1 medium red bell pepper

1 1/2 pounds green and gold Romano beans, sliced 1 inch on the bias (about 4 cups)

Optional: 3-inch sprig of fresh winter savory

8 to 10 leaves butter or leaf lettuce

1/2 to 2/3 pound fresh tuna fillet

To make the dressing: In a small bowl, whisk the olive oil, lemon juice, salt, and pepper together until they emulsify and set aside.

To make the salad: Put the onion slices into a small bowl, cover them with cold water, and add the salt. Mix together and let them sit for 1 hour to remove some of the bite.

Meanwhile, roast the pepper over the flame of a gas stove, or under a broiler until charred. Place the charred pepper into a brown paper bag and let it cool. When it is cool enough to handle, remove the seeds, scrape off the skin, and cut the pepper into 1/2-inch strips. Set them aside.

Steam the beans with the (optional) savory over simmering water about 5 minutes or until just tender. Drain the beans, discarding the savory. Shock the beans in ice water until they are chilled and drain again. Drain the onion slices. Arrange the butter lettuce leaves on a serving platter or in a large flat bowl. Arrange the beans, onion slices, and peppers over top.

Meanwhile, preheat the grill. Brush the tuna with one tablespoon of the dressing mixture. Over high heat, grill the tuna to medium rare for about 7 minutes on each side. Cut the fish on the bias into 1/2-inch-thick slices and arrange them on the vegetables. Drizzle the remaining dressing over the tuna and the vegetables. Serve immediately.

Serves 4.

Riot of Color Salad

How about a really colorful salad for a special occasion? Use your imagination and the prettiest edible flowers from your garden.

For the dressing:

> 1 ¹/₂ tablespoons white wine
>   vinegar
> 3 to 4 tablespoons sunflower oil
> 1 tablespoon clover or wildflower
>   honey
> Salt and freshly ground black pepper

For the salad:

> 1 large head romaine lettuce
> 1 head butter lettuce
> 1 small head frisée
> 4 to 6 young leaves of yellow chard
> About a dozen edible flowers such
>   as yellow and blue violas, pur-
>   ple pansies, nasturtiums, yellow
>   calendulas, and red dianthus

To make the dressing: In a small bowl, combine the vinegar, sunflower oil, honey, salt and pepper. Set aside.

To make the salad: Arrange the romaine lettuce, butter lettuce, and chard leaves on a large colorful platter. Separate the flowers into petals, reserv-ing some whole. Sprinkle the greens with flower petals and garnish with the whole blossoms. Bring the salad to the table and let diners dress their own salad.

Serves 4.

Rainbow Party Slaw with Chard

For a party dish this slaw is fairly low in calories. Serve it with grilled vegetables, fish, or as part of a buffet selection.

For the dressing:

Juice of 1 lemon

2/3 cup white wine vinegar

1 teaspoon salt

3/4 teaspoon celery seeds

1/3 cup vegetable oil

3 to 4 tablespoons frozen apple
    juice concentrate

Freshly ground black pepper

For the Salad:

1 large green cabbage, finely sliced
    (about 8 cups)

1 cup thinly sliced chard leaves

2 cups finely sliced carrots (about 4
    carrots)

1 small sweet onion, thinly sliced

1 cup thinly sliced red chard stems
    (about 4 chard stems)

To make the dressing: In a small bowl, combine the lemon juice, vinegar, salt, celery seeds, oil, apple concentrate, and pepper. Stir until well blended. Set aside.

To make the salad: Place the cabbage in the bottom of a large salad bowl. Creating a decorative pattern, arrange the chard leaves, the carrots, the onions and finally, the chard stems on top of the cabbage.

Pour the dressing over the sliced vegetables and serve. The salad may be refrigerated for a few hours, but the dressing will separate and the red chard stems will lose some of their color if it sits too long.

Serves 8 to 10.

Red, White, and Green Radish Salad

This recipe is another imaginative creation from Renee Shepherd, of Renee's Garden, and Fran Raboff who work together to develop novel recipes.

For the dressing:

1 tablespoon fresh lemon juice

1 tablespoon raspberry vinegar

1 teaspoon stone-ground mustard

1 teaspoon sugar

3 tablespoons extra virgin olive oil

Salt and freshly ground black pepper

For the salad:

2 bunches Easter Egg radishes,
    thinly sliced

1/4 cup chopped red onions

3 tablespoons chopped fennel leaves

1 fennel bulb, diced

1/2 cup thinly sliced scallions,
    including part of the green

1 large unpeeled green apple, diced

1/4 cup dried currants

Garnish: 1/3 cup coarsely chopped
    toasted walnuts

To make the salad: Combine the dressing ingredients and whisk until blended.

In a salad bowl, combine the radishes, onion, fennel leaves, fennel bulb, scallions, apple, and currants. Pour the dressing over the salad, tossing until mixed. Refrigerate the salad for several hours before serving. Garnish the salad with the chopped walnuts before serving.

Serves 6.

Rainbow Beets Vinaigrette

I like to make this recipe with beets of many colors: gold, red, white, and pink. I steam rather then boil them, so the red and gold beets do not bleed all over the pink and white ones. The greens are delicious too. Steam them separately and they can be served on the same plate with the beets.

6 medium beets, of assorted colors

3 tablespoons balsamic vinegar

1/3 cup extra virgin olive oil

1/2 teaspoon minced fresh tarragon
    or dill

Salt and freshly ground black pepper

Wash the beets and steam them for about 40 minutes, or until they are just tender. Cool then peel and slice them.

In a bowl, put the vinegar, oil, herbs, and seasonings and stir. Pour the dressing over the beets and let them marinate for about 1 hour. Serve hot or cold. Serves 4.

Garden Celebration Salad

This dish is a busy assembly project and takes lots of bowls, but it requires little in the way of technique. It provides plenty of room for creativity and makes a spectacular party salad. Some of the vegetables work best when cooked, others when raw. As with any good garden recipe, the ingredient list is fluid and can be varied by the season and by what's in the garden.

The salad has 5 layers of colors, each layer with a slightly different flavor combination. Suggested vegetables and herbs for the orange/gold layer include slivered carrots, chopped orange peppers, gold beets, and sliced gold tomatoes; for the yellow layer: yellow zucchini, wax beans, chopped yellow peppers, and sliced yellow tomatoes. For the green layer choose among: chopped lettuces, cabbages, baby spinach, snow pea pods, scallions, and any of the herbs: parsley, chives, basil, fennel, or savory. For the red layer I suggest: red beets, tomatoes, and peppers; and for the purple layer: chopped red cabbage, magenta radicchio, and blue potatoes.

I've given directions for stacking the prepared vegetables in a glass trifle bowl to reveal the colors through the sides of the bowl, but the same ingredients can be laid out on a large colorful platter instead. If you use a clear glass bowl, the moisture from the vegetables will condense on the bowl when you add hot ingredients or when you bring it out of the refrigerator. Let the bowl stand at room temperature before serving time to give the condensation time to evaporate.

For the garlic vinaigrette:

2 garlic cloves, minced

1 tablespoon Dijon mustard

1/2 cup extra virgin olive oil

1/4 cup white wine vinegar

Freshly ground black pepper and salt

For the salad:

1 pound yellow zucchini, sliced

1 pound yellow wax beans cut in 2-inch sections

1 medium yellow sweet pepper, chopped

1 pound green zucchini, sliced

1 pound green beans cut in 2-inch sections

4 tablespoons chopped scallion greens

1/2 teaspoon minced fresh savory

1 small red cabbage, shredded

1 medium red sweet pepper, chopped

3 red paste tomatoes, sliced

1/3 teaspoon red pepper flakes

1 medium orange sweet pepper, chopped

3 orange paste tomatoes, sliced

3 medium golden beets, steamed 30 minutes, peeled and sliced

For the honey vinaigrette:

1/4 cup extra virgin olive oil

1 teaspoon honey

2 tablespoons white wine vinegar

1/8 teaspoon red pepper flakes

To make the vinaigrettes: In two separate bowls, whisk together the ingredients for each of the vinaigrettes and set them aside.

To prepare the salad layers: Bring a large pot of salted water to a boil. First cook the yellow zucchini, then the yellow wax beans for 3 minutes each, or until just tender. After each batch is done remove the vegetables from the cooking water with a slotted spoon and refresh them for a couple of seconds in a bowl of ice water to keep their color. Drain the vegetables and put them in a small bowl. Add the yellow pepper and toss with 1/4 cup of garlic vinaigrette.

Repeat the process with the green zucchini and green beans. When the vegetables are at room temperature, toss the contents of the bowl with 1/4 cup more of garlic vinaigrette. Set aside to marinate for about 10 minutes, then sprinkle with the scallions and savory.

Mix the shredded red cabbage with the remaning garlic vinaigrette and set it aside.

In a fourth bowl, combine the red pepper, red tomato, and red pepper flakes.

In a fifth bowl combine the orange pepppers, the orange tomatoes, and the golden beets.

To assemble the salad: You will need a glass bowl 5 inches wide and 8 inches deep. A traditional footed trifle bowl works well. Each layer of vegetables needs to be about 1 inch thick.

Build the salad by first layering the marinated yellow vegetables 1 inch deep on the bottom. On top of this create a green layer. Create the third purple layer with the red cabbage.

Cover with the red layer and finally the orange layer. Glaze the top of the salad with the honey dressing. Serve immediately.

Serves 12 to 14 for a buffet.

Red, White, and Blue Potato Salad

This potato salad is an eye-catching addition to luncheons, particularly around the Fourth of July and elections. If you have no blue potatoes in your garden, they are occasionally available from specialty produce markets. Select only the deep blue-fleshed potatoes as the light and medium blue-fleshed ones turn an unappetizing gray when boiled. Blue-fleshed potatoes can be used in any potato salad recipe, but the color is best featured when a clear dressing is used.

For the dressing:

2 tablespoons rich chicken stock

1/4 cup white wine vinegar

2 tablespoons dry white wine or white vermouth

Salt and freshly ground pepper to taste

1/2 cup extra virgin olive oil

1 tablespoon chopped parsley

1 tablespoon fresh chopped tarragon

For the salad:

4 medium white boiling potatoes

4 medium deep blue-fleshed potatoes (or 2 blue- and 2 red-fleshed potatoes)

1/2 cup thinly sliced red bell peppers

1/2 teaspoon freshly ground pepper

To make the dressing: In a small bowl, mix the chicken stock, vinegar, wine, salt, and pepper until the salt is dissolved. Slowly, whisk in the olive oil. Add the parsley and the tarragon and stir well to combine.

To make the salad: In two separate pots, boil the 2 or 3 colors of potatoes for 20 to 30 minutes until just barely tender when stuck with a fork. While still warm, peel the potatoes and slice them into 1/4-inch-thick slices.

Place the potatoes in a large salad bowl, alternating layers of blue and white potatoes with the red peppers. Pour the dressing over the still-warm potatoes and sprinkle with the pepper. Toss gently so the dressing gets evenly dispersed and the potatoes don't fall apart. (If the potatoes are overcooked or the mixing is too vigorous it will cause the separate colors of potatoes to mingle and the result will be a muddy looking salad.)

Let the salad sit for 3 or 4 hours so the flavors will meld. Serve the salad at room temperature or chilled.

Serves 4 to 6.

Multi-Colored Tomato Wedges

This salad is a simple but elegant way to show off the kaleidoscope of tomato colors in your garden.

For the vinaigrette:

1 1/2 tablespoons balsamic vinegar

1 teaspoon chopped fresh thyme leaves

1/4 cup extra virgin olive oil

Optional: salt and pepper

For the salad:

3 red paste tomatoes

2 orange gold paste tomatoes

1 yellow tomato

2 Green Zebra tomatoes

1 purple tomato

Garnish: sprigs of fresh thyme

To make the salad: In a small bowl, combine the vinaigrette ingredients and whisk until they emulsify. Set aside.

Cut the tomatoes into equal-sized wedges. Arrange them in a shallow round or oval bowl so the skin sides of the tomatoes are showing. Drizzle them with the vinaigrette and garnish with the fresh thyme sprigs.

Serves 6.

Braised Red Cabbage

This dish is most often associated with northern France and Germany. The brilliant red color is achieved by adding acidic vinegar and red wine to the cabbage. Serve this cabbage dish with roast chicken or pork and mashed potatoes.

2 tablespoons butter

1 onion, thinly sliced

1 medium red cabbage, shredded
(about 8 cups)

1 tart apple, peeled, cored, and
sliced

1 tablespoon sugar

1 tablespoon red wine vinegar

1/2 cup good red wine

1 bay leaf

Salt and freshly ground black
pepper

Melt the butter in a Dutch oven or a soup pot. Add the onions and sauté them over medium heat until they are soft, about 7 minutes. Add the cabbage, apple, sugar, vinegar, red wine and the bay leaf. Stir the ingredients together and simmer on low for 30 to 40 minutes, or until the cabbage is tender. Remove the bay leaf and season with salt and pepper.

Serves 6.

Grilled Red and Gold Peppers with Melted Anchovies, Garlic, and Basil Sauce

This is one of Renee Shepherd's favorite recipes. Once I made it I had to agree. She developed it when working with her cooking partner Fran Raboff. Accompany the peppers with slices of crusty bread.

2 large sweet peppers, one red and
one yellow

1 tablespoon extra virgin olive oil

1–2 ounce can anchovies, drained
and coarsely chopped

6 garlic cloves, minced

2 tablespoons balsamic vinegar

1/2 cup chopped fresh Italian
parsley

1/2 cup chopped fresh basil

Preheat a charcoal grill. Remove the seeds and membranes from the peppers and cut them lengthwise into 1-inch-wide strips. Brush them with olive oil and grill them over charcoal until they are slightly charred and tender, from 5 to 7 minutes. Put the peppers aside.

In a heavy skillet, heat one tablespoon of olive oil. Add the chopped anchovies and the garlic and cook over low to medium heat, stirring, until the anchovies melt and the garlic is fragrant, about 2 to 3 minutes. Stir in the balsamic vinegar. Add the parsley and basil and remove from the heat.

Arrange the grilled pepper strips on a serving platter and spoon the sauce over them. Serve immediately.

Serves 4.

Golden Tomato Tart

This spectacular tart can be served as an appetizer or as an entree for a light lunch. It is quite dramatic, made with gold tomatoes or any combination of colorful homegrown luscious tomatoes. Any leftover marinade can be used as a base for a vinaigrette dressing.

For the marinated tomatoes:

> 4 to 5 medium gold tomatoes, thinly sliced
> 6 to 7 gold cherry or pear tomatoes, halved
> 1/2 cup extra virgin olive oil
> 1 to 2 garlic cloves, crushed
> 2 tablespoons chopped fresh parsley
> 1 tablespoon minced fresh chives
> Freshly ground black pepper

For the filling:

> 1 cup soft goat cheese or natural cream cheese
> 3 to 4 tablespoons heavy cream
> 1 tablespoon minced fresh rosemary
> 1 9-inch prebaked pie shell

Put both kinds of tomatoes into a bowl. In another bowl combine the ingredients for the marinade. Set aside 1/4 cup of the marinade and pour the rest over the sliced tomatoes. Marinate them for at least 1 hour.

In a mixing bowl, combine the cheese with the cream and work them into a smooth, creamy consistency that will spread easily. Mix in the rosemary and spread the cheese mixture over the cooled pie crust.

Arrange drained tomato slices in a single-layered circular pattern over cheese mixture, using the large slices for the outside and one slice for the middle. Fill in between the rows of large tomatoes with halved cherry tomatoes. Refrigerate until ready to serve. Just before serving, glaze the tomatoes with a 1/4 cup of the marinating mixture.

Serves 6 as an appetizer.

Grandma Alice's Summer Vegetables

This recipe was given to me by Renee Shepherd of Renee's Garden. Renee's Grandma Alice made this dish for her when she was a kid after she let her pick all the vegetables. Renee loved all the colors. Here, the onions and carrots add sweetness while the fresh squash tastes quite nutty and creamy.

When I tried it I used small squash cut in pieces, as Renee recommends. Subsequently, I have also made it using only the tiniest baby squashes, such as pattypans, crooknecks, and zucchini, along with baby carrots. In that case, the squash and carrots should be left whole to really enjoy their beauty.

4 to 5 cups green and gold summer squashes, cut into 1-inch pieces (4 to 5 medium squashes)
1 cup sliced carrots (2 medium carrots)
1 large onion, coarsely chopped
1 cup rich chicken stock
2 tablespoons butter
2 1/2 tablespoons chopped fresh dill
1 tablespoon chopped fresh Italian parsley
Salt and freshly ground black pepper
2 tablespoons freshly grated Parmesan or Asiago cheese

In a 3-quart Dutch oven, combine the vegetables with the chicken broth and the butter. Bring the mixture to a boil and then reduce the heat and simmer for about 8 to 10 minutes or until the carrots and squash are just tender.

Remove the pan from the heat and mix in the dill, parsley, salt and pepper. Serve immediately with the freshly grated Parmesan or Asiago cheese.

Serves 6.

Show-Off Barbecued Vegetables

One of the tastiest and showiest ways to prepare summer vegetables is a quick and easy adaptation of the ever-popular barbecue. Although meat, fish, or poultry can be a nice complement, the vegetables are so good cooked this way; one is tempted to dispense with the rest.

If you are limited by the size of your grill you may have to cook the vegetables in more than one batch. Also consider that some of the vegetables cook at different rates. Peppers need the least amount of time, followed by the eggplant, squash, and onions.

For the seasoned oil:

- 1 cup extra virgin olive oil
- 2 garlic cloves, crushed
- 1/4 cup minced fresh basil or 1 tablespoon minced fresh rosemary

For the vegetables:

- 2 (medium to large) eggplants, cut into 1/2-inch-thick rounds
- 2 to 4 assorted colored summer squash, depending on their size (if large, cut diagonally into 1/2-inch-thick slices; if small, slice lengthwise into halves or leave whole)
- 4 small red onions whole, or 1 large onion, quartered
- 2 to 4 sweet red or yellow peppers, halved and seeded
- Salt and freshly ground black pepper

To make the seasoned oil: In a small bowl, mix the olive oil, garlic, and herbs and let them marinate at least 2 hours. (Refrigerate them if they are left to stand much longer).

To make the vegetables: Prepare the barbecue with charcoal and preheat. Meanwhile, place the vegetable slices on a cookie sheet and brush them with the seasoned oil. When the coals die down and are ready, spread them evenly around the bottom of the barbecue kettle. Place the vegetables oiled-side down on the grill. Brush the top sides of the vegetables with the oil and turn them when they are starting to brown.

Cooking time will vary in accordance with heat, distance from coals, and size and density of the vegetables. Over medium coals, expect average cooking time to be about 4 minutes on the first side and 3 minutes on the second side, but watch them carefully. Cook the vegetables until they are just tender, as they will fall apart if they are overcooked. Sprinkle with salt and pepper and serve.

Serves 4.

Cauliflower Mold with Lemon-Leek Béchamel Sauce

This is a fun way to feature different colored cauliflower.

For the mold:

> 1 head each of yellow, white, and
> Romanesco cauliflower (about 1
> pound each)
> 1 teaspoon butter

To make the mold: Cut equal-sized florets off the cauliflower. In a large pot bring 3 cups of water to a rolling boil. First cook the white cauliflower for 4 minutes and then the yellow and Rom-anesco. Drain the florets and reserve about $1/2$ cup of the cooking water.

Butter a rounded stainless steel or glass bowl (about 8 inches wide and 5 inches deep). Line the bowl with alternating cauliflower colors, starting with a cluster of Romanesco in the center, then a ring of white, then yellow, and so on, until the bowl is filled. All the florets should have their stems pointing inward and their florets pressed against the bowl.

Fill the center with smaller pieces and sprinkle with salt and pepper. Cover the mold with buttered parchment paper and press down lightly to compact.

For the sauce:

> 2 tablespoons butter
> 1 leek, light green parts only, sliced
> and cleaned (about 1 cup)
> 2 tablespoons all-purpose flour
> 1 cup milk
> $1/4$ cup cooking water from the
> cauliflower

> 2 tablespoons fresh lemon juice
> Dash of freshly grated nutmeg
> Salt and freshly ground black pepper

To make the sauce: In a saucepan melt the butter and over medium heat sauté the leeks until tender, about 10 minutes. Add the flour and cook for another 2 minutes while stirring.

Add the milk a little at a time, continuing to stir until the sauce is free of lumps. Add $1/4$ cup of the cauliflower cooking water, the lemon juice, a grating of nutmeg and the salt and pepper to taste. If the sauce is too thick, add a little more cooking water and reserve.

Before serving, reheat the mold in a hot water bath for 10 minutes. To serve, place a warm plate on top of the mold and invert the mold with the plate. Gently remove the mold. Serve with the lemon-leek béchamel sauce.

Serves 6.

Yellow Tomatoes Stuffed with Shrimp and Salsa

not as easy to hollow out without having them rip.

> 4 large yellow stuffing tomatoes
> 1 medium avocado
> 1 teaspoon fresh lemon juice
> 1/2 pound cooked baby shrimp
> 1 cup fresh salsa, or your favorite commercial salsa
> Garnish: sprigs of fresh cilantro

This is quick, but zesty first course for a summer dinner. The unusual tomatoes will throw your guests for a loop. Stuffing tomatoes have an extra large cavity and fairly solid walls. Other large tomatoes can be used for this recipe but they are just

Cut the top off the stuffing tomatoes and remove the seeds and liquid from the cavity. Stand them upright on a serving plate. If they are not even on the bottom, carefully slice a little off the bottom to make them level, but careful to not cut through the outside wall.

Cut the avocado into 1/2-inch cubes, place in a bowl, sprinkle with the lemon juice and stir. Add the baby shrimp and the salsa and gently mix the ingredients together. Stuff the tomato cavities with the filling and garnish with the cilantro leaves.

Serves 4.

Sunny Delight Squash Blossom Omelet

Squash blossoms can be combined with red peppers and yellow zucchini for a colorful and especially tasty entree. Choose from Sunny Delight, Gold Rush, Golden Dawn, Sunburst, and Yellow Crookneck yellow summer squashes for the brightest colors.

For the filling:

> 2 tablespoons extra virgin olive oil
> 1 medium red onion, thinly sliced
> 1 garlic clove, minced
> 1 medium red bell pepper, seeded
>   and chopped
> 6 baby yellow and green summer
>   squash, cut in half lengthwise
> 6 large squash blossoms
> 2 tablespoons chopped fresh basil
> 1/2 teaspoon salt
> Freshly ground black pepper

For the omelet:

> 1 teaspoon olive oil
> 6 large eggs
> 4 tablespoons grated Parmesan
>   cheese
> Garnish: 2 tablespoons snipped
>   fresh chives and extra whole
>   squash blossooms

To make the filling: In a large nonstick sauté pan, heat the olive oil and sauté the onions over medium heat until soft, about 7 minutes. Add the garlic and bell peppers and cook for 5 minutes or until tender. Remove the onion mixture to a bowl and set it aside. Put the yellow and green summer squash in the same pan and sauté them until lightly browned. Combine the onion mixture with the squash in the pan.

Carefully open the squash blossoms and remove any possible critters. Remove the stamens and pistils and coarsely chop the flowers. Add the chopped blossoms and the basil to the zucchini pan, season with the salt and pepper, cover and set aside.

To make the omelet: In a small mixing bowl, mix 3 of the eggs using a fork. In a nonstick 8- to 10-inch sauté pan, heat the olive oil until hot, but not smoking. Pour the eggs into the pan (they should sizzle). Tilt the pan in a few directions to assure that the mixture evenly coats the pan. Give the mixture a gentle shake to make sure it is not sticking. With a spatula, gently lift sections of the cooked portions and let a little of the uncooked egg flow underneath.

When most of the egg is set but the top is still moist, sprinkle 2 tablespoons of the Parmesan cheese over one half of the omelet. Spoon half of the vegetable filling over the cheese. With a spatula make sure the omelet is not sticking and then gently fold the other half of the omelet over the filling.

Slide the omelet onto a preheated plate, garnish with the chives and squash blossoms. Repeat the process for the second omelet.

Serves 2.

Rainbow Pepper Pizza with Pesto

Colorful wedges of peppers arranged in a color shift on a pesto base makes this pizza party fare. It can be made with only one or two colors of peppers and in any pattern, it will taste the same.

For the pesto:

- 2/3 cup extra virgin olive oil
- 4 tablespoons pine nuts
- 4 garlic cloves, minced
- 2 1/2 cups loosely packed fresh basil leaves
- 2/3 cup freshly grated Parmesan cheese
- Salt and freshly ground black pepper

For the pizza:

- 1 tablespoon extra virgin olive oil
- 1 large yellow onion, thinly sliced
- 1/4 teaspoon red pepper flakes, or to taste
- 1/2 cup fresh basil leaves, chopped
- 1/2 teaspoon dry oregano leaves
- 1 cup plus 1/2 cup grated mozzarella cheese (about 6 ounces)
- A combination of red, yellow, orange, ivory, and green bell peppers cut into thin strips with colors kept separate (about 1/3 cup of each color)
- 1 12-inch prebaked commercial pizza shell

To make the pesto: In a blender or food processor, place 3 tablespoons of the olive oil, the pine nuts, garlic, and the basil. Process for 1 minute or so, stopping the machine occasionally to push the basil leaves down and clean the sides of the container. Continue processing, adding the rest of the olive oil. Process until the mixture is smooth. Transfer the pesto to a bowl, stir in the Parmesan cheese and season to taste with salt and freshly ground black pepper.

To make the pizza: Preheat the oven to 450°F. Spread the pesto evenly up to 1 inch from the edge of the pizza shell.

In a large nonstick frying pan, heat the olive oil and sauté the onions over medium heat until translucent, about 7 minutes. Spread the onions evenly over the pesto base.

Sprinkle the pepper flakes, chopped basil, oregano, and 1 cup of mozzarella cheese evenly over the onion mixture.

Place the orange and red pepper slices in a single layer in the frying pan used for the onions and gently sauté until they are limp but not brown. Add a little oil if they start to stick. (To simplify the recipe, all the peppers can be cooked together. If you want to achieve a rainbow effect, however, you need to separate the red and orange peppers from each other and the other colors as their pigments bleed.)

Repeat the process, cooking the yellow, ivory, and green peppers together. To give the rainbow effect, keep the red peppers separate and arrange them over a fifth of the pizza in a wedge pattern. Repeat the process with the orange, yellow, ivory and green bell peppers, covering the whole pizza shell in a wedge pattern. Sprinkle the remaining 1/2 cup mozzarella cheese evenly over the peppers.

Bake for 12 to 14 minutes, or until the cheese has melted and started to brown.

Serves 4.

Technicolor Nachos

Tortilla chips and peppers come in many colors. This recipe is a variation on a tried-and-true restaurant dish.

- 12 ounces corn tortilla chips (red or blue or a combination of both)
- 1 pound of pepper Jack cheese, grated
- 1 1/2 cups roasted pepper strips, of all different colors
- 1 teaspoon ground cumin
- 2 tablespoon freshly chopped cilantro
- 1 cup fresh salsa, or your favorite commercial salsa

Preheat the oven to 350°F. Place one layer of chips in a baking dish. Sprinkle with 1/3 each of the cheese, the pepper strips, and the cumin. Repeat with a second and third layer. Bake until the cheese has melted and started to brown, about 3 to 5 minutes. Watch carefully to avoid burning the chips. Garnish the nachos with the cilantro and serve with the salsa.

Serves 4.

Kaleidoscope Tacos

These unusually colorful tacos are best served "do-it-yourself" style. Every diner assembles their own, according to taste.

For the guacamole:

- 1 ripe avocado
- 1 teaspoon fresh lime juice
- 1 teaspoon sour cream
- 1/2 teaspoon chile powder

Cut the avocado in half; remove the pit and the peel. In a small bowl, mash the avocado with a fork, add the lime juice, sour cream, and chile powder. Mix until smooth and creamy. Place in a small bowl, cover with plastic wrap, and refrigerate until ready to serve.

For the salsa:

- 2 yellow or orange tomatoes, chopped
- 2 tablespoons chopped red onion
- 1 small avocado, peeled, pitted, and chopped
- 1 teaspoon minced jalapeño pepper
- 1 tablespoon minced fresh cilantro
- 2 tablespoons fresh lime juice
- 2 tablespoons extra virgin olive oil
- 1/4 teaspoon ground cumin
- 1/8 teaspoon salt
- Freshly ground black pepper

In a bowl, combine the tomatoes, red onion, avocado, jalapeño pepper, and the cilantro with the lime juice, olive oil, cumin, and salt and pepper. Cover with plastic wrap and set aside.

For the taco filling:

- 4 ears Ruby Queen corn, husked
- 1 (15-ounce) can black beans
- 1/2 pound French feta cheese, sliced
- 1 yellow or orange bell pepper, sliced
- 6 leaves romaine lettuce, chopped
- 12 corn tortillas (1 14-ounce package)

Cook the ears of corn in the microwave on high for about 2 minutes each. (Cooking them in the microwave will preserve the red color.) With a sharp knife, cut off the kernels. Set them aside in a small bowl.

Drain the beans into a sieve; rinse them with cold water and set aside in a small bowl. Place cheese, peppers, and lettuce in separate bowls.

To make the tacos: Preheat the grill. Toast the corn tortillas on the hot grill for 10 to 20 seconds on each side. Present the guacamole, salsa, and the filling ingredients in bowls at the dining table.

Each diner should fill a tortilla with about 1 tablespoon each of guacamole, salsa, corn kernels, and the black beans, then add several slices of feta cheese and bell pepper and the romaine and then fold them together to eat.

Serves 4.

Mystery Marinara

This dish can really confuse guests. If
you do not tell them it's made with
tomatoes, they rarely guess correctly.
The light-colored tomatoes are generally sweeter than the red ones and have
an elusive taste of their own. Serve this
meal with a salad and a crusty French
baguette.

2 pounds white or cream-colored
   tomatoes: Locerno's Ivory Pearl,
   or White Beauty
1 tablespoon butter
1 small onion, minced (about 2/3 cup)
2 garlic cloves, minced

1/2 teaspoon dried herbs: choose a
   combination of marjoram,
   thyme, rosemary, and oregano
Salt and freshly ground black pepper
1 pound fresh spinach fettuccine
1/3 cup heavy cream
Grated Parmesan cheese

Put the tomatoes into a large saucepan
and pierce their skins with a sharp
knife. Cover and bring to the boil, then
simmer for about 5 minutes, or until
the tomatoes are soft. Transfer them to
a food mill and strain out the seeds and
skins (I use the food mill attachment to
my stand mixer).

In a sauté pan, melt the butter and
sauté the onions and garlic over low
heat for about 7 minutes or until the
onions are translucent.

Return the tomato puree to the
saucepan and add the onion and garlic
mixture and the herbs. Simmer the
sauce over low heat till it has reduced
to 1 1/2 cups, about 40 minutes. (Most
light-colored tomatoes are quite juicy
and need to be cooked quite a long
time.) Season with salt and pepper
to taste.

Meanwhile, cook the fettuccine
according to the directions on the
package. Drain and put them into a
warm serving bowl. Add the cream to
the sauce and stir. Heat the sauce to
serving temperature, but do not boil or
it will separate. Pour the sauce over the
fettuccine and serve with grated
Parmesan cheese.

Serves 4 to 6.

Golden Chard Dessert Tart

It is not unusual in Italy to have ricotta cheese in a tart. This version is enriched with golden grapes and chard. It makes a lovely, not-too-sweet finale to a meal.

For the crust:

    2 cups all-purpose flour
    1/2 cup ground blanched almonds
    1/4 cup sugar
    3/4 cup butter, cut in small pieces,
        at room temperature
    1 egg yolk

For the filling:

    3 eggs
    15 ounces low-fat ricotta cheese
    1/4 cup honey
    1/4 cup dry white wine
    Dash of grated nutmeg
    2 cups finely chopped golden chard
        leaves and tender stems, (about
        5 medium leaves)
    1 tablespoon chopped fresh mint
    1 1/2 cups grated yellow squash,
        (about 1 large squash)

To make the crust: In the bowl of a stand mixer combine the flour, almonds, and sugar and stir. Add the butter and the egg yolk to the dry ingredients. Using the paddle attachment, beat on medium speed until the mixture is the texture of coarse corn meal. Gather into a ball, wrap in plastic wrap and refrigerate the dough for 15 minutes.

Preheat the oven to 375°F. Press the dough evenly into a 9-inch tart or pie pan. Cover it with parchment paper or aluminum foil and chill the crust for 15 minutes. Before prebaking the shell, fill its cavity with dry beans or rice to weigh down the crust so it will not bubble up. Bake for 10 minutes. Remove the paper and the beans and rice used as weights and reserve.

To prepare the filling: In a mixing bowl, blend the eggs with the cheese, honey, wine and nutmeg. Then fold in the chard, mint and squash. Pour the filling into the warm pie shell and bake it on the middle shelf of the oven for 50 minutes or until golden brown. The filling should be set when a toothpick inserted in the center comes out clean.

Serves 6 to 8.

Sunshine Zucchini Pancakes with Salsa

Most often, I serve these pancakes with salsa for a light supper; but for breakfast I omit the onions and serve them with maple syrup. This is a fun dish to make with children. If they want to do it all by themselves, a package of corn muffin mix works well. Follow the directions for cornmeal pancakes and add the vegetables to the wet mixture.

3/4 cup all-purpose flour, sifted

2 1/2 teaspoons baking powder

1 tablespoon sugar

1 1/4 cups yellow cornmeal

3/4 teaspoon salt

1 egg

1 cup milk

2 tablespoons vegetable oil

1 cup grated yellow summer
squash or yellow zucchini,
(about 1 1/2 medium)

3 tablespoons yellow bell pepper,
seeded and chopped fine

3 tablespoons finely chopped
onion

1 cup fresh salsa, or your favorite
commercial salsa

In a medium bowl, put flour, baking powder, sugar, cornmeal and salt. Blend with a spoon. In another small bowl, put the egg, milk, oil, squash, pepper, and onion. Mix the wet ingredients with a spoon. Pour over the dry ingredients and stir lightly until just barely moist.

Heat a nonstick frying pan or griddle, then cook 2 or 3 pancakes at a time over medium heat until both sides are golden brown and the insides are firm. Keep the pancakes warm in a low oven until all are cooked. Serve the pancakes with the salsa.

Makes 8 to 10 3-inch pancakes.

88

True-Blue Pancakes

These delicious, hearty pancakes get their lovely blue-green hue from the blue cornmeal and, of course, the blueberries.

3/4 cup all-purpose flour, sifted

2 1/2 teaspoons baking powder

1 tablespoon sugar

1 1/4 cups blue cornmeal

3/4 teaspoon salt

1 egg

1 cup milk

2 tablespoons vegetable oil

1 cup fresh blueberries

Garnish: more fresh blueberries

In a medium bowl, put the flour, baking powder, sugar, cornmeal, and salt. Blend with a spoon. In another small bowl, put the egg, milk, and oil. Mix the wet ingredients with a spoon and pour them over the dry ingredients and lightly stir until the batter is just barely moist. Fold in the blueberries.

Heat a frying pan or griddle, lightly grease it, then cook 2 or 3 pancakes at a time over medium heat until both sides are golden brown and the insides are firm. Keep the pancakes warm in a low oven until all are cooked.

Stack the pancakes and serve them with maple syrup and more fresh blueberries.

Makes 8 to 10 3-inch pancakes.

edible art of salad gardens

How limited my salads have been throughout the years! Seeing a salad in the hands of someone with a completely different vision amazed me. It was sometime in the early 1980s, and I had just entered the kitchen at the Farallones Institute in California in time to see artistic salads being put together for an evening meal. First Doug Gosling and Mimi Fry went out to the garden carrying big baskets to choose a little of this and a little of that. It was late spring, and what a selection! This garden contained every herb, edible flower, baby vegetable, and salad green you could imagine. I think deciding what to

include each night must have been the hardest part.

Doug and Mimi brought everything back and washed and spin-dried it. Next they set up five pottery bowls—some as big as two feet across—along a large counter, and then went to it. First Doug lined two of the bowls with baby leaves of 'Russian Red' kale, one with baby red lettuces, one with romaine lettuce, and a final one with frilly frisée. Mimi broke up five or six kinds of lettuces, some radicchio, and some endive and started adding their leaves to a few of the bowls. Into one salad

went a little fennel, into another a little chervil, and into another went red orach or some slices of baby kohlrabi. The decisions weren't random; Doug and Mimi had done this many times before and had their favorite combinations. To garnish the salads, Doug julienned some stalks of red chard and sprinkled them over some chartreuse lettuces. Onto one of the simple lettuce salads Mimi scattered miniature roses, pea blossoms, borage flowers, and mustard blossoms. Deep red nasturtiums were artfully placed on one, calendula petals scattered over another. Sunflower seeds went into one, pecans into another, and on and on went the assembly process. Within an hour the buffet table was covered with fabulous salads, and the appreciative diners were feasting.

Since watching Doug and Mimi, I have turned up many other creative salads made with many unusual garden ingredients and in many styles.

After years of debate, out came the back lawn and in went a spring salad garden (*left*). In the space under the bedroom window (foreground) I planted red cabbages, Japanese red mustard, and ornamental cabbages. I then lined the path with chamomile, and created crescent-shaped beds near the patio for succession plantings of salad greens.

Obviously, there is more to making a salad than tossing together a piece of iceberg lettuce and a few slices of tomato. From Andrea Crawford, at the Chez Panisse restaurant in Berkeley, California, I learned about baby cutting lettuces. From Shep Ogden in Vermont I learned about growing specialty lettuce varieties—he and his wife, Ellen, served me a salad in February made of just-sprouted greens from their greenhouse. From Bruce Naftaly and Robin Sanders, chef-owners at Le Gourmand in Seattle, I learned about wild greens, fancy vinegars, and olive oils. But I gathered the most information over the past decades from the salad garden in my own front and backyard gardens. Here my day-to-day experimentation with a large number of ingredients has added dramatically to my repertoire of salads.

Before I go much further, it's important to mention that although just about any vegetable can be made into a salad, in this book I have chosen to concentrate on green, leafy salads in their myriad forms. This means that I set out to examine in detail most of the aromatic herbs and leafy domestic vegetables used worldwide in salads. I have included very few wild greens, however, since that subject could amount to a book in itself.

In doing my research, I have certainly widened my definition of a salad, and I hope you will too. But in learning a great deal about salad greens, I also came to appreciate an important fact: nowhere else in your from-the-garden cooking does fresh-

This is another look at my patio salad garden (*above*), this time from the other side and in the summertime. In the beds are a small pool of 'Australian Yellow' lettuce, two pepper plants, and some basil. Because salad greens generally grow poorly in the heat of midsummer, I've planted a number of ornamentals including impatiens and begonias to fill it in.

ness and quality result in such dramatic improvement as with greens and herbs. In this regard, I discovered that most of the chefs in this country long for garden-fresh produce and have no commercial access to it. As Seppi Renggli, onetime chef of the Four Seasons restaurant in New York, told me, "I have a garden at home and get used to all these special fresh vegetables and unusual herbs, but I can't get many commercially for the restaurant." To treat yourself, and eat like royalty, put in a small salad garden.

The leaf lettuces 'Black-seeded Simpson,' 'Marvel of Four Seasons,' and a crisp head variety grow in old wooden buckets on my front retaining wall (*below*). They are surrounded by California poppies and orange calendulas.

how to grow a salad garden

My front yard vegetable garden (*right, top*) is filled with salad ingredients. In the middle bed, from left to right, are beets, crisp head lettuces, a small bed of mesclun seedlings, curly endive, and onions. In the back bed are sprouting broccolis and 'Ruby' chard. My assistant, Wendy Krupnick, harvests romaine, leaf, and butter lettuces, parsley, and chervil from my back patio salad garden (*right, bottom*).

Salad gardening is largely cool-weather gardening. Our ancestors eagerly looked forward to the first greens of spring. After spending a winter eating root vegetables and dense cabbages, they savored those first succulent leaves of lettuce or, more often, wild greens as a precious tonic to the body and soul. In the late 1800s refrigerated railroad cars began transporting California-grown iceberg lettuces to the East Coast, and these out-of-season crunchy greens became the rage among Victorian hostesses. For decades iceberg-type lettuces dominated the American salad, in both the market and the home garden. To our benefit, in the 1970s the concept of a salad began to change dramatically. Travelers and chefs went abroad and brought back a hunger for different greens like arugula, Shanghai baby bok choys, and mesclun baby salad greens. Concerned citizens in the 1980s pushed for better nutrition, and along with organic produce they discovered the power of leafy greens and the extra vitamins in sprouts. Meanwhile, chefs were busy creating a world cuisine that fused the foods not only of other continents but of other times as well. Heirloom salad greens like orach, miner's lettuce, dandelions, and other wild greens were brought back to the repertoire. Today the concept of a salad is quite grand, and thanks to modern transportation, we enjoy them year-round. Therefore, the cool-weather preference of these leafy vegetables is less obvious. But as you harvest your greens, you will find the majority of your salad-garden production will come in the spring, fall,

and, with extra protection, the winter.

Most gardeners start salad greens early in the spring, though some species and varieties are better started in the summer or fall since their flavor is richer and sweeter when they mature in cool weather. All salad greens need rich, moist, well-drained soil, and the majority benefit from regular applications of compost, small amounts of nitrogen, and supplemental watering. The secret to growing succulent greens is keeping them growing vigorously; otherwise, most get bitter or tough or go to seed prematurely. You can plant salad greens in rows or cast the seeds over a well-prepared bed no more than four feet across. A wider bed is too hard for most people to reach across comfortably and too difficult to weed and harvest.

Most greens are rarely bothered by pests and diseases. The major exceptions would be slugs on ground-hugging greens like lettuces and sorrel, caterpillars on cabbages and bok choys, and leaf miners on spinach and chard.

It is possible to have a wide selection of salad greens growing throughout most of the year through sucession planting. This is a technique for keeping a constant supply of young plants coming along by continually seeding in flats or containers and then using transplants to fill in the holes left by harvested plants. Most of the major seed companies in this country carry a nice selection of lettuces and greens, but for the more unusual species and varieties you will probably want to obtain seeds from the companies listed in the "Resources" section on page 198.

94

Baby Greens and Salad Mixes

No discussion of salad gardening would be complete without an in-depth look at baby greens and salad mixes. The only salad greens that don't make sense to me to harvest as babies are Belgian endive and some radicchios (they'd be too bitter) and most cabbages (they'd be tough and a waste of expensive seed). That leaves hundreds of different varieties of greens. When reading about growing baby salad greens, you'll come across a number of terms, which I will run through here to clear up a few misconceptions. As the name implies, baby salad greens are immature plants less than four inches long and usually less than six weeks old. Sometimes they are but the thinnings of greens being salvaged from the seedling row, but more often they are grown specifically with immature harvest in mind. These baby greens can be harvested either in their entirety or in what's called a cut-and-come-again bed by either scissor-cutting or by picking each leaf by hand. The latter are techniques by which the gardener harvests individual leaves off the baby plants, leaving the crown or growing point to regrow so that new leaves can be harvested again in a few weeks. (For detailed information on growing lettuces by the cut-and-come-again method, see the interview with Andrea Crawford on page 100.)

A bed of baby greens may be grown with only one type of green, say, all romaine lettuces, or the bed may contain a mix. Such a mix might include, say, three different lettuce varieties, arugula, a curly endive, and cress, all together in one bed to be harvested at one time. To grow baby greens in a mix, it's critical that they all grow at the same rate and taste great in combination. Many mixes have a long tradition in France, where they are called *mesclun*, and in Italy, where they are called *misticanza*. In the past few decades gardeners have taken the baby-salad-mix concept and created entirely new mixes. A nontraditional mix might contain the heirloom greens orach, 'Russian Red' kale, and miner's lettuces in combination with bok choys and lettuces, or a wild-greens mix.

Another option is to plant the different baby greens in their own small beds and then mix them in the salad bowl. With this method, you don't need to be concerned about whether the greens are culturally compatible. While most salad greens grow well together in a mix, some of the choice baby greens do not. Two that come to mind are tatsoi and mâche. Tatsoi grows in a ground-hugging rosette and would be shaded by many taller greens, and mâche grows quite slowly and would never catch up with the rest of the greens. The information in the "Encyclopedia of Salad Greens" (page 113) covers which plants grow well as baby greens and which don't, as well as which ones work well in a mix.

Seed mixes can be purchased at your local nursery or from specialty seed companies. Many of the seed mixes used by the seed companies are based on the traditional mixes. For instance, mesclun Provençal is popular in the Provence region of France and consists of various mixes of lettuces, arugula, finely curled endive, and chervil. This is a popular mix carried by a number of seed companies and is a good choice for beginners. *Misticanza* (or *saladini*), is usually a combination of lettuces and chicories. If formulated in a traditional manner, it would be too bitter for the American palate; however, seed companies in the United States choose a milder blend. The mail-order seed companies Cook's Garden, Johnny's Selected Seeds, Nichols Garden Nursery, Shepherd's Garden Seeds, and Territorial Seed Company all carry a number of mesclun mixes.

My kitchen assistant, Gudi Riter, steps away from her recipe testing to plant a small bed of baby salad greens, often called mesclun, in my front garden. First (*right, top left*) she prepares the soil by applying four inches of compost and a few cups of blood meal and bonemeal, and working them into the soil with a spading fork. Once the soil is light and fluffy and the nutrients are incorporated, she sprinkles the seeds over the soil so that the seeds average from one half to one inch apart. She then spreads a half inch or so of light soil or compost over the bed, pats down the seeds and the compost to ensure that the seeds are in contact with the soil (*right, top right*), and labels the bed with the name of the seed mix and the date. Gudi then waters the seeds in gently with a watering can until the soil is thoroughly moist (*right, bottom left*) and places a piece of floating row cover (*right, bottom*) over the bed to prevent critters from destroying it. To make sure the row cover won't blow away, and pests can't get in under it, secure it tightly by putting bricks or stones at the corners and also along the edges if birds are a problem in your garden.

Of course, you can design your own salad mix. Just buy seeds of your favorite baby greens (remember that the plants need to grow at the same rate), stir all the seeds together in a container, and spread them in rows or in a wide bed. No matter how you grow the baby greens, an intensely grown garden bed of about fifty square feet will provide a very generous amount of baby greens for two people.

Prepare a small bed in full sun by working organic matter and soil amendments into the soil. (The information in Appendix A, page 182, covers soil preparation in its entirety.) Sow the seeds over the bed as you would grass seeds—the goal is to plant the majority of the seeds a half to one inch apart. Lightly rake the area to cover the seeds with a little soil. Pat the seeds in place with your hand, water the bed well, and cover the bed with a floating row cover to keep out marauding birds and digging cats. Secure it at the corners with stones, bricks, or boards. (For information on row covers see Appendix A.) Keep the bed moist but not soggy. Within seven to ten days the seeds should sprout. Water occasionally to keep the soil moist; as a rule, no fertilizing or thinning is needed. Within thirty-five to forty-five days the greens will be large enough to harvest.

Containers of young Asian greens (*right, top*) including pac choi, shungiku, and mixed mustards are ready for harvest. Japanese red mustard, grown as a cut-and-come-again crop, is also ready for harvesting (*right, middle*). A harvested mix (*right, bottom*) of baby greens and edible flower petals. A seedling bed of mesclun greens that are about two weeks old sits between a row of heading lettuces and curly endives (*far right*).

Andrea Crawford

Many people grow lettuce, but few do so with as much passion as Andrea Crawford. Andrea, who for years has grown lettuce for some of the best restaurants in the country—among them Chez Panisse in Berkeley, Spago's in Los Angeles, and the Four Seasons in New York—takes pride in producing the incredibly succulent and dewy lettuces critical to the restaurants' reputations for using fresh, seasonal ingredients.

Andrea oversees these gardens devoted to what she considers the best vegetable varieties, the most important culinary herbs, and the tastiest edible flowers. Her real specialty, though, is lettuces. After many years of gardening experience, she has perfected a productive growing technique of leaf-picking baby lettuces. She recommends this method or another referred to as scissor-cutting, or cut-and-come-again, because she feels that home gardeners can obtain high-quality lettuces using this approach.

Andrea is eager to share her techniques for growing and harvesting baby lettuces. "People ask why I don't grow lettuce in the standard manner, why I bother with this intensive technique," she said. "My immediate answer is, aesthetics. People in restaurants love baby lettuces, and my method allows them to preserve the shape of individual leaves. Garden lettuce is beautiful to look at; you can enjoy the lobed blades of 'Oak Leaf,' the undulations of 'Salad Bowl,' and the frills of 'Lollo Rossa.' If you're going to grow your own lettuces, why not enjoy them to the fullest? Big lettuces taste great, but baby varieties, while milder and usually more tender, taste good too. This method is also an efficient way to produce lettuce in a small area.

"To grow baby lettuces using my methods, it's critical to start with optimum exposure and weather conditions and, most important of all, very rich soil. At the gardens I work with, we place a premium on compost, making it as rich as possible by composting continually and digging in at regular intervals. Three times a year we add soil amendments: blood meal and bonemeal or cottonseed meal. I think organic soil amendments are best for growing anything—particularly lettuces, because lettuce can be very bitter if not grown in rich, humusy soil. We never have bitter lettuce because we use so much organic matter—and because the weather never gets very hot in my garden.

"The only pests we have are aphids and slugs. For the aphids we use an insecticidal soap. Slugs aren't a problem most of the year because we're there all the time to control them, but when they're really active, we use slug bait on the perimeter of the garden, never touching the food plants.

"For our intensive method of growing lettuce, we don't let plants get much bigger than three or four inches tall. When we sow the seeds, we space them about a quarter inch apart; then we never thin them. Because we pick them so fast and so often, we never have crowding problems as we would if we just left them to choke themselves and eventually self-thin.

"Optimum exposure and weather conditions are also essential to producing the best baby lettuce, so we take care to protect the plants in all weather. In cold weather we create tunnels of clear plastic film spread over PVC [polyvinyl chloride] tubing hoops; the plastic is attached to the hoops with giant plastic clips available from plumbing-supply houses. In warm summer weather we shade the beds with commercial shade cloth. Of course, winter weather doesn't drop much below thirty degrees in either Berkeley or Los Angeles, and our summers are mild, but in cold-winter areas you could do the same thing in a greenhouse or cold frame.

"Because we produce so much lettuce for the restaurants, I've decided through the years against scissor-cutting; leaf-picking is easier on plants because the plants regenerate faster that way. We pick only the biggest leaves, which are still only two to three inches long, and leave the crowns to produce new leaves.

"Home gardeners can choose whichever method appeals to them, though. If you prefer the cut-and-come-again method of harvesting, take a knife or scissors and just go snip, snip across the plant about an inch or two above the crown. This won't kill the plant, because enough energy and growing information is left in the crown for it to produce new leaves. New growth will occur in a short time if the weather is right—not too cold or too hot. Cut as much as you need and then separate the damaged leaves from the good ones. Scissor-cutting is great for home gardeners because it's fast, but we leaf-pick each plant for restaurants and sort as we go so only the perfect leaves end up in the tub.

"Washing is an important part of the final presentation. Put the lettuce leaves in a sink filled with water, gently slosh them up and down, and then spin several turns in a salad spinner until the leaves are quite dry. It's important to dry baby lettuces thoroughly because they'll collapse under the weight of any water left on them. Put the leaves between damp towels and refrigerate immediately. Later, be careful to dress them very lightly with a delicate oil-and-vinegar mixture so they won't sag under the weight of a heavy dressing."

When asked which lettuce varieties she prefers most, Andrea said, "I think all varieties are interesting. There are all kinds of lettuces, and they're fun to grow because they all look and taste slightly different. I've decided that the final product depends not as much on which varieties you choose as on how you grow them. There's no such thing as a bad lettuce or a terrific lettuce; it's entirely personal. Aesthetics are important; color, taste, and texture depend on what you want. If you like smooth, buttery, tender lettuces, go with 'Limestone' and 'Bibb' lettuces. For something slightly more crunchy and succulent, try the Batavians. Finally, in general, the reds may be a little more strongly flavored than the greens. All in all, it's entirely up to your individual taste."

harvesting from the salad garden

My salad gardens produce far more greens than I and my husband could ever use. Jesse Cool (*right, top*), chef at the nearb Flea Street restaurant, visits and leaves with a few giant leaves of Japanese red mustard and a handful of lettuce leaves. Jody Main (*right, bottom*), my gardenmanager, harvests extra lettuces for a food bank.

Salad greens may be harvested in many ways. The differences are dictated by the age of the plant, the method used to grow it, and the variety. Let's first look at the different stages of a salad green's life and see how to harvest each one. When you start seeds for most greens, you need to plant extra to make sure you have a full flat or bed of greens. Generally many more plants sprout than will fit in a mature bed, and selected baby plants need to be pulled out to prevent overcrowding. This process is called thinning. Once your plants have three or four leaves, you can thin them by cutting the baby plants off at soil level, or just pull the entire plant out of the ground. (This applies to some other vegetable seedlings besides salad greens too. Thinnings of beets, radishes, turnips, scallions, and peas are also good salad material.) Simply remove the root end, wash the baby plants, and add them to a mixed salad.

The method you choose to grow your greens also affects how you harvest them. If you grow a wide bed of baby greens, once the plants are three or four inches tall you harvest the greens either with scissors or with your fingers. You cut at least an inch above the crown so the plant will not be killed. Put the baby greens in a basket and bring them into the kitchen to be washed and served. After you pick your baby greens, fertilize the bed with fish emulsion; if the weather is suitable, they will resprout and be ready for a second harvesting in a few weeks. Sometimes they resprout a third time.

There is yet another method for growing varieties that head-up forming crisp, tight heads and rosette-type greens. Plant these varieties—such as lettuces, spinach, tatsoi, endive, escarole, kale, arugula, and mustards—in conventional rows. Your first harvest would be of the thinnings; then as the remaining plants became established (with six or eight leaves), you can harvest an outer leaf or so from each plant. Depending on the type of plant, once your plants reach mature size, you can either harvest the whole plant or continue to harvest individual leaves over a few months. As a rule, mature heading lettuces, cabbages, tatsoi, spinachs, curly endive, escarole, mâche, and arugula are harvested as entire plants. If you let them get too mature they will get bitter and develop a flowering stalk; this is called bolting. You can harvest individual tender young leaves off leaf lettuces, amaranths, Swiss chard, kales, and orach over a fairly long season. The perennials, dandelions and sorrel, are harvested over a number of years, either by picking a few leaves at a time as needed or by cutting back the entire plant a few times a year so new leaves will emerge a few weeks later. See the individual vegetable entries in the "Encyclopedia of Salad Greens" (page 113) for more specific harvesting information, especially for greens such as radicchio, escarole, and Belgian endive, which need special treatment.

All in all, a salad garden makes a wonderful beginner's garden and provides a good selection for busy cooks. Few edible gardens can be as beautiful or as useful in the kitchen.

the Creasy salad garden

My first official "salad garden" was in my backyard in 1984. In the middle of my small backyard is a huge but fruitless mulberry tree. For years I would stand staring at it and ask myself the same question: With all that shade and all that root competition, what edible plants can I grow under that tree? That spring it occurred to me that the area would be a perfect place for a salad garden. Leafy salad greens would grow in the cool sun of winter and spring, when the leaves were off the tree, and would do fine most of the summer and fall, when the shade of the tree would protect them from the heat. The problem of the mulberry's invasive roots could be solved over time if I continued to dig up the roots and amend the soil every time I did a major planting beneath the tree.

I was right. A salad garden turned out to be the perfect solution to the problem. Not only did the salad vegetables grow well, but leafy greens interplanted with annual flowers also made a beautiful garden next to the patio. As a bonus, with a salad garden right off the kitchen, I found myself using many more salad greens than in the past, since it was so easy to harvest leaves as I needed them.

To prepare the area for the lettuces and herbs, I had the soil dug up under the part of the tree where the salad greens would go so as to remove as many mulberry roots as possible (something that is possible only when you have a mature specimen of a vigorous species). Then I added lots of compost and put in some low, pop-up sprinkler heads. To ensure a continuous supply of salad greens, my assistant at the time, Wendy Krupnick, set up a nursery area with starter flats so she could replant lettuce every six weeks or so. (We also bought seedlings from the nursery on occasion.) We found that starting lettuce plants by seeds in place in the garden sometimes resulted in spotty germination. Also, in watering the seedlings twice a day in the warm weather we were overwatering the tree and the more mature plants and contributing to fungus problems on the lettuces.

For more than two years we planted different lettuces and salad herbs recommended to me by restaurant gardeners and seed company folks. In the cool seasons all the lettuces, the chervil, the mâche, and the arugula did very well. On the other hand, for a short time in the hottest weather most of the greens did poorly; only the parsley and the 'Oak Leaf,' 'Summer Bibb,' and 'Australian Yellow' lettuces held up, but they needed to be harvested very young, or they would turn bitter.

It was certainly handy to have a salad garden right off the kitchen, but even handier was the method of lettuce harvesting that Wendy showed me. First thing in the morning, when the lettuces are dewy and the temperature is cool, she goes out and harvests enough salad greens for one or two days. She brings them in and washes and dries them in a salad spinner. (The salad spinner, a basket inside a plastic bowl, with a cover equipped with a spinning device, has to be one

of the most useful modern kitchen inventions.) Then she dumps the salad mix into a plastic bag and puts it in the refrigerator. By picking the lettuces at their peak in the cool of the morning you ensure that your greens will be crisp and flavorful, and by washing them you make them available for use anytime, whether you're grabbing a few leaves for a sandwich at lunch or making a salad in the evening.

At some point your baby lettuces will stop resprouting because the weather is too warm or because they are played out. You can prepare the bed for the next crop in two ways. The first is to simply turn the lettuces under, after which they will decompose quickly. The other way, which I prefer, is to leave the lettuces in place and gently plant your summer crops, like tomatoes and peppers, around them. This is called the "no till" method, and its benefits are that it cuts down on erosion and is easier on your soil structure. Another bonus is that the decomposing lettuces will feed your next crop.

After growing my backyard salad garden I became so enamored with these greens that in 1995 I designed a large garden full of them. It consisted of beds arranged between an array of

My front yard "magic circle" salad garden in late spring (*right*) provides us with copious amounts of greens, but also creates an exciting welcome to my home. There are salad greens in the containers by the tea house and rows of lettuces, endives, and scallions around the paths at the left. The beds at the right contain mâche (now in bloom and covered with tiny white flowers), nestled up to chives with their lavender flowers.

106

planks encircling a birdbath. This garden became the focal point for the front yard. The salad greens and herbs were grown mostly in rows encircling what finally became called the "magic circle." The rosettes of dozens of varieties of lettuces were interspersed with scallions, chives, spinach, mâche, and edible and purely decorative flowers. Of course, this garden produced much more than my husband and I could ever have consumed; it fed many of the neighbors, and we even had extra to take to the food bank. By growing so many salad greens at one time, though, I finally had a chance to compare many varieties and see how they tasted and held up to growing conditions in my microclimate. Alas, that garden is now gone—it went on to become a new garden, one filled with American heirloom vegetables and

flowers. I still grow many salad greens, however. They are interplanted among my other beds, in containers, and sometimes back under the tree near the patio.

After years of growing hundreds of salad greens, I've found that I really enjoy mâche, miner's lettuce, spinach, perpetual spinach, dandelions, many of the Oriental greens, and most lettuces. I'm less enamored with the strong-flavored arugula and shungiku greens, preferring to use them as herbs rather than as a chief ingredient in salads. Further, I find I seldom plant some of the heirloom chicories, as they are so unpredictable, and I still haven't developed a taste for purslane (I'm put off by its slippery texture). In contrast, I've yet to meet a lettuce I don't like. They are all so lovely and tasty, and each gives its own look to a salad. The

romaines have a crisp texture, the butterheads are velvety, and the leaf lettuces are beautiful and tender. If forced to grow but a few, I guess I'd choose 'Oak Leaf,' the Batavians, and the velvety 'Buttercrunch'; still, I'd miss all the others for all their great shapes and colors.

The magic circle (*above*) is made of three-foot-long tapered boards that are connected by two concentric circles of bender board. After the greens were planted, laser drip tubing was snaked among the plants. Spray heads were used to irrigate the blue star creeper ground cover among the boards. The same area (*right, top*) as viewed from the front walk is shown about ten weeks later, after the greens have filled in. The garden looks different when viewed from the tea house looking toward the front walk(*right,bottom*). Here rosemary, Japanese red mustard, Vietnamese coriander, and the blue flowers of an ornamental campanula create a background for the greens.

Shepherd Ogden

Shepherd Ogden and his wife, Ellen, run a seed company in Londonderry, Vermont, where they specialize in salad vegetables and carry the seeds of more than forty varieties of lettuce. Shep's family has grown vegetables for many years, and his enthusiasm for salad greens is obvious when he talks about them.

At one time Shep supported himself while writing poetry by driving a cab in Cambridge. Then in the early 1970s, during a summer visit to his grandfather, Sam Ogden, a garden writer who had a small market garden, Shep planted the garden for him. The work was so satisfying that he took over the garden the next year and sold produce to local restaurants and vacationers. Unable to obtain some of the specialty lettuces he wanted from other American companies, he started his own seed company a little while later.

Shep talked to me about the different types of lettuces, dividing the many varieties into categories. First he discussed forcing lettuces, which are grown in greenhouses or cold frames. "We plant forcing lettuces in our heated greenhouse in mid-February and transplant them to the outdoor tunnels in mid- to late March," he said. "In Vermont that means harvesting in the middle of May. These types will grow in temperatures as low as fourteen degrees because they'll actually freeze, unthaw, and recover. My favorite for forcing is

'Magnet,' a butterhead that forces exceptionally well.

"Most lettuces are spring lettuces—except for the overwintering types," Shep explained. Spring weather is ideal for growing lettuces, and even summer and fall lettuces can be grown in the spring, although some spring lettuces will not tolerate the heat of summer or the cold of fall or winter.

"I like the big beautiful heads of 'Red Sails' and 'Black-Seeded Simpson,' which grows fast and tastes good. 'Red Grenoble,' another of my favorites, is a vigorous grower and can be cut as loose-leaf lettuce or left to head up. 'Four Seasons' is a good red butterhead and seems to grow a little longer into the summer than some around here do.

"For the summer 'Esmeralda' is a great butterhead with big, beautiful heads. We've had good luck with that even in the middle of the summer. Of course, our summers aren't as hot as many; they're usually in the seventies with some days in the low eighties. Occasionally we get temperatures in the nineties, but they don't last long enough to really hurt the lettuce. And we always have cool nights.

"Other summer lettuces I like are 'Matchless' and 'Buttercrunch,' which have very nice heads; 'Matchless' is the darker of the two and has unique, triangular leaves. 'Red Riding Hood' is nice—it's similar to 'Four Seasons' but darker and holds better in the heat. Of course, I must mention 'Sierra,' a butterhead type with a bronze tinge, as it's the most heat-tolerant of all the varieties. 'Craquerelle du Midi' also holds well in the heat and is like 'Buttercrunch' but more open-hearted. I don't care for the texture that much, but it's popular among people in warm climates. People even write to us from Florida to tell us how well it does there.

"'Diamond Gem,' another summer variety, is my personal favorite at the moment. I planted a lot of it and found it did really well. It's very heat-resistant—so heat-resistant that it almost fouls up our successions, because it can sit in the heat longer than most of the other lettuce varieties in the same bed without going to seed. But that makes it a good home variety, and it's the best sandwich lettuce I know of.

"Of the fall/winter lettuces, I like 'Winter Density.' That's like a large 'Diamond Gem,' but with row covers it overwinters here—or it grows well in the summer. 'Brune d'Hiver,' another nice winter lettuce, is more brown than red and is real hardy. That one overwinters here with no problem, but it has to be planted late in the summer to prevent bolting.

"Of the cutting lettuces, I like 'Royal Oak Leaf,' 'Salad Bowl,' and 'Red Salad Bowl.' I grow large amounts of these three side by side because they're so beautiful and look so good in salads. The 'Royal Oak Leaf' gets bitter easily, though, and it's more susceptible to disease than the others are. There is a red form, too, called 'Brunia.'

"For other greens, we do fine with escaroles and endives, but chicories, which should be planted in the fall for a spring harvest in a Mediterranean climate, are really chancy here. 'Sugar loaf,' 'Ceriolo,' 'Spadona,' 'Puntarella,' and 'Dentarella' are all chancy, as are red chicories, the radicchios. We grow them on a spring/fall schedule rather than a fall/spring schedule, and I always leave some in the ground because I've discovered that they occasionally will survive the winter. We've tried forcing various radicchios as you would 'Witloof,' but they haven't done well.

"Obviously, rocket [arugula] also needs to be included on the list of other greens," Shep continued. "Its spicy flavor is a good addition to salads. I have no use for 'White Mustard,' on the other hand; it has a hairy leaf. I much prefer 'Miike Purple,' 'Osaka Purple,' or mizuna. Mizuna has beautiful cut foliage and a mild flavor. I also like all of the cresses. I sow the seeds often and harvest when they're very small. I like mâche too. I prefer the big-leaf kinds like 'Piedmont' or the cup-leaved 'Coquille.' Then there is the whole range of minor greens that really make a mesclun mix stand out: miner's lettuce [*claytonia*], golden purslane, minutina, shungiku, orach—the list goes on—we grow about forty kinds."

As Shep's strong ideas about varieties indicate, there are lots of options. Deciding which lettuces are best for your garden depends on your climate and season and on which ones enchant you the most!

encyclopedia of salad greens

The following detailed list of green vegetables gives the particulars for growing a lifetime's worth of salads. For more detailed information on soil preparation, mulching, fertilizing, composting, and pests and diseases, see Appendixes A and B (pages 182-197). Many can be grown as baby greens and harvested in the cut-and-come-again method—and those I have so noted. See the Andrea Crawford interview (page 100) for more information on this method of growing and harvesting baby greens. Of course, most of these greens can also be cooked, but the "How to Prepare" instructions here focus on using them raw in salads.

There are many hundreds of salad

greens. For this section I have chosen my favorites. The encyclopedia entries include the Latin plant names so that you can identify plants properly. Some of the species and varieties are quite popular and will be readily available, many, however, are only available through specialty mail-order houses. I have listed the seed companies that carry the largest selections of greens in the Resources section on page 198. You will need to obtain at least three or four catalogs to get the best selection of greens.

'Marvel of Four Seasons' is a lush spring leaf lettuce that originated in France. It is sometimes sold under its French name: 'Merveille des Quatres Saisons.'

Amaranth 'Sensation'

AMARANTH

Amaranthus hypochondriacus,
A. tricolor

AMARANTH LEAVES CAN BE
green, red, cream, or a combination of
all three, depending on the variety.
The young shoots and leaves are tender and mild enough to eat raw in salads. From the land of the Incas, this
nutritious green has traveled a bit: in
Africa and the Caribbean it is known
as callaloo, and in China a leaf type
called Chinese spinach is grown.
Amaranth is one of the few salad
greens that glories in warm weather.
Young leaves from the leaf-type varieties can be used as a substitute for
spinach.

How to grow: Start amaranth
seedlings after all danger of frost has
passed. Plant seeds ⅛ inch deep, 4
inches apart in full sun and in rich,

well-drained soil, and keep the bed
fairly moist. Thin the plants to 1 foot
and mulch to preserve moisture and
prevent weeds. Generally, amaranth
seeds and seedlings grow with great
enthusiasm. The leaf types grow to 2
feet, some of the showy varieties to 3
feet. If cucumber beetles or other chew-
ing insects are a problem, protect the

plants with floating (polyester) row
covers. Harvest the tender leaves when
they are quite young.

Varieties

'Burgundy': 105 days, spectacular reddish purple plants to 8 feet tall,
grain type
'Green Leaf Vegetable Amaranth': 50
days, oval green leaves, 18 inches
tall, leaf type, the best for salads
'Joseph's-Coat': a tricolor variety (red,
cream, and green leaves), spectacular plants, leaf type, great as a garnish
'Merah': 80 days, crinkled bicolored
green-and-red leaves, leaf type
'Puteh': 80 days, light green leaves, 18
inches tall, mild flavor, leaf type
'Red Leaf Vegetable Amaranth': 50
days, bicolored green-and-red
leaves, 18 inches tall, leaf type

How to prepare: Select young, tender leaves and use them raw in salads
or as spectacular garnishes.

A leaf-type Oriental amaranth

114

Arugula grown as a cut-and-come-again crop.

ARUGULA

(rocket, roquette)

Eruca vesicaria

(E. sativa, Arugula sativa)

RUSTIC ARUGULA

(wild arugula, rucola)

E. selvatica

(Diplotaxis tenuifolia)

ARUGULA LEAVES ARE LOBED, pungent, and nutty; they taste a bit like horseradish. The most common arugula is the domesticated one. However, there is another, usually called rustic arugula, that is perennial and has a more intense flavor.

How to grow: The standard arugula is grown in cool weather in early spring and again in the fall. The plants are short-lived; they get quite spicy and bolt in hot weather. Rustic arugula is a tender perennial that if started in spring and kept cut back, grows throughout the summer and fall and will winter over in mild-winter areas. Common arugula is planted in the fall for a winter harvest in these same mild climates. Broadcast seeds of both types over rich soil in a sunny area of the garden and lightly cover the seeds with soil, or plant them in flats and transplant the seedlings out into the garden. In the fall in cold climates, plant common arugula in a cold frame or greenhouse for winter salads. For succulent growth, keep arugula well watered and fertilize lightly. Both arugulas have few pest and disease problems. Harvest individual leaves or cut back the plant and leave a few inches of growth for a cut-and-come-again crop. Common arugula comes back more quickly than rustic does. Arugula flowers attract beneficial insects, so I usually keep some going for much of the spring. If allowed to go to seed, both arugulas reseed readily in your garden.

Varieties

Arugula: 40 days, lobed green leaves, plants grow to 1 foot tall, white flowers

Wild rustic arugula (Italian wild arugula, 'Sylvetta'): 55 days, finely cut leaves, plants grow to 8 inches, yellow flowers

How to prepare: When they're only 2 or 3 inches tall and very mild, arugula leaves can be used in fairly large amounts to add a peppery and nutty flavor to a salad. Combine them with other assertive greens, especially the fall and winter ones such as cresses, mustards, or chicories, and complement them with strong cheeses, meats, and fruits. Later, as the leaves become much more pungent, use arugula as an herb in a mixed salad, dressing, or main course. Good companions are anchovies, duck breast, chicken livers, capers, olives, and fruity olive oils—in other words, think "gusto." Long after the leaves become too strong, the flowers are great in salads or as a garnish.

CABBAGE AND CHINESE CABBAGE

Brassica oleracea, var. capitata, and B. rapa, var. Pekinensis

I FIND THE CABBAGES TO BE quite splendid in all their variety. The puckery Savoy types with their handsome crinkled leaves and rich texture are real eye-catchers, as are the red and purple ball-like smooth cabbages. Then there are the Chinese cabbages, which are tall and stately and have a milder flavor and a more tender leaf than their cousins. The ornamental cabbages, which look like giant reclining peonies, are spectacular: their foliage is crinkled and comes in shades from pink to purple.

How to grow: Cabbages are best grown as cool-season annuals and will bolt and go to seed in extremely hot weather. In cold climates cabbage is started in early spring or early summer, depending on the variety. In the South and warm-winter parts of the West, it is started in late winter or midsummer. The colorful flowering cabbages prefer a frost or cool nights to turn their deepest purple, so they are best planted in summer for a fall display. Cabbages need full sun, although they prefer light shade in hot climates. Plant seeds ¼ inch deep, 4 inches apart in rows. (Cabbage seed does not

Ornamental cabbage and the edible 'Alaska' nasturtiums make good bed mates in a fall garden.

Savoy cabbage

germinate well in cold temperatures.) Or buy small plants at a local nursery, or start seeds indoors about eight weeks before your last average frost date. Transplant your seedlings out into the garden in rich soil about two weeks before the last average frost date. Seeds or plants can also be planted in midsummer for a fall crop. Space small varieties 12 inches apart, and larger ones 24 inches apart, in rows spaced no closer than 2½ feet. When transplanting cabbages, place them lower in the soil than you would most transplants—up to their first set of true leaves (the first leaves after the seed leaves). As these plants tend to be top-heavy, planting them too high results in plants that are not sturdy enough to support their interior weight as they develop. Chinese cabbages do not transplant well, tending to bolt if disturbed. As they grow best in fall, you should probably start them from seeds planted directly in the garden in midsummer so they can mature

in the cool weather. Cabbages are heavy feeders and need soil that contains a good deal of organic matter; in addition, add a balanced organic fertilizer: 1 cup worked into the soil around each plant at planting time. Cabbages need regular and even watering. They seem to grow best where the soil has the capacity to hold on to the large amounts of moisture they require for

'O-S Cross' giant cabbage

the development of firm heads. Mulching helps retain this necessary moisture. The biggest problem in growing cabbage is keeping ahead of the pests, and the Chinese types seem to get more than their share. The white cabbage butterfly has flitted its way across the entire continent, and its green caterpillar offspring chew on cabbages all season long. As soon as the plants are in the garden, prevent the butterfly from laying eggs by covering your cabbages with floating row covers. If you get a severe infestation, the pesticide *Bacillus thuringiensis* (Bt) controls the caterpillars very effectively, but it also can kill all other types of butterflies (as any kind of caterpillar eating the Bt would be affected). Instead, I usually pick the eggs off the underside of the foliage, where the butterfly deposits them every few days. These eggs are cream-colored and about the size of a large pinhead. Cabbage root fly is another troublesome pest. You can use floating row covers to prevent the fly from laying her eggs on your plants, or you can prevent the larvae (maggots) from entering the soil by placing a 12-inch square of tar paper or black plastic directly over the roots of the plant. To do so, cut a slit about 6 inches long from one edge directly to the middle of the square and then slip it around the plant. Cutworms often attack young cabbage plants. A good preventive measure is to place a collar of cardboard around each seedling. Club root is a serious fungus disease of the cabbage family, as are black rot and aster yellows. Good garden hygiene is your best prevention here. Buy disease-free plants and do not accept plants from friends who have had the problem. Rotate members of the cabbage family with other vegetable families so that they do not grow in the same area for more than one year. And pull up all cabbage family weeds; mustard and shepherd's purse are the most common. Harvest head cabbages anytime after they have started to head up well and before they become so large that they split. Mature cabbages can take temperatures as low as 20°F, so do not rush to harvest all of them before a frost. The Savoy types are the most hardy. If a hard freeze is expected, harvest all the cabbages and store them in a cool place, stacking them in straw if possible.

Varieties

There are many different types of cabbages: red-leafed ones; Savoy types with their crinkly leaves; diminutive varieties suitable for one meal; Chinese cabbages, both the tight cylindrical heads called Napa cabbages and the looser-growing ones that look like romaine lettuce, referred to as lettuce types; and the multicolored flowering cabbages. For planting in early spring, choose early and midseason varieties of standard and Savoy cabbages; for fall crops and winter storage, choose midseason, Chinese, and ornamental varieties. Also look for varieties that are resistant to some of the cabbage diseases.

Chinese Cabbages

'Blues': 50 days, hybrid Napa-type Chinese cabbage, bolt- and disease-resistant

'Lettucy Type': 45 days, thin tender leaves, tall open-top Chinese cabbage

'Market Prize': 70 days, light green crinkled leaves, Napa-style, cylindrical heads

Ornamental Cabbages

'Tokyo Mix': 60 days; mix of white-, pink-, and red-centered ornamental cabbages, very cold-tolerant

Savoy Cabbages

'Chieftain': 83 days, well-savoyed 4- to 5-pound heads, mild taste great for slaw, stands in garden well without splitting

'Julius': 75 days, blue-green savoyed round heads, 4 to 5 pounds

'Savoy Ace': 80 days, hybrid, good quality, almost round, up to 4½ pounds, highly resistant to fusarium wilt and insect damage

Standard and Red Cabbages

'Columbia': 73 days; midseason; round 3- to 5-pound, blue-green heads; resistant to fusarium wilt

'Dynamo': 70 days, hybrid, one-meal-size, 2½-pound green heads that resist splitting, plant spring and again in fall, resistant to fusarium wilt

'Early Jersey Wakefield': 63 days, green heading type with pointed head, longtime favorite, resistant to fusarium wilt, fine flavor

'Green Glitter': 80 days, hybrid, dark green 3½-pound heads, holds up well in the garden for winter harvest

'Red Express': 63 days, early, round red compact heads up to 4 pounds, split-resistant

'Ruby Perfection': 80 days, popular round red cabbage

How to prepare: The taste of all types of cabbages is similar. The Chinese and young Savoy cabbages are among the mildest-flavored of the group and the most versatile for mixed green salads. Heading cabbages are great for coleslaw. The Oriental cabbages are great alone or mixed with other Oriental greens with dressings containing rice wine vinegar, grated ginger, and sesame oil. In Mexico, cabbages are often used in all types of salads, and in the Southwest they are used in a classic taco salad. Red cabbage and flowering cabbage add color and texture to mixed salads.

Chard with stems of many colors

CHARD

(Swiss chard, leaf chard)

Beta vulgaris var. *cicla*

CHARD IS A CLOSE COUSIN of the beet and a mild-flavored green that tolerates a lot more heat than most salad greens. There are two types, stem or Swiss chard with its wide crunchy and sometimes colorful ribs and large leaves, and another less well-known type, variously called leaf chard, leaf beet, or perpetual spinach, which looks more like a light green tall spinach. Both have their place in salads.

How to grow: Start both chard types in early spring in hot-summer areas and through late spring in mild-summer areas. Gardeners in areas where winters have but a few frosts can plant them in spring, and if the weather's not too hot, the plants will produce until the next spring when they finally go to seed. In these areas chard may also be planted in late summer for fall and winter crops. Swiss chard grows upright and straight, even to 4 feet tall when it bolts. Its strong supporting midribs can be white, pink, cherry red, orange, coral, or yellow, and its deep green leaves are usually ruffled and rich-looking. They are one of the most spectacular vegetables you can grow. These colorful chards look handsome when planted with other greens or edible flowers that complement their colors.

Plant chard seeds ¼ to ½ inch deep in full sun, in neutral soil with lots of added organic matter. Chard seeds are actually fruits containing four to eight seeds, so plant them 4 to 6 inches apart, then thin them to a foot apart. When you plant the colored mixes, because they are predominately red and white, seed a full flat and wait until the plants are 4 inches tall to select out yellows and oranges. For tender succulent leaves, keep plants well watered but not soggy. Mulch with a few inches of organic matter to inhibit weeds and preserve moisture, and add organic matter to the soil. When plants are about six weeks old, fertilize them with ½ cup of balanced organic fertilizer for every 5 feet of row. A few pests and diseases bother chard, namely slugs, snails (especially when chard is young), and leaf miners, a fly larvae. Leaf miners tunnel through chard leaves in early summer in northern climates and all spring and most of the summer in the West, disfiguring leaves by causing patches of dead tissue where they feed. To harvest chard, remove the outside leaves at the base so tender new leaves can keep coming throughout the season.

Varieties

There are numerous varieties of chard: many are from France and Italy; others are old American favorites. The leaf chard is often listed in the spinach section of a seed catalog, not with the chard.

'Argentata': 55 days, a large Italian green-and-white heirloom chard, plants are widely adapted and among the most cold-tolerant

'Bright Lights': 60 days, a large chard with colorful midribs of yellow, orange, red, pink, coral, cream, and white, with some streaked plants in the mix. This variety was selected to have a higher proportion of yellow and orange plants than usual in mixes

'Five-Color Silver Beet': a large chard with colorful midribs of yellow, orange, red, pink, cream, and white, with some streaked plants in the mix

'Fordhook Giant': 60 days, the standard American green chard with white ribs, fairly cold-hardy

'Paros': 55 days, a French green-and-white traditional-type chard with

'Perpetual Spinach' chard

milder and more tender stalks than some domestic varieties

'Perpetual Spinach' ('Spinach beet'): 60 days, small ribs, provides a very long harvest of especially tender leaves from spring through winter in most climates, good for baby greens, especially well suited for greenhouses and cold frames

'Ruby' ('Rhubarb'): solid red, sometimes dark pink stems with dark green leaves; an heirloom variety that is widely available

How to prepare: Young chard leaves are tender and mild; they're used as a staple in mixed green salads or as a bed for fruits and other vegetables. The leaf chard is especially suited for this treatment. As chard leaves are large, remove the long, crisp ribs and chop them separately from the greens; or if they're too tough and stringy, use the ribs in soups instead. Before adding them to salads, rip or cut the greens into bite-size pieces or cut in a chiffonade. Do this close to serving time because the leaves and ribs, especially of the colorful varieties, discolor once they're cut. To keep the color, I've found that julienning the stems just before serving makes a colorful confetti to sprinkle on a salad; if you sprinkle the julienned stems with lemon juice or vinegar they will hold their color longer in a slaw or mixed salad. To accentuate the bright-colored chards in a salad, I sometimes combine red chard with red beets, and the yellow chard with yellow beets.

'Bright Lights' chard

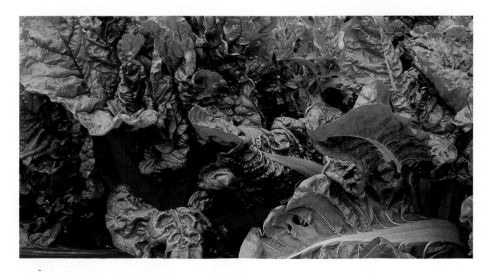

CHICORIES
Cichorium intybus

CHICORIES ARE A COOL-WEATHER salad staple in parts of Europe. The quintessential Italian cutting chicories, the burgundy-colored heading radicchios, and the elegant Belgian endive are all covered here. Curly endive and escarole, well-known chicories associated with France, are covered in their own entry (see page 125). All chicories have in common a mildly bitter taste that can be mitigated by blanching, and by weather conditions. Blanching

is a process whereby you exclude light from the new shoots so they emerge creamy white and lose a lot of their bitterness.

How to grow: Generally chicories are easy to grow, though they prefer cool growing conditions and often perform poorly in very hot-summer areas. Plant all chicory seeds ¼ inch deep in good soil filled with organic matter and in full sun. (Or start seeds inside and transplant them out when they are a few inches tall.) Thin seedlings to 8 inches apart and keep them fairly moist to produce healthy plants that

have few pests and disease problems. The challenges to producing some of the chicories are in the timing and the pre- and post-harvest treatment. And it's here that there are major differences by type.

Let's start with the easiest chicories to produce, the non-heading ancient Italian chicories, called cutting chicories. Plant them in early spring or sixty days before the onset of cool fall weather. They are easily harvested by cutting them with scissors and inch above the crown when the plants are 3 to 4 inches tall. If the weather stays cool, they can be cut again a few weeks later. That's all there is to it.

In contrast, producing the beautiful ruby red and white radicchios and the silky chicons (tight new shoots) of Belgian endive is another matter. While they are not difficult to grow, knowledge and timing are needed. To produce the chicories Americans call radicchios, choosing the proper variety and planting time is the first step. If you are new to growing radicchios, choose modern varieties; they are much easier to grow in most climates than the old ones, as they pretty reliably head up and self-blanch in the garden. (The heirloom varieties are generally climate-specific to Italy and are much more temperamental about heading up.) Even so, you may have to try a few different modern varieties to see which ones do best in your climate before you get a reliable crop. In cold climates plant the modern varieties in late May or early June. If they don't form round

Young red radicchio

heads on their own, cut the plants back around Labor Day; they will resprout and be ready for harvest four to six weeks later. In parts of the country where the winters stay above 10°F, plant radicchios in late June for a fall crop, or in fall for a harvest in the spring. The red radicchios are a bit unnerving; young plants start out with loose green leaves, then round heads form and the inner hearts turn red at maturity. When harvested, the outer green wrapper leaves are removed, revealing a center that is a deep, dark wine color with white midribs.

Belgian endive is something else again; it is always blanched by hand before you eat it. In cold climates start seeds in late June and dig up the plants after the first frost. In mild areas start plants in July and dig them up in late October. The roots are then blanched. Once plants are out of the ground, cut back the foliage to within an inch of the crown and cut the roots back to 8 to 10 inches. Bury the roots in a crate or bucket 18 inches to 2 feet deep in about a foot of damp sand, packing them fairly close together. Store the roots in a dark cellar where it stays between 40 and 50°F. Check occasionally to make sure the sand stays moist, and water sparingly when it gets dry. Within a month or so the crowns start to resprout and produce chicons, which are harvested as they get 4 or 5 inches tall. (The newest varieties maintain a tight head without being held in place by the sand. Old varieties must have 4 or 5 inches of damp sand packed around the emerging shoots to hold them in a tight chicon.) The plants

Radicchio

usually resprout at least once, and sometimes you can harvest them a third or fourth time. In mild-winter areas Belgian endive can also be blanched in the garden. Start the plants in midsummer and cut them back in the fall. Put a lightproof container over the crowns or build a frame around the roots and cover the endive bed with 4 to 6 inches of sand.

Varieties

Italian Cutting Chicories

'Catalogna Frastagliata': 65 days, Italian variety with bright green and frilled leaves

'Ceriolo' ('Grumulo'): 120 days from fall planting, a green cutting chicory for spring harvest

'Spadona': 40 days from spring planting, green cutting chicory with smooth leaves

Radicchios

'Chioggia Red Preco No. 1': 60 days, modern round red radicchio that is widely adapted

'Firebird': 74 days in the North; modern round red radicchio

'Giulio': about 90 days; spring planting type; modern round red radicchio

'Medusa': 65 days; modern round red radicchio hybrid for spring or fall planting

'Rossana': 90 days; early-maturing; modern round red radicchio hybrid; reliable

Belgian Endive

'Flash': 110 days, hybrid Belgian endive bred for forcing without sand or soil around the shoots

'Witloof Zoom': a new hybrid Belgian endive for forcing without sand or soil around the shoots

How to prepare: In salads all types of chicories are usually sliced or torn into bite-size pieces and eaten raw in mixed and mesclun salads or used as a bed for cooked vegetables and meats. The red radicchios can also be added to a salad after it has been braised or roasted. If you wish to cut the bitterness, shred raw radicchio fine and use a dressing with a little fruit juice or honey in it. Red radicchio is most prized for its gorgeous color in a fall or winter salad and for the bittersweetness it gives green salads. Belgian endive is most often used as a bed for or in salads with other vegetables, seafood, and meats. The individual leaves are removed from the chicon and placed on a platter, with other ingredients arranged on them.

CRESSES

WATERCRESS
Nasturtium officinale

GARDEN CRESS
(pepper grass)
Lepidium sativum

LAND CRESS
(Winter cress)
Barbarea verna

CRESSES AS A GROUP GROW best in cool weather and have a pleasant sassy bite and mustardlike flavor that can turn hot and sulfurous in hot weather.

How to grow: The most familiar cress, watercress, has dark green leaves and white flower rosettes similar to sweet alyssum. If you are lucky enough to have a stream with cool, pure, potable water, you will enjoy harvesting watercress for years once you establish a planting in it.

However, watercress also grows in soil that's kept moist; it can be planted in a container, which is then set in a shallow dish of water. Under such conditions, it grows best in the cool part of the year in some dappled shade. Watercress is well suited to cool greenhouses. Start it from seeds or from grocery-store cuttings, which can be rooted in water inside and then planted out in the garden. Two other cresses that are popular with gardeners and cooks both have segmented medium-green leaves. The first, called garden cress or pepper grass, has both a smooth-leafed and a curly-leafed variety. There's also a similar cress known as land or winter cress (called Creasy greens in the South). Both are easily grown and reseed themselves in most gardens. They are most popular grown as baby greens, as a cut-and-come-again crop.

How to prepare: Cresses add spice to salads, and their frilly leaves add texture and visual interest when they're part of a mesclun or mixed salad. Cress works well as a bed for sliced tomatoes, beets, or roasted vegetables.

DANDELION, COMMON
Taraxacum officinale

DANDELION GREENS ARE flavorful and add a slightly bitter richness and lots of nutrition (especially iron and vitamin A) to a salad. You can grow your own dandelions or gather them from wild areas early in the spring, but make sure that the area has not been treated with herbicides.

How to grow: Dandelions prefer full sun and slightly acidic soil. Plant these perennials as seeds ½ inch deep directly in the soil in rich, fertile loam in the spring or fall and keep them fairly moist. Thin to 8 inches apart. Mulch seedlings to control weeds, conserve moisture, and add organic matter to the soil. Dandelions have very few pest and disease problems. Start harvesting them after three months. Harvest only the youngest, tender leaves. For the most delicate flavor, blanch the leaves by tying them up at the top as you would escarole. Do not let dandelions go to seed, or they will become a nuisance.

Varieties

'Pissenlit': 92 days, notched leaves usually blanched, French strain popular in Europe

'Thick-Leaved Improved' 95 days, large leaves good as potherb, blanched leaves good in salads

Watercress (*back*), curly cress (*left*), and smooth-leaved cresses(*right*)

Dandelion

How to prepare: When harvested very young and blanched, dandelions can be used in large amounts; but if they are strong-flavored, they should be used sparingly. Dandelion greens can be eaten raw or cooked. They are assertive-tasting greens and are best known for going well with hot bacon dressing or bold cheeses, garlic, nuts, and nut oils.

ENDIVE, CURLY
AND
ESCAROLE
Cichorium endivia

ENDIVE IS THE NAME GIVEN to a group of plants that fall into two primary categories most commonly referred to as curly endive (the finely cut ones are also known as frisée or frisée lettuce) and escarole. Both groups are popular in fresh salads or cooked as greens. (Do not confuse curly endive with Belgian or French endive, also known as Witloof chicory, which is actually the blanched sprouts of another species, *Cichorium intybus*. See "Chicories," page 122.)

Curly endive has narrow, finely cut, curled and twisted leaves. The outer leaves are usually dark green, fading to a paler color toward the center of the head. The plant is rather shaggy and low growing. Escarole is a larger, more upright plant with longer and broader leaves, also twisted at the base, and a less pronounced pale interior.

How to grow: Curly endive and escarole are cool-season crops, so in temperate climates plant them in early spring or late summer. In northern and cool-summer climates plant them in June for a fall crop and in late summer for greenhouse growing as baby greens. In mild-winter areas fall plantings thrive all winter. Under warmer conditions success is possible if you grow curly endive as a cut-and-come-again baby green. Plant seeds ¼ to ½ inch deep in full sun in rich, fertile loam. Curly endive and escarole get bitter if the soil dries out, so water the plants regularly; try to water the soil (drip irrigation is perfect), not the plants, as they also tend to rot easily. Thin to 9 to 12 inches apart. Thinnings may be used in salads. Mulch the seedlings to control weeds, conserve moisture, and add organic matter to the soil. Fertilize the plants with an organic nitrogen fertilizer, such as fish emulsion, during the growing season.

Most varieties of curly endive and escarole are best if blanched so the creamy golden center becomes tender

Finely curled endive (frisée)

and less bitter. Many curly endive varieties develop a light heart without extensive blanching, especially if they are planted closer together than usual so that they shade one another's leaves. To blanch, some gardeners lay boards across the top of the endive and escarole rows a few weeks before harvesting; other times small plastic containers are inverted over the plants' centers. Other gardeners secure the leaf tops together with a rubber band during the last two weeks. In all cases, make sure the leaves are dry first. If you use rubber bands remove them after a heavy rain, or, again, the plants may rot. Curly endive and escarole are vulnerable to very few pests, though aphids, flea beetles, slugs, and snails are occasional problems.

Harvest your spring crop while it's young, before hot weather sets in, as curly endive and escarole become tough and bitter and often go to seed in hot weather. For a fall crop, a light frost actually sweetens the leaves. The heads can be harvested a few leaves at a time as needed or in their entirety.

Varieties
Curly Endive

'Galia': 45 days, finely cut curly endive from France, smaller than usual varieties

'President': 80 days, a curly endive that holds up to winter cold better than most

'Très Fine' ('Fine Maraîchère'): 50 days, very finely cut leaf endive, elegant small plant, good for individual servings, use young for baby greens and mesclun

'Salad King': 45 days, curly endive, heavy producer, early, slow to bolt

Escarole

'Coral': 48 days, partially self-blanching escarole that is slow to bolt

'Coronet d'Anjou': 80 days, a French escarole that needs to be blanched

'Grosse Bouclée': 50 days, a French escarole that is early and self-blanches

'Perfect': 80 days, a mild escarole that is very winter-hardy

'Sinco Escarole': 80 days, leaves fold around a closely bunched heart

How to prepare: Both curly endive and escarole leaves have a slightly chewy texture and a bitter taste that may appeal only to adults. Curly endive is often harvested very young, and its attractive leaves are frequently added to mesclun mixes. Curly endive and escarole broken into bite-size pieces are excellent when used sparingly in mixed salads, to which they add variety to the texture, taste, and color. The texture and flavor are assertive enough to hold up to strong-flavored ingredients. Anchovies; bacon and spicy sausage; garlic; feta, Parmesan, dry Jack, and blue cheeses; and olives all combine well with endive and escarole to make hearty salads.

Escarole 'Sinco'

KALE AND ORNAMENTAL KALE

Brassica oleracea,
var. *acephala*

A MEMBER OF THE CABBAGE family, kale is beautiful as well as tasty, but its show-off cousin, ornamental kale, while not as flavorful, puts most flowers to shame. Both can be enjoyed in the early spring but are at their best in fall and winter; neither does well in warm weather. Ornamental kale (also known as flowering kale) will not produce its brilliant purple foliage without some cold, and the flavor of both types of kale is improved by frost. Kale is one of the staples of the winter salad, as it is very hardy, even poking up through the snow.

How to grow: During warm weather these leafy vegetables may need partial shade. Kales may be started from seed in early spring, but most gardeners start them midsummer, or three months before the first expected frost in the fall. Sometimes nurseries carry them as seedlings at that time. Seeds or transplants should be planted in rich, fertile loam and kept fairly moist. Plant seeds ½ inch deep, 1 inch apart, and thin plants to 12 to 18 inches apart; thinnings are great for salads. Mulch to control weeds, conserve moisture, and add organic matter to the soil. Fertilize with an organic nitrogen fertilizer, such as fish meal,

during the growing season. As kales are members of the cabbage family, they are occasionally plagued by the same pests. (See "Cabbages," page 116.) Kales improve in flavor and color after a frost, and they winter over in most climates. In the very coldest areas cover them with floating row covers or poly tunnels. For salads, young green kale and ornamental kale leaves can be harvested a few at a time as they are needed.

One kale, 'Russian Red' ('Ragged Jack'), and its variations are particularly well suited for salads because they are the most tender and have lovely frilly red leaves. 'Red Russian' is more heat-tolerant and less hardy than most kales. It is sometimes used when mature but is most often used in mesclun mixes and grown as a baby green in a cut-and-come-again bed by itself or with other greens.

Ornamental kale

Varieties

Choose from the tasty dwarf, green, curly-leafed types; colorful, ornamental ones sometimes called salad Savoy; or the distinctive 'Russian Red.'

Green, Curly-Leafed Kale

'Dwarf Blue Curled Vates' ('Scotch'): 55 days, a blue-green standard kale with curly leaves, for fall planting, very hardy

'Verdura': 60 days, green curly-leafed hybrid Dutch standard kale, more tender than most standard varieties

Ornamental Kale

'Red Peacock': 28 days immature, 60 days mature; spectacular ornamental kale with red feathery leaves for garnishing; when immature, can be used for baby greens or for mesclun mixes

'Russian Red' Kale

'Russian Red' ('Ragged Jack'): 30 days immature, 60 days mature; heirloom kale with frilly red-veined leaves; not very winter-hardy; a strain of 'Russian Red' is 'Winter Red' (50 days), which colors more readily and has more red than the standard; it is great for baby greens and mesclun mixes

'Winter White': 59 days, similar to 'Red Russian' but has white variegations instead of red, hardier than 'Red Russian,' good for baby greens

How to prepare: Kale is very nutritious and contains large quantities of calcium, iron, and potassium. The tender new growth of the standard varieties are good raw in salads, especially in winter. Unless they're very old, mature leaves of the more tender-leafed kales can be eaten in salads.

Baby kale is great in a mixed or mesclun salad. Kale can be combined with lettuces for a light salad or with heavier greens for a heartier fall or winter salad. The ornamental types add welcome color to a green salad in winter and are spectacular when the leaves are used to line a salad bowl or platter. Yellow kale flowers are tasty and colorful in a salad or as a garnish.

Russian Red kale underplanted with lettuce

Lettuces and scallions

LETTUCES
HEAD, ROMAINE, AND LEAF
Lactuca sativa

LETTUCES ARE THE BACKBONE of salads. They are versatile in all types of salads and come in a fabulous array of forms: frilly red lettuces, silky-smooth green rosettes, and varieties with exaggerated undulated leaf shapes. Some lettuce varieties, namely iceberg and romaine (cos), are crisp; others, like 'Bibb,' are soft and buttery. These decorative edibles grace both the flower border and the table.

How to grow: Lettuces can be categorized in different ways—by the form of the plant, say, or even by the season, or even by the way they are grown. While all lettuces grow best in cool weather, some tolerate no hot weather and are referred to as spring lettuces; more heat-tolerant ones are called summer lettuces. Those that adjust well to cold frame or greenhouse growing are quite hardy; they are called winter lettuces.

Lettuce is a cool-season annual crop that can be grown in most areas of the country. Most varieties go to seed or become bitter rapidly when hot weather comes, although leaf lettuces can take more heat than the heading types

can. In warm weather lettuce does better with some afternoon or filtered shade. In mild-winter areas lettuce grows through the winter. In cold-winter areas you can grow forcing lettuces in a greenhouse or a cold frame for winter salads (see "Cold Frames" in Appendix A, page 188, and "Forcing Lettuces" under "Varieties," below) or you can plant hardy overwintering types in the fall if your temperatures stay above 25°F.

Most lettuces are easy to grow when their requirements are met. They prefer loamy soil, rich with organic matter; need regular moisture; and profit from quarter-strength feedings of a fish emulsion type of fertilizer every

'Formiliana' lettuce

'Royal Oak Leaf' and 'Red Oak Leaf'
lettuce

few weeks to keep them growing vigorously. Sow seeds outdoors, start seeds indoors in flats, or buy transplants. Lettuce seeds germinate at quite low temperatures, but most varieties will not germinate if the soil temperature is above 80°F. In summer, shade the seed bed with a sheet of plywood or start seeds inside.

Grow transplants inside on a sunny windowsill three or four weeks before setting them out. This way you can keep an eye on them. You can start lettuces outside in place as soon as you can work the soil in spring. Plant seeds 2 inches apart for mature lettuces, ½ to 1 inch apart for baby lettuces. In all cases, plant the seeds ⅛ to ¼ inch deep. Keep the seed beds uniformly moist until seedlings appear. Lettuce seeds planted indoors in flats or in containers usually germinate within a week. Outdoors, if the soil is cold, germination can take two weeks.

When seedlings growing in flats get their first set of true leaves (after their initial seed leaves), space the plants 2 inches apart in larger flats. Fertilize them with quarter-strength fish emulsion. For example, if the recommended rate is 2 tablespoons per gallon, cut the amount to ½ tablespoon. When transplanting them outdoors, first harden them off for a few days, then put them out, spacing them about a foot apart. Fertilize transplants with quarter-strength fish emulsion.

If you have seeded the lettuce directly, thin the seedlings to between 6 and 12 inches apart, depending on the variety and size you prefer for harvesting. No thinning is needed for baby let-

'Cerice' iceberg lettuce

tuces because they are harvested when so small. But for lettuces harvested at maturity, failure to thin seedlings can result in disease problems and small, stunted plants. Use the thinnings in your salads. In arid climates mulch to conserve moisture.

Succulent young lettuce leaves are ambrosia to birds, slugs, snails, aphids, and cutworms, so until they get fairly good sized, protect your seedlings with floating row covers and hand pick the pests. Where slugs are a problem, do not mulch, or you will give them more places to hide. Under cool, humid conditions, botrytis, a gray mold fungus disease, can cause the plants to rot off at the base. Downy mildew, another fungus, causes older leaves to get whitish patches that eventually die. In both cases, practicing good garden hygiene is the best medicine. Rotate your lettuce plantings with other vegetables and keep the plants spaced well apart for good air circulation. Water

'Black-Seeded Simpson'

'Ice Queen' Batavian lettuce

Staggering the crop during the growing season is the tricky part of ensuring a constant supply. It usually takes a few years to get the timing down for your climate and your family's consumption. The secret is to keep small amounts of lettuce coming along. This is best done by sowing a few seeds every ten to fourteen days throughout the optimum growing seasons.

Varieties
Spring Lettuces

Once the ground can be prepared—usually February or March in mild climates, late May in the coldest climates—you're ready to plant spring lettuces. However, most varieties (with the exception of overwintering types) do well, even best, with early spring planting.

'Bibb' ('Limestone'): 57 days, heirloom classic butterhead lettuce, bolts readily in hot weather

'Black-Seeded Simpson': 46 days, light green and ruffled, delicious, one of the earliest lettuces

'Deer Tongue': heirloom green lettuce with unusual spear-shaped leaf, texture similar to spinach, slow to bolt

'Freckles' ('Trout Back'): a lime green romaine lettuce, good for cut-and-come-again

'Ice Queen' ('Reine des Glaces'): 62 days, beautiful frosty green head of deeply notched leaves, early plantings yield best results

'Lollo Rossa': 56 days, mild-flavored loose leaf, distinctive, a real eye-catcher, frilly leaves and red margins fading to pale green at the heart, good for cut-and-come-again harvesting

'Marvel of Four Seasons' ('Four Seasons'): 60 days, known in France as 'Merveille des Quatres Saisons,' striking, with bright red outer leaves, pale pink and cream interior, tender yet crisp

'Nevada': 60 days, a lovely Batavian lettuce that combines the crispness of iceberg with the flavor of leaf lettuces, tall mint green heads resistant to downy mildew and heat-tolerant

'Red Sails': 52 days, red-fringed leaves, fast-growing, heat-tolerant, slow to bolt, deepens in color as it matures

'Rosy': red to burgundy-colored iceberg-type lettuce, slow to bolt

the plants in the morning, wetting the soil but not the leaves, and try not to handle the plants when they are wet.

Lettuce can be harvested for baby lettuces in three to four weeks. From then on, you can harvest lettuce at any stage. If possible, harvest during the cool of the day. Leaf lettuces can be harvested one leaf at a time, as needed, rather than harvesting the entire plant. Although you can pick a few outer leaves from heading lettuces, generally they are harvested a full head at a time, whether half grown or mature, by cutting off the head at the soil line. (Seedlings can be transplanted into empty spaces left by harvested plants.)

In some regions you can grow lettuce almost all year long. Exceptions would be in the hottest summer conditions generally in the South and the Southwest (AHS Heat Map zones 7 through 12). In cold climates you can grow lettuce in a cool greenhouse or cold frame in all but the coldest areas.

'Rouge d'Hiver' lettuce

'Ruby': 47 days, ruby red, savoyed and frilly leaves

'St. Blaise': small, bright green romaine, good for spring plantings under row covers

'Simpson Elite': 48 days, a more bolt-resistant variety of 'Black-seeded Simpson'

'Summertime': heat-resistant iceberg type, more tolerant of heat than most icebergs

'Tom Thumb': 47 days, solid butterhead about the size of a tennis ball; can be served whole as individual salad, ideal for containers or other small spaces

Summer Lettuces

Summer lettuces can tolerate a little more heat than most but should still be planted soon after the last frost, to get them well on their way before the hot weather sets in. Plants should be har-vested before full size to be sweet. Seed every week or so for continuous har-vesting. Water plants lavishly during hot months.

'Buttercrunch': 60 days, deep green compact head, crisp and juicy, toler-ates heat better and is larger, than 'Bibb'

'Craquerelle du Midi' ('Craquante d'Avignon'): open-hearted cos type, well suited for warm climates, simi-lar to 'Buttercrunch'

'Little Gem' ('Sugar Cos'): 60 days to baby lettuce, 80 days to maturity; delicious, trouble-free; miniature, deep green cos-type head with very few outside leaves; moderately frost-tolerant, slow to bolt in hot weather

'Sierra': butterhead type with bronze tinge, heat-tolerant

Fall/Winter Lettuces

For a fall harvest, plant these after the heat of summer. However, when shortened days bring temperatures down to the forties or below, most lettuces deteriorate. To flourish in such conditions, special varieties have been bred. They should be sown from about Labor Day until the first frost. If you plant them ear-lier, they may bolt prematurely.

'Brune d'Hiver': 56 days, French heirloom variety, bronzy red-edged leaves tapering to green at the cen-ter, butterhead, one of the hardiest varieties

'Rouge d'Hiver': 60 days, another French heirloom, loose romaine, deep red leaves in cold weather, resistant to heat and cold, lovely in both the garden and the kitchen

'Winter Density': 60 days, hardy green variety, semi-cos type, resembles a tall buttercrunch, can be grown

'Mantilia' butterhead lettuce

Romaine lettuce

heat well

'Royal Oak Leaf': 50 days, large deep green rosettes with oak-leaf-shaped leaves, holds well in the garden, a beautiful complement to any salad

'Salad Bowl': 45 days, lime green, deeply lobed, fairly heat-resistant, easy to grow, great mixed with 'Red Salad Bowl'

How to prepare: Baby lettuces are a traditional part of a mesclun salad and are served with vinaigrettes of all types. Mature lettuce leaves have hundreds of uses, as their flavor is mild and their shapes and textures many. The crisp heads, including the iceberg types, and the hearts of romaine and Batavian lettuces hold up to creamy dressings and combine well with crispy rice noodles and taco chips for ethnic salads. They lend themselves beautifully to a chiffonade that can be used as a bed for fish or meat. The frilly-leaf lettuces in their many colors and textures are as versatile as a salad green gets. Their flavor is neutral and can be mixed with assertive greens to tone them down or made into a light-tasting salad on their own. They are spectacular when used to line a platter and can take any type of filling imaginable. The soft, velvety "butter" lettuces are lovely by themselves with a simple vinaigrette or combined with raspberries or sliced pears, or in combination with any of the leaf lettuces. All in all, there are so many uses for lettuce, it's almost impossible to list them all.

nearly year-round in mild climates

'Winter Marvel': 68 days; if planted in fall, produces large, pale green head in early spring; very hardy

Forcing Lettuces

These lettuces grow well in greenhouses, poly tunnels, or cold frames and can survive colder temperatures better than many varieties. Forcing lettuces should be planted in flats about a month before you plan to transplant them under cover.

'North Pole': pale green butterhead, ideal size at onset of winter is 4 to 6

inches

'Valeria': 'Lollo Rossa' type, red coloring on frizzy edges, cold-tolerant

Cutting Lettuces

These vigorous, loose-leaf lettuces are usually grown to produce mature heads. However, if you sow the seeds continuously and thickly, you can have a continuous crop of baby lettuce. Harvest them by scissor-cutting leaves when the lettuces are about 4 inches high.

'Red Salad Bowl' ('Red Oak Leaf'): 50 days, pale red color increases to deep red with maturity, withstands

133

MÂCHE

(fetticus, Feldsalat,
lamb's lettuce, corn salad)

Valerianella locusta

MÂCHE IS A LITTLE, LOW PLANT
whose leaves grow from a central
rosette and produce soft and tender
spoon-shaped greens with a delicate
nutty flavor. You will want to let some
of your mâche go to flower, as its tiny
white flowers attract beneficial insects
and can also be picked for bouquets. In
the garden mâche looks lovely planted
with spring edible flowers like pansies,
calendulas, and Johnny-jump-ups.

How to grow: Mâche is an easily
grown annual that grows best in cool
weather. Plant seeds ½ inch deep, 1
inch apart, in rich, fertile loam in full
sun. Thin plants to 4 inches apart in
rows or wide beds. Directly seed most
varieties in late summer for a fall harvest, or in fall for winter and spring
harvests in mild-winter areas. In cold
climates directly seed in cold frames in
fall, about the time of your first
expected frost, for winter use. A few
big-seeded types tolerate summer
weather if it's not too hot. Mâche seeds
germinate poorly in warm weather, so
shade the seed bed until they germinate. The seeds germinate unevenly
and grow slowly but steadily. Keep the
seed bed and seedlings moist. Once
established, mâche usually reseeds
itself. Mâche has few problems with
pests, though mildew is sometimes a
problem. Choose resistant varieties

Mâche growing wild in my garden

when possible. The harvest starts in
forty to seventy days, depending on the
variety and the season. Pick individual
leaves or the whole head, either when
they're tiny (six to eight leaves) for
baby mâche or when they're mature.
Mâche is cold-tolerant, and frost
enhances the flavor of your fall crop.

Varieties

Though the flavor is not too variable,
some varieties grow better in one sea-
son than another; others resist mildew.
'Elan': upright plants, resists mildew
'Gayula': 70 to 80 days, oval leaves,
French variety, very hardy
'Piedmont': large, pale, spoon-shaped
leaves; good heat resistance

'Verte de Cambrai': 75 days, fine-textured little plant with flat leaves and exceptional tenderness, hardy variety for overwintering

'Vit': 50 days, elongated glossy leaves, vigorous, mildew-tolerant, hardy

How to prepare: Mâche's small, dark green leaves can be used in mixed salads or by themselves with a light vinaigrette. These greens are popular served with cooked beets or potatoes and are sometimes garnished with hard-cooked eggs that have been forced through a sieve. They are particularly nice with raspberry vinegar, pears, and a hazelnut or walnut oil dressing.

Note: Many salad greens reseed themselves readily in the garden if you let them go to flower and set seeds. Most of the time I welcome these volunteers as they save the time and effort of yearly planting. Further, the flowers of most of these plants attract beneficial insects and the extra seeds feed the birds. Among the most reliable "self-seeders" are the amaranths, mâche, arugula, minutina, Japanese red mustard, mizuna, orach, purslane, and miner's lettuce. If they sprout where I want to grow another plant, I simply weed them out or move them to another bed. To prevent self-seeding in an area, I remove the plants before they go to seed.

Minutina

MINUTINA

(Buck's horn plantain, *erba stella*)

Plantago coronopus

MINUTINA IS A STRIKING PLANT with narrow, dark green spiky leaves that emerge in a rosette. A native of the Mediterranean, for eons it has been gathered in the wild to be a part of the Italian *misticanza* (along with arugula, lettuces, and chicories).

How to grow: Even though minutina is quite tolerant of warm and very cold weather, the tastiest and most tender leaves are produced in the cool of spring and fall and from young plants. Plant seeds ¼ inch deep, 2 inches apart in rows or wide beds of good organic soil in full sun in the spring or fall. Thin seedlings to 4 to 6 inches apart. Keep the bed evenly moist. Apply fish emulsion when the plants are about a month old. Harvest minutina in a few months, before the plant blooms, by cutting the young leaves an inch above the crown. The plant will regrow and be ready for another harvest in a few weeks. Minutina can also be grown for baby greens, by themselves or in a mesclun mix, or as a cut-and-come-again crop. If allowed to go to seed, minutina often reseeds itself in your garden.

Varieties

'Minutina': 50 days, cold-hardy, narrow-leafed green, for spring, fall, and winter salads

How to prepare: While it has a mild flavor, minutina is valued in salads for its unusual shape, which adds interest to a mesclun or mixed green salad. The neutral-tasting leaves can be used in just about any salad green combination or bed for raw or cooked vegetables, meats, and seafood. When minutina is used in a mesclun with other baby greens, a light vinaigrette is used because the delicate leaves would be weighed down by cheeses and creamy dressings.

'Red Giant Mustard'

MUSTARD

(India mustard)

JAPANESE RED MUSTARD, SPINACH MUSTARD, AND TATSOI

Brassica juncea, B. spp.

There are a number of greens that are referred to as mustards. These stout-hearted members of the cabbage family are often eaten cooked but are spicy and crisp when eaten raw and make a wonderful addition to hearty salads. Some are also suitable to be grown as baby greens in a cut-and-come-again method, either by themselves or in a mesclun mixed bed. The mustard used as a condiment comes from the ground-up seeds of plants in this family. Prepared mustards are made from white mustard, *Brassica hirta*, or black mustard, *B. nigra*. The young leaves of these plants can be used as potherbs. To make condiment mustard, allow these plants to go to seed and harvest them when the pods turn yellow. Put the seeds in a blender with wine vinegar, black pepper, allspice, salt, and water if needed. (See "Mustards" on page 154, for more information.)

How to grow: Mustards are cool-season crops and are grown in the same manner as most garden greens. Plant seeds ¼ inch deep, 2 inches apart in full sun in rich, fertile loam in the early spring or in the fall. Thin seedlings to a foot apart if you're growing them to maturity. All mustards need sufficient moisture while growing, or they become too hot to eat. Mulch to conserve moisture, control weeds, and add organic matter to the soil. All mustards are members of the cabbage family and may occasionally be plagued by the same pests that bother that family. (See "Cabbage," page 116.) Harvest a few leaves at a time as needed. Generally, the younger the mustard leaf, the less bite it has. Japanese red mustards (such as 'Red Giant' and 'Osaka Purple') can be grown as baby greens and harvested in the cut-and-come-again method. You can also mix them with komat-suna and mizuna (see "Oriental

136

Greens," page 138, for information on these), growing all three together. Mustard flowers are edible well after the leaves are too strong to eat, and they attract beneficial insects.

Varieties

Some varieties have a rich mustard flavor, and others are peppery. Mustards can also be put in salads to add a range of textures and colors.

'Green Wave': 50 days; American mustard with hot, mustardy flavor; used in small amounts in salads; slow to bolt

'Osaka Purple': 40 days, milder and more compact than the more common 'Giant Red,' purple leaves with white veins, great for baby greens

'Red Giant Mustard' ('Giant Red'): 45 days, deep purple-red savoyed leaves, tangy, great for baby greens

'Tendergreen' (Mustard spinach): 45 days, smooth-leaved, easier to clean, tastes less hot than others, flower shoots may be used in salads too

How to prepare: The mature mustards have a zesty flavor that adds body and a little bite to a mixed salad. Use them sparingly in light salads or pair them with other strong-flavored greens in a heartier fall or winter salad with a rich dressing. Adding Dijon or other prepared mustard accents the mustard flavor. The baby mustards are fairly mild and can be used to add texture, color, and a slight tang to mesclun salads. Use the flowers in salads and on cream soups.

ORACH
Atriplex hortensis

THIS ATTRACTIVE "GREEN" has either blueish green or reddish purple spade-shaped leaves that left unpruned grow to 6 feet tall. It's an old-fashioned potherb that can be enjoyed in a mixed salad.

How to grow: Plant orach seeds ¼ inch deep in good soil six to eight weeks before your expected last spring frost. Thin plants to 18 inches apart and mulch to conserve water and add organic matter to the soil. Keep plants moist but not soggy. Start to harvest leaves in about six weeks. If plants are kept pinched back, they produce well into summer. If not pruned, they will go to seed. Orach has few pests and diseases.

Varieties

Orach (Green Orach): 37 days, green leaves, plants to 6 feet tall

Baby red orach

Red Orach: 37 days, red leaves, plants to 6 feet tall

How to prepare: Harvested leaves can be used to add color to mixed salads. The flavor is mild and is a good foil to strong-flavored greens.

Red orach

ORIENTAL GREENS

CELTUCE

(stem lettuce, Chinese lettuce, asparagus lettuce)

Lactuca sativa var. *asparagina*

GREEN IN SNOW MUSTARD

(snow cabbage, serifon),

Brassica juncea var. *multiceps*

KOMATSUNA

(Japanese mustard spinach)

B. rapa var. *perviridis*

(B. rapa var. *komatsuna)*

MIBUNA

(mibu greens)

B. japonica

MIZUNA

B. japonica

BOK CHOY

(pak choi, pac choy, pac choi, boy choi, baak choi)

B. rapa var. *chinensis*

SHINGIKU

(edible garland chrysanthemum, chop suey green, shungiku)

Chrysanthemum coronarium

Japanese red mustard, mizuna, and bok choy in a cut-and-come-again bed with 'Russian Red

TATSOI

(rosette pak choi, flat cabbage, spoon mustard)

B. rapa var. *rosularis*

GROWING ORIENTAL GREENS will open up a whole new world of tastes and textures. There's a further advantage to growing Oriental greens, as most of these plants are so attractive that they can be successfully interplanted in a flower border.

Celtuce, which tastes like lettuce, its close relative, looks like a loose head of lettuce on a tall stalk about a foot high. Both the leaves (which have a high vitamin C content) and the peeled stems are eaten. Oriental mustards are mild

to pungent loose-leafed vegetables that grow one to several feet in height. Some mustards can be slightly bitter; others have a hot bite. Green in Snow mustard (as its names implies) is a highly cold-tolerant Chinese mustard, making it an excellent winter green. Komatsuna, a Japanese mustard that is typically used for its glossy dark green leaves, tender stalks, and flower shoots, and tatsoi (a flat bok choy) are also quite cold-tolerant. Mizuna (a potherb mustard) is a strikingly beautiful cut-leafed vegetable related to mustards and is very popular in Japan. The mild-flavored leaves of mizuna are dark green on top and silvery white underneath. Mibuna is a mild-flavored Japanese green with a pleasant mus-

tardy taste. Mibuna plants, which can grow up to 22 inches, are multi-stemmed with slender, smooth leaves at the end of each stem. Bok choy is a delightful nonheading type of green that looks something like Swiss chard. Bok choy varieties differ with regard to leaf shape: some leaves are sword-like, some spoonlike, and others open and flat. The most common bok choys have white stems, but less common varieties have green stems. Some have been bred for their flowering leaf stalks and buds. Shingiku is an annual edible chrysanthemum that is grown mainly for its tangy-tasting leaves and stems. The yellow, white, or orange flower petals of shingiku can also be eaten and are sprinkled over salads or

soups or used as a garnish. There are three main types of shingiku: large leaf, small leaf, and round leaf.

How to grow: Oriental greens need fertile soil, with sufficient nitrogen, and good drainage. Work plenty of aged manure or compost into the soil before planting, to increase fertility and moisture retention. Oriental greens are fast-growing, cool-weather plants as a rule, so sow seeds in the spring or early fall. Komatsuna is slow to bolt and quite cold-tolerant, so it may also be planted in summer for a winter crop. Bok choy tends to get stringy in hot weather. Some bok choy varieties, however, are heat-tolerant. Bok choys are shallow-rooted, so water them frequently and lightly. Celtuce and mizuna are grown like lettuces; see "Lettuces," page 129. Celtuce tolerates a wide range of growing climates. It can be grown as a cool-season plant; or to grow it like a warm-season lettuce, germinate celtuce seeds in a cool area (as they do not germinate well at hot temperatures) and transplant the seedlings into the garden. Komatsuna, mizuna, shingiku, and some of the bok choys (such as 'Joi Choi' or 'Shanghai Pac Choi') may be grown as single plants, or the seeds may be broadcast and the plants harvested as a cut-and-come-again crop. An added advantage to this is that they can be grown all mixed together. Tatsoi can be treated as a cut-and-come-again crop but must be planted in a bed by itself, as it grows in a flat rosette that would be crowded out by the other greens.

Plant all Oriental greens in full sun, or in light shade in hot climates; give them plenty of water. Mulch with a couple of inches of organic material to conserve water, control weeds, and add organic matter. If your soil does not drain well, consider planting the greens in raised beds. Give a half-strength feeding of liquid nitrogen fertilizer, such as fish emulsion, when planting, and another supplemental feeding of liquid nitrogen about a month later, and again at the beginning of head development. Most Oriental greens are members of the cabbage family and may be bothered by the same pests and diseases as cabbages. (See "Cabbages," page 116.) Bok choys tend to be less susceptible to disease than other Chinese cabbages, and Green in Snow mustard is highly resistant to pests and diseases.

Harvest shoots, individual leaves, or the whole plant of most of these greens, or use the cut-and-come-again method with some. As a rule, the younger the plant, the more tender it is. And tangy-tasting plants, such as the mustards, are milder when younger too. The flowering types of bok choys are grown for their flower buds and flower stalks, so harvest them when the buds form. Komatsuna flower shoots may be harvested; they are sweet and succulent when young but get hotter as they mature. Begin harvesting celtuce leaves in about six weeks, and the stems in two to three months.

Varieties

Celtuce

There are no named varieties of celtuce. Only generic seeds are available.

Green in Snow Mustard

50 days, excellent winter green, grows to about 20 inches

Komatsuna

'Summer Fest': 35 to 55 days, chartreuse loose heads, mild and tender, heat- and disease-tolerant, good for baby greens

Mibuna

'Green Spray': 40 days, most robust of the mibunas, has a crunchy texture and a mild flavor

Mizuna

'Kyona Mizuna': 45 days, finely cut and notched foliage, milder than most mustards, good for baby greens

Bok Choy

Green-leafed, white-stemmed bok choy

'Joi Choi': 45 days, vigorous, long-standing bok choy hybrid; heavy yielder of crisp and tender white stalks with deep green leaves

Green-stemmed Bok Choy

'Chinese Bok Choy': 65 days; fast-growing, cold-resistant, compact plant; delicious glossy leaves and crisp stems

'Mei Qing Choi': 45 days, a baby bok choy, bolt-resistant, uniform

'Shanghai Bok Choy': 40 to 50 days,

Tatsoi grown for cut-and-come-again harvesting.

Shingiku greens

to fall

Flowering Bok Choy

'Autumn Poem': 35 days; green flower stems and leaves; succulent stems, leaves, and flower buds

Flowering Bok Choy: 50 days, light green leaves, grown for flowering stalks and tops

Shingiku

Named varieties of shingiku are usually not available. The large-leaf type has milder, more tender leaves that lend themselves well to salads; however, the small-leaf type can also be used. Harvest the plants when small for salads.

Tatsoi

'Tatsoi' ('Tat Soi'): 45 days, deep green spoon-shaped leaves forming a tight rosette, mild mustard flavor, great for baby greens

How to prepare: Oriental greens are great in salads and sandwiches and as garnishes. Use celtuce leaves and stems in tossed salads. Before the stem is used, its bitter, tough skin must be completely peeled off. Add the red mustards sparingly to salads and sandwiches for their pungent, wasabi-like taste and red color; add the leaves of mizuna and mibuna to salads for their texture and mild flavor; use young Green in Snow mustard leaves in salad—they become too hot when mature. I enjoy bok choy raw in salads—by no means a traditional use, but delicious. Young shingiku leaves are excellent raw in a mixed green salad. Shingiku leaves can also be blanched in boiling water for a few seconds, which gives them a dark green color. Quickly cool the leaves in cold water after blanching them, then add them to the salad. Enjoy tatsoi raw in salads or quickly wilted. While young, komatsuna leaves, stems, and shoots may be added to salads.

PURSLANE

Portulaca oleracea var. *sativa*

A WILD FORM OF THIS low-growing fleshy herb, one that many gardeners know as a pest, is pigweed. However, cultivated purslane can be a tasty green and is enjoyed in many cultures, including France, where it's known as *pourpier*, and Mexico, where it is called *verdolagas*. This easily grown green is high in vitamins and those famous Omega-3 fatty acids we are all supposed to consume.

How to grow: Start seeds of this annual plant either in warm garden soil in the spring or inside and then transplant the purslane out when the weather warms up. If you are sowing the plants in place, sow the seeds ¼ inch deep and an inch apart, then thin and harvest the seedlings, leaving the remainder about 4 to 6 inches apart. Purslane also grows well in a cold frame in the spring and fall. The object of growing purslane is to produce tender, succulent leaves, so keep the plants well watered and cut them back often to 2 inches above the ground to force new growth. Harvest thinnings and young leaves. Remove the flower stalks as they form, or the leaves will become tough and the plants might go to seed and become a nuisance.

How to prepare: The leaves of purslane have a slightly tart taste and are juicy, bordering on slippery. Purslane leaves are small and quite succulent. Use tender young leaves and shoots in raw mixed salads for a contrast of texture and flavors.

Varieties

'Golden Leaf' ('Goldberg'): 50 days, 1½ inch greenish gold leaves on upright plants

'Green Leaf' ('Garden Purslane'): 60 days, green leaves, much larger leaf than wild purslane and an upright habit

'Green Leaf' purslane

SORREL

Rumex acetosa, R. scutatus

SORREL IS A SLIGHTLY lemon-flavored green perennial herb used as a delightful tangy salad green.

How to grow: There are two types of sorrel: garden sorrel, *Rumex acetosa*, often mistakenly called French sorrel, and the true French sorrel, *R. scutatus*, sometimes called buckler sorrel. Garden sorrel is a fairly coarse-looking plant growing to 2 feet tall with 6-inch-long sword-shaped leaves. True French sorrel is a much smaller and refined plant, growing to only 6 inches with leaves an inch or so across. Both are very hardy perennial plants and flourish in all but the most extreme climates. Sorrels are generally planted from divisions, though they can also be planted from seeds in the spring. Locate plants in full sun or with some afternoon shade in rich, well-drained soil that is kept fairly moist. As sorrel can sometimes spread and become a weed, put your plants in a place where they can be contained by paths or retaining walls, or grow them in containers. Fertilize in spring, and again in summer if the plants look pale. Divide plants every three years to renew them. Protect the plants from slugs and snails, which relish the tender leaves.

How to prepare: Sorrel leaves are used to add a citrusy tang and acidic note to mixed greens. Accent their flavor further by adding lemon juice to the dressing or by garnishing the salad with orange or tangerine sections. Honey or fruit juices help ameliorate the acid if the sorrel is especially strong.

Note: Many salad plants: including spinach, chard, sorrel, and purslane, while filled with beneficial vitamins also contain oxalic acid. Oxalic acid in large amounts ties up calcium in the intestines that is then excreted. Further, consuming too much oxalic acid can cause oxalate crystals to form in the kidneys and clog the urinary tract. As with all dietary recommendations, moderation is the key. To be safe, avoid a heavy diet of these greens and make sure you eat foods high in calcium.

Garden sorrel

SPINACH
Spinacia oleracea

SPINACH IS A HEARTY GREEN great for salads. It is also very nutritious, as it is chock full of vitamins (especially vitamins A and B₂) and minerals such as iron and calcium.

How to grow: If the weather is cool and the soil is rich and filled with humus, spinach is easy to grow. Since spinach is a cool-season crop, many varieties quickly bolt (go to seed) if the weather is too warm. Sow the seeds in early spring or fall, or in winter in mild-winter areas. Plant seeds ½ inch deep about an inch apart in full sun in rich, well-drained soil. Keep them fairly moist. Thin seedlings to 3 inches apart and use the thinnings in salads. Make successive sowings every two or three weeks to extend the harvest. Spinach has occasional problems with slugs and leaf miners, plus downy mildew under fall and winter conditions. Harvest the leaves a few at a time as they are needed, by cutting or pinching them off, or harvest the entire plant.

Varieties

Spinach varieties vary in leaf type—smooth or savoyed—heat tolerance, mildew resistance, and taste. As a rule, smooth-leafed spinaches tolerate heat better than savoyed ones, and savoyed leaves are harder to clean.

'Bloomsdale': 48 days, old-time variety, savoyed leaves, heavy yielding, slow to bolt

Spinach

'Hector': 37 days, mild flavor, smooth leaves, slow to bolt

'Melody': 42 days, hybrid, large adaptable plants resistant to downy mildew and mosaic virus

'Olympia': 45 days, dark green smooth leaf, slow to bolt, mildew-resistant

'Tyee': 45 days, hybrid variety, dark green wrinkled leaves, upright vigorous growth, slow to bolt, tolerant of mildew, good in most seasons

'Wolter': 45 days, rapid growing, tender, smooth-leafed, developed by Dutch breeders, resistant to mildew

How to prepare: The deep green leaves, with their slightly metallic taste, can be used alone with a fairly heavy dressing (such as blue cheese or the traditional bacon), or more sparingly combined with lettuces for a light salad. The flavor of spinach is complemented by rich olive and nut oils. Use spinach as a bed for roasted root vegetables, blanched green beans, or grilled tuna; for a change of pace, steam spinach and serve it at room temperature with a drizzle of olive oil and garlic in the Italian manner. And a spinach salad with raw mushrooms and artichoke hearts is nearly a meal in itself.

WILD GREENS

CLAYTONIA
(miner's lettuce)
Claytonia perfoliata

CHICKWEED
Stellaria media

SHEPHERD'S PURSE
Capsella bursapastoris

VIOLETS
Viola odorata

A WIDE ARRAY OF WILD PLANTS can be used in salads. Many cultures regularly harvest from the country-side, particularly in Europe. Here I have focused on only a few of the most common greens, as the use of wild plants is a study in itself. These wild plants, usually referred to as weeds, are so widespread that you may already have them growing in or around your garden. Before you intro-duce them intentionally, see if you can find them in your own or a neighbor's yard. Make very sure you can properly identify these greens; consult an expert if you have the slightest doubt. If you are gathering your greens from the wild, to avoid lead contamination, make sure they're not growing by a heavily traveled road.

How to grow: Miner's lettuce is native to the West Coast but grows readily in most parts of the country. Grow it in partial shade in rich, moist soil. The stems, which grow to about 6 inches, emerge from the base and produce round, flat, fleshy leaves about 2 inches across that wrap around the stem. Little clusters of white flowers emerge from the center of the leaves. Seeds are available from a few seed companies. Plant the seeds in the spring in the garden or in late summer for winter use in cold frames or greenhouses. In mild-winter areas the plants take light frosts and winter over or appear in early spring from seeds planted in the fall. When har-vesting, gather whole young plants or individual leaves. You can harvest young or mature leaves a few at a time or cut back the whole plant to an inch above the ground and treat it as a cut-and-come-again crop as you would lettuce.

Chickweed (I know of no source of seeds) is another common garden weed. Its light green leaves grow on a rather disjointed stem that sprawls across the ground. It appears in the spring and dies back in the hot weather.

Shepherd's purse is a low-growing plant (to 2 inches) with cut leaves. It

Miner's lettuce

produces a little seed stalk that has a spike of tiny heart-shaped seed pods.

The common violet that grows so readily in shady parts of many gardeners' yards has both edible heart-shaped leaves and edible purple flowers. Harvest the leaves in the spring when they're tender and use them as you would most greens. Miner's lettuce, chickweed, shepherd's purse, and violets have few pest and disease problems. For chickweed, harvest only the very young leaves.

How to prepare: Miner's lettuce has very succulent leaves and a slightly "grassy" taste. For chickweed, the very young leaves are tender, a little tangy, and have that characteristic "grassy" taste as well. Shepherd's purse has a taste all its own, with a slightly sulfurous overtone. Violet leaves have a slight tang. Use all of the wild greens in a mixed salad with other greens and edible flowers.

Miner's lettuce grown as a cut-and-come-again crop

Violets and dandelions

145

favorite
salad
recipes

If you occasionally enjoy pulling off a memorable coup when you entertain, a salad garden should be in your arsenal. Frankly, I've been known to purr when folks ooh and ahh over my salads, and someday I'm bound to get caught gloating. The discussion around the table can get quite animated. "Miner's lettuce—what's that?" Or "Look, I have a pea blossom. And what do you suppose this is?" And "Wow, this tastes great!"

A truly masterful salad is a work of art and is best achieved with a garden a few feet from the kitchen. To orchestrate a well-blended green salad, many experts recommend you limit yourself to only a handful of ingredients; that way diners can savor the tang of the sorrel, the slight bitterness of the radicchio, and the buttery texture of the lettuces. The idea is to give clear flavors and not produce a muddy mix.

That's very fine advice for most of your salad making, but if "show biz" is what you want, I say once and a while throw out the rules. Try using, say, four or five varieties of red and green baby lettuces, some serrated burnet leaves ("What's this?" they'll ask), some tiny pink 'Ragged Jack' kale leaves, a little arugula, some tiny dandelion leaves, and a little purslane or miner's lettuce. Make a ceremony of it. Bring to the table a big bowl of your greens, a decanter of vinegar (maybe with a few raspberries in it), some light-green olive oil, and a small bowl of flower petals and dress the salad at the table. Once the salad is anointed, sprinkle the petals over the greens. Voilà! A happening! It's fun when you can use food to please the eye as well as the palate. And sometimes an animated discussion of food is the perfect icebreaker for a dinner party.

Obviously, your everyday salads are not going to be as grandiose as the one described above. Simpler salads and clear flavor combinations wear better on a daily basis. Nothing beats the lettuces as the backbone of your salad garden. Simple green salads made primarily with lettuces can be dressed up one day with dill, another with nasturtiums, and yet another with Roquefort

---

A salad (*left*) of ornamental kale, curly endive, and Batavian lettuce or chèvre. The pristine fresh lettuces of all types can be used in an infinite variety of combinations. To the lettuces you can add some of the radicchios, endives, and chervil to create your own mesclun mix or gather wild greens and edible flowers for a completely different dish. As you experiment, you might try some combinations that other cooks have enjoyed. For instance, serve the basic mesclun salad with garlic-rubbed croutons or smoked duck or quail. Try an autumn salad made with frisée combined with nutty arugula, mâche, and sliced russet apples and sprinkled with chopped hazelnuts. Other classics are a spinach or young dandelion-green salad topped with a hot bacon dressing, and the bitter chicories with a honey vinaigrette.

Before you begin creating your salads, take a look at the general guidelines on how to integrate a salad into the meal in the profile of Bruce Naftaly and Robin Sanders (page 150), and to refresh your memory, you may wish to read the descriptions of the tastes and complementary flavors of the greens, herbs, and edible flowers in the "Encyclopedia of Salad Greens."

To start making your salad, scan the garden to see what's looking best, or what needs to be picked, and taste as you go along. Has the arugula or mustard gotten too hot? If so, try some of their flowers instead. Does the kale or chard need thinning? The little leaves are wonderful. Think of flavors to combine, but also visualize the colors and shapes you want in your salad. The greens, served with a simple dressing, can be the end in themselves

Salads come in many different styles. Here is a large garden salad, a Caesar's salad, and a composed salad of cucumbers and yellow tomatoes. At the side is a head of curly endive.

or the foundation to build on and the vehicle for featuring baby beets, fresh pears, or even grilled tuna.

Look beyond the salad garden to the rest of your vegetables for ingredients. Have the radishes gone to seed? The pods are good in salads. Are the peas growing well enough so that you

can harvest a few of the sweet young shoots? Do you have fava beans growing vigorously? Their young leaves are tender and flavorful. Is the apple tree in bloom? The flowers are a rare treat. If you have nasturtiums, pick a few tangy leaves or flowers. And, of course, look over your "weeds." Are the edible ones young and succulent? As you can see, the boundaries of the salad garden really encompass the whole yard, and a "salad awareness" can stimulate you to look at your yard with new eyes.

Once you have chosen your salad ingredients, you need to prepare them. Wash the greens; it is critical to remove the grit and occasional insect that might have taken up residence there. The easiest way to wash a reasonable amount of greens is to fill a large container half full of cool water and gently slosh the greens up and down so the grit sinks to the bottom. You might need to do this a few times. Then dry the greens well. (Wet greens will shed the dressing and make it watery.) By far the easiest and most efficient way to dry greens is to use a salad spinner. If you don't have one, pat the greens dry

with paper or tea towels. Place your clean and dry greens in a plastic bag or between damp paper towels and refrigerate until you are ready to serve them. Keep any flowers you may have picked separate, because they are fragile; most should be preserved by putting their stems in water or between damp towels.

If you are using only small baby lettuces and greens, once you wash and dry them, they're ready to serve. (Remember to have them very dry and dress them only lightly, as the dressing will easily weigh them down.) If you are using mature, full-sized greens, most people prefer that they be bite-size; tear them gently so as not to bruise them. Alternatively, serve whole leaves, as is the custom in some cultures. The diner is then expected to dexterously

fold an individual leaf around a fork and eat it in its entirety or to cut the salad with a knife and fork.

The presentation of your salad can be anything as simple as putting the bowl with the dressed salad on the table and having everyone help themselves or a downright ceremonial presentation with all the trimmings. You can mix the greens together or arrange them on individual serving plates to accentuate the leaf shapes or colors. The choice is up to you, the artist. Some cooks prefer to dress the salad themselves; others let the diners dress their own.

The greens laid out on this basket include (*clockwise from the top*) young ornamental kale, spinach, mâche, arugula and baby 'Russian Red' kale, and in the middle miner's lettuce.

Bruce Naftaly and Robin Sanders

Fifteen years ago, while visiting the Seattle area to explore new developments in vegetable cookery in the Northwest, I was told about Le Gourmand, a restaurant known for its creative use of fresh vegetables and local specialties. While there I met with chef-owners Bruce Naftaly and Robin Sanders. They had begun experimenting with a variety of unusual greens, herbs, flowers, and wild edibles in the seventies, years before greens became fashionable, and have accumulated a vast knowledge of salad greens, producing dishes like asparagus with sweet cicely herb butter and salads of miner's lettuce, or pristine young dandelions, or the mixed flavors of kale, anise hyssop, and preserved duck, dressed with balsamic vinegar.

Over the years Robin and Bruce have cultivated a network of hobby and market gardeners who supply them with fancy greens, fresh herbs, and flowers, and they've developed their own ideas about what makes a good salad. "First, it's a question of taste," said Robin, "Just as with colors— some people like red, others blue—if you like it, it's right. Next I ask, What's the purpose of the salad? To cleanse the palate after a meal? To balance a heavy course? And what comes next? If it's a light dessert, you don't want a pungent, heavy salad; that would be more appropriate as a luncheon meal or before a rich game dish. Finally, what's the high point of the meal: the salad or the entrée?"

"A salad is a mixture of textures and tastes," Bruce said. "You need to taste everything, maybe even take notes on the characteristics of various ingredients for later combinations." For example, he explained, you should be aware of ways in which ingredients complement one another. Mustard brings out one flavor in greens, vinegar accentuates another, and orange juice and honey have still different effects. "Notice everything," said Bruce. "Are the greens smooth or fuzzy? Crisp or soft? Hot and spicy, bitter or sour?"

Most cooking is improvising, combining textures and flavors in ways that please, Bruce and Robin believe. "We all get better with practice," Robin added. "You shouldn't be afraid to try different combinations; don't be afraid to make a mistake. Of course, you don't want to get carried away, filling a salad with everything in sight either; too many ingredients tend to muddy the flavors. Try featuring just a few greens."

I asked Bruce and Robin what salad greens they like to use and how they might combine them. For a rich salad they suggest arugula and/or slightly spicy mustard greens; rich and tender mizuna, bitter radicchio, and/or edible chrysanthemums; and a small amount of slightly sweet anise hyssop. This kind of salad is best served with a fruity olive oil and balsamic vinegar or other heavy dressing.

For light salads they suggest lettuces, very young dandelions, grassy-flavored chickweed (used sparingly), and mâche (corn salad), a favorite because

it's neutral, nutty, and slightly sweet. They also like lamb's-quarters and purslane because, as Bruce explained, "they're not very strong, and they give interesting flavor and texture contrasts—very nice with lettuces."

Onc of Robin's personal favorites is arugula—if it's not too sharp. "When it's really strong, I sometimes chop it up and use it like an herb in a dressing. But when it's not too strong, it has a full, nutty taste, and it's spicy. It makes my mouth come alive."

Bruce especially likes French sorrel. "It's lemony—tart, but still springy," he said. "It's one of the first greens to come up in the spring, so I often use a little in my spring salads." Bruce also likes anise hyssop, which he maintained "has an interesting licorice taste. It's a little fuzzy, and the flowers are very pretty and tasty as well. I like to use hyssop sparingly in warm salads, maybe with some kale and preserved goose or duck. It's nice with a balsamic vinegar; then it has a sweet-and-sour flavor that I like a lot."

Both Robin and Bruce like mild mustard greens in salad. They combine the mustard with heavy greens, add pork or lamb cured with red currant juice or red currant vinegar (which is very tart but fruity), honey, and a warm dressing. Served warm,

this salad makes a light main course—or a nice appetizer if served in a small quantity.

Just as Bruce and Robin have personal favorites, they also have personal dislikes. Both, for example, avoid combining sweet dressings with members of the Brassica family. "We think that brings out the worst in Brassicas," they said. "Instead, we use a simple oil and wine vinegar dressing—not a sweet balsamic, but a dry sherry."

"Through the years we've experimented," Bruce concluded, "and we've enjoyed creating all types of salads. We've put nasturtium leaves, tips of young pea vines, young leaves of salad burnet, and sweet cicely in our salads, and we've garnished them with chive, dandelion, and broccoli flowers."

After I left Le Gourmand, I felt compelled to look beyond my salad garden and start harvesting more from my flower border. I looked at my weeds in a new light and scrutinized my vegetable garden to find other parts of the plants to use in my salads. Bruce and Robin, part of a new breed of cooks, have not only diverged from routine produce selection; they have broken the shackles of the vegetable garden to include wild and ornamental plants in their edible horizon.

delicious dressings

While I've given much attention to the salad greens and herbs, another key ingredient to a masterful salad is the dressing. Dressings have traditionally been a blend of some sort of oil, an acidic liquid such as vinegar or lemon juice, and flavorings. Nowadays nonfat ones are popular too. Here the main ingredient is often non-fat yogurt, or fruit or vegetable juice. The dressing is an important element in a salad; it serves to meld the many flavors and textures and to highlight the greens. It is important that the dressing ingredients, like your greens, be fresh, fresh, fresh and of the best quality. Off-tasting stale oils and vinegars undo the delicate and sweet flavors of the greens and defeat the purpose of serving superior salad vegetables.

For your dressing use cold-pressed oils and high-quality vinegars (discussed in detail below) whenever possible. Note that these ingredients must be stored well to maintain their freshness. Once opened, oils and vinegars should be kept in a cool, dark place or, if used infrequently, in the refrigerator. While some authorities disagree with putting oil in the refrigerator, I recommend that you do so with oil that will be kept more than six months. However, some oils solidify when refrigerated and need to be brought up to room temperature to be used. Check your oil before using it, as a rancid, off-tasting oil will ruin your salad.

The secret to making a good dressing is to keep the proportions right and match the ingredients to the particular combination of salad makings. A vinaigrette is a time-honored and versatile dressing. You can dress it up or down and vary it from day to day. Most recipes for a vinaigrette call for three or four parts oil to one part vinegar. If you use too much oil, the dressing will be bland and slick; too much vinegar makes it too sharp.

For other dressings the proportions and ingredients vary according to personal taste, the types of oils and vinegars used, and the kind of dressing intended. For example, a rich or creamy dressing is nice with the heartier greens; it might be made with an egg yolk, a heavier olive oil, or a cheese. Sweeteners such as honey, apple juice, white grape juice, and the many types of citrus juice are especially nice to accompany tangy salads made with sour or bitter greens. Fresh garden herbs also enrich your salad palette, giving a dressing a minty tang one day and a dusky dill flavor another. For some reason, I used to be intimidated by the idea of making my own salad dressings, and for years I purchased bottled ones. Nowadays I find making dressings quite simple, and the results greatly improve my salads, especially since I use my own herbs. If you're hesitant, start with a vinaigrette, which is easy, and use the lighter oils and vinegars.

Oils

Oils are used in salads to coat the greens and carry the flavorings. They add richness and, in many cases, their own flavors. Many different

Flavored olive oils (*above*) add richness to a salad.

kinds of oils are used in salads; they range from the heavy, fruity olive oil to the light, almost neutral safflower oil. While the choice of an oil is basically a matter of taste, the olive oils and some of the nut oils are most often used on strong-flavored greens. For everyday salads the lighter oils are the most versatile. Whatever your choice, try to buy cold-pressed oils (check the label), which means they have not been heated and are consistently of high quality. Heating can destroy some of the vitamins in an oil. Store oil in a cool place.

Olive oils: There are many informal grades of olive oil. They range from "extra-virgin" (first cold pressing) and "pure virgin" to "pure" and "fine." Though the latter sound distinctive, olive oils in these categories often have a lighter and sometimes off taste. Generally, the extra-virgin and pure virgin olive oils have been cold-pressed and the oil poured off, the pure and fine oils are sometimes made from imperfect olives, and/or are extracted by boiling or chemical means. Oils of higher quality are generally green in color and have varying flavors. You'll need to taste many different kinds to determine your own flavor preferences.

Salad oils: The so-called salad or vegetable oils available in the market are quite tasteless, adding only a slippery quality to your salad at best and an off taste at worst. However, the light-tasting ones like safflower, corn, and canola oils available at natural-food stores have a light, clear flavor. They can be used with some of the lighter-flavored greens and combine

nicely with the nut or olive oils in varying amounts to taste and take added flavoring (as with chilies, garlic, or herbs) very well.

Nut oils: Many oils are made from nuts, including walnut, almond, sunflower seed, and hazelnut oils, and they are usually pressed in the fall and are best used very fresh. These oils are elegant with some of the hardier greens or with mâche, where their nutty flavors really come through. Walnut oil is particularly nice with bitter salad greens or combined with raspberry vinegar and served over a mixed lettuce salad. Or try it with some lemon juice in a spinach salad. The hazelnut and almond oils are particularly nice with avocados and with spinach. For all the nut oils, the taste is heightened by garnishing the salad with a few roasted nuts.

Vinegars

Basically, vinegar is fermented fruit juice or, as with Oriental rice wine vinegars, grain. A good vinegar should be sharp but not harsh, mellow but not anemic, and have a fruity aroma. The best vinegars have complex flavors similar to fine wines. The acidity level for most commercial vinegars is between 5 and 7 percent.

Wine vinegars: Wine vinegars, either white or red, are among the most flavorful and popular for mixed green salads. White wine vinegars are the most versatile for making herb vinegars or flavoring with fruits.

Balsamic vinegar: Balsamic vinegar

(*aceto balsamico*) is a rich-tasting vinegar. It is slightly sweet and quite rich. There can be confusion surrounding balsamic vinegar. The traditional balsamic vinegars are made in small batches and aged for decades in wooden vats, and a bottle is priced like that of the best red wines. For the few times they are used in a salad dressing, they are generally combined with a superior red wine. In contrast, there are numerous mass-produced, moderately priced brands of balsamic vinegar available. Each brand has a slightly different taste, and the more expensive ones are generally more mellow and have a more complex flavor. Try a few to find your favorite.

Cider vinegar: Cider vinegar, made from apples, is a fairly mild vinegar. It combines well with light oils and apple juice and in sweet-and-sour dressings.

Oriental vinegars: Another type of vinegar I like to keep on hand is an Oriental rice wine vinegar. Oriental vinegars come in many forms and flavors, but most are quite a bit milder than European vinegars. Oriental vinegars are particularly nice when combined with a little soy sauce and ginger, and used to dress Oriental greens.

Flavored vinegars: Flavored vinegars can be made at home or are available from specialty stores. These are made by steeping fruit (for instance, raspberries), herbs, hot peppers, flower petals, or garlic in the vinegar. To make a fruit vinegar, start with a good wine vinegar and use two parts fruit to one part vinegar. Soak the fruit in the vinegar for a few weeks and then strain the vinegar. Put the strained vinegar in a sterilized bottle, cap it, and refrigerate. To make herb vinegars, use the same process, but fill the bottle with a large handful of your favorite fresh herb, cap it, and then let it sit for a few days until the flavor suits your taste. Pour it through a strainer, put it in a bottle and cap it. Herb vinegars do not need refrigeration.

Mustards

One of the most common flavorings for salad dressings is mustard. Like vinegar or lemon, it adds sharpness to a dressing, but has a zesty flavor as well. Mustard is made from the ground-up seeds of the white- (yellow) or brown-seeded mustard plants, *Brassica alba* and *B. nigra*. Both mustards, in fact, can be grown in your garden. Plant the seeds and grow as you would standard mustard. After the plants flower and go to seed, harvest the yellow pods and thresh; then win-

now to remove the chaff as you would with grains and strain through a kitchen strainer with holes just large enough to let the seeds go through. To make into a grainy mustard, grind up the seeds in a blender with a liquid such as wine or vinegar and then mix with other flavorings such as honey or spices.

The most common type of mustard used in salad dressings is commercial Dijon-type. Use mustard sparingly in your salad dressings and add to taste. Once opened, keep your prepared mustard in the refrigerator. It is best used within six months.

Vinaigrettes and Other Blends

The dressing we all need in our repertoire is the basic vinaigrette. This ageless combination of ingredients is elegant in its simplicity, and its

quality depends on superior ingredients. Once the basic vinaigrette is mastered, it has endless variations. And then there all those wonderful creamy dressings—some are made with yogurt, others with cheese, cream, or buttermilk. They are also valuable in the salad repertoire. Newcomers to the dressing world are low-fat and nonfat ones. Salads are so much a part of a healthy diet that it makes sense to lower the caloric content for day-to-day salads. With the help of a lot of talented cooks, we now have an ever expanding choice of tasty low-calorie dressings. Let's start with a basic vinaigrette.

Basic Vinaigrette

Though the proportions of ingredients in a basic vinaigrette differ from cook to cook, the following is a representative recipe. It makes enough to dress a salad for four to six people. As vinaigrettes keep well for a few days, I generally double the amounts to make enough for two salads, refrigerating half.

> 1½ to 2 tablespoons wine vinegar
> ¼ teaspoon salt
> Dash of freshly ground black pepper
> 5 to 6 tablespoons extra-virgin olive oil

Mix the vinegar, salt, and pepper and with a whisk blend in the oil to taste. Drizzle most of the dressing over 4 to 6 handfuls of mixed greens, toss gently, and taste. Add more dressing, if needed, and serve.

A salad of Oriental mustard, tatsoi, and lettuces is garnished with mustard flowers

The beauty of a vinaigrette is that it has hundreds of variations. Different oils and acidic ingredients can be substituted for the oils and vinegar. The most common substitutions are lemon juice for the vinegar, and corn or safflower oil instead of olive oil. Beyond that, there are numerous seasonings that can be added. The most popular are minced garlic or shallots, prepared mustard, and chopped herbs. Most cooks have their own favorite combinations. For example, Robin Sanders and Bruce Naftaly favor using extra-virgin olive oil and a twenty-five-year-old sherry vinegar for mild, tender greens such as lettuces, mâche, young mizuna, and miner's lettuce. Herbs that can be used on these salads include chopped fresh parsley, basil, chervil, tarragon, and thyme. Robin and Bruce use the heavy kalamata (Greek) olive oil and balsamic vinegar for hardier autumn and winter greens such as chard, kale, and chicory. Rose geranium leaves, rosemary, oregano, marjoram, and other strong-flavored herbs can also be used with these greens, though with discretion.

An elegant vinaigrette I really enjoy is from Annie Somerville, executive chef at Greens Restaurant, San Francisco's premier vegetarian restaurant. The slightly sweet dressing is a great foil to some of the tart or bitter hearty greens. Annie suggests serving the vinaigrette over a bed of radicchio, creamy hearts of escarole, and other assertive winter greens topped with fresh orange or grapefruit sections. She also uses this vinaigrette over a salad of arugula, mizuna, and red mustard, to

which she adds slices of fresh figs and melon. In this case she cuts the amount of vinegar in half.

Vinaigrette with Blood Oranges and Champagne Vinegar

½ teaspoon finely minced orange zest

2 tablespoons freshly squeezed blood orange or tangelo juice

1 tablespoon champagne vinegar

¼ teaspoon salt

3 tablespoons extra-virgin olive oil

In a small bowl, whisk together the orange zest, juice, vinegar, and salt. Once the salt dissolves, whisk in the oil.
Makes ⅓ cup.

Oriental Vinaigrette

Oriental greens seem to cry out for their own dressing. I like to use a basic vinaigrette but substitute Oriental ingredients and seasonings to complement the "cabbagy" flavor. This rich (but very low-cal) and flavorful vinaigrette is perfect on all sorts of mixed Oriental greens. I love to sprinkle a teaspoon or so of toasted sesame seeds over the salad after it is dressed, to accentuate the flavors. You can add all sorts of steamed vegetables to the salad and cooked chicken as well.

½ teaspoon honey

¼ teaspoon freshly grated ginger

1½ tablespoons rice wine vinegar

2 tablespoons commercial low- or nonfat defatted chicken or vegetable stock

½ teaspoon tamari or soy sauce

½ teaspoon chili oil

1 tablespoon cold-pressed toasted sesame oil

1 tablespoon fresh chopped cilantro (optional)

In a small bowl, mix the honey and ginger. Slowly add the vinegar, whisking it in to incorporate the honey. Slowly add the stock, whisking it in. Add the tamari and oils and stir to blend.
Makes ½ cup.

Vinaigrettes don't always need to be used as a dressing drizzled over a salad; they can also be used to marinate vegetables that are then served cold, by themselves or over greens. Chef John Downey, from Downey's in Santa Barbara, California, likes to use a vinaigrette filled with lots of garden-fresh herbs to marinate lightly cooked vegetables for appetizer salads. For this he uses a light combination of olive and corn oils and cider vinegar to let the flavors of the greens and herbs predominate. The recipe makes enough to use as a marinade or to use for two or three green salads.

Vegetable Marinade

¼ cup cider or wine vinegar

1 to 3 teaspoons high-quality mustard

1 to 2 tablespoons minced shallots, dried or green onions, garlic, or a combination of all three

⅓ cup finely chopped fresh herbs such as basil, dill, fennel, parsley, or thyme

Salt and freshly ground black pepper

1 cup oil

In a bowl, combine all the ingredients except the oil or process them briefly in a food processor. Slowly whisk in the oil or add it to the processor. Let the mixture stand for ½ hour to allow the flavors to blend; check the seasoning. Refrigerate the unused portion and use within a few days.

Makes 1½ cups.

Creamy Dressings

Creamy dressings are at their best served with crunchy, crisp lettuces and with assertive greens. As a rule they are not used with baby greens, because they weigh down the greens and overpower the delicate flavors.

Garden Ranch Dressing

This creamy dressing is great on all types of lettuces and mixed greens. Beets and croutons would be great additions to the salad. This recipe makes enough for at least two large salads and will keep in the refrigerator for up to ten days.

- 1 tablespoon grated shallots or sweet onion
- 1 garlic clove, minced or pressed
- 1 cup buttermilk
- ½ cup mayonnaise
- 1 teaspoon honey
- 1 teaspoon white wine vinegar
- ¼ teaspoon hot sauce
- ¼ teaspoon salt
- ¼ teaspoon freshly ground black pepper
- 1 tablespoon finely chopped fresh parsley
- 1 tablespoon finely chopped fresh chives
- 1 teaspoon chopped fresh thyme
- 1 teaspoon chopped fresh chervil
- ½ teaspoon chopped fresh tarragon

In a mixing bowl, combine all the

ingredients, blending them together well. Refrigerate before serving.

Makes 1½ cups.

Light Roquefort Dressing

No dressing made with Roquefort can be truly low-cal; however, this version cuts out much of the fat but not the flavor of the classic version. You can also substitute Gorgonzola or Maytag blue cheese, one of the few domestic blue cheeses that works in this recipe. The dressing keeps for up to ten days in the refrigerator.

- 1 garlic clove, minced or pressed
- 1 tablespoon lemon juice
- 1 tablespoon extra-virgin olive oil
- 4 ounces Roquefort cheese, crumbled
- ⅓ cup nonfat plain yogurt
- ⅔ cup low-fat sour cream
- 3 tablespoons nonfat milk
- ¼ teaspoon hot sauce
- ¼ teaspoon salt
- ¼ teaspoon freshly ground black pepper

In a small mixing bowl, blend the garlic, lemon juice, oil, and Roquefort with a fork until creamy. Add the yogurt, sour cream, milk, hot sauce, and salt and pepper. Whisk until the mixture is well blended. Refrigerate until ready to serve.

Makes 2 cups.

Sauce Verte

Here is a variation of the classic French *sauce verte* and the *German Grüne Sosse* traditionally served over cold cooked vegetables. It can also be used as a dip for cooked or raw vegetables.

- ½ cup fresh blanched and drained spinach
- ¼ cup chopped fresh watercress leaves (or ⅛ cup fresh young arugula or nasturtium leaves)
- ¼ cup fresh chopped parsley leaves (preferably Italian)
- ¼ cup fresh chopped sorrel leaves
- 1 scallion or 1 shallot or 2 tablespoons snipped chives
- 1 small garlic clove, crushed
- 2 tablespoons minced fresh tarragon, dill, or chervil
- 1½ cups mayonnaise
- ½ cup sour cream or yogurt

Blend all the ingredients in a blender or food processor. Makes about 2½ cups.

Low-Calorie Dressings

There are a number of ways to cut down on fat and calories in salad dressings. Most of the calories come from the oil, which gives a rich flavor and a slippery "mouth feel" to dressings. You can still get the same effect by reducing the amount of oil and substituting vegetable or chicken stock instead. The amount you substitute is a matter of personal taste. I've given proportions that I like; you may want more or less oil. Some cooks recommend substituting a little corn syrup or honey for the oil, to help add viscosity. To add rich flavors to a dressing, try adding stock, fruit juice, or tomato juice or substitute some of the richer-flavored nut oils for a milder olive or vegetable oil. The Oriental Vinaigrette (page 155) is one such recipe; here are a few more.

Basic Low-Cal Vinaigrette

This dressing is to my salad repertoire what my jeans are to my wardrobe. Always there, always comfortable. It's at home with any mixed or mesclun salad, and I often substitute my favorite herb of the day for the fennel.

    3 tablespoons commercial low- or nonfat
        chicken stock
    1 tablespoon fresh lemon juice
    1½ tablespoons extra-virgin olive oil
    1 teaspoon chopped fresh fennel (or
        chives, basil, dill, or tarragon)
    ⅛ teaspoon salt
    ⅛ teaspoon freshly ground black pepper

Pour all the ingredients into a small bowl and whisk to blend them. Use immediately or refrigerate for up to a week.

Makes ½ cup.

Sun-Dried Tomato Dressing

I met David Hirsch, chef at the Moosewood Restaurant in Ithaca, New York, and author of *The Moosewood Restaurant Kitchen Garden*, while visiting the restaurant. I asked him if he'd share a salad dressing recipe that was low in fat. David suggests serving this robust thick and creamy dressing with greens "that are more than delicate," such as crunchy romaine, endive, arugula, radicchio, lightly steamed vegetables, and potatoes. The dressing looks best when made with sun-dried tomatoes that have retained some of their red color. The carrots also add

color as well as sweetness, fiber, and nutrition.

    5 dry-packed sun-dried tomatoes
    ⅓ cup raw grated carrot
    1 garlic clove, minced or pressed
    2 tablespoons extra-virgin olive oil
    1½ to 2 tablespoons cider vinegar
    1 tablespoon minced fresh parsley
    1½ tablespoons minced fresh basil

Soak the tomatoes in boiling water to cover for about 15 minutes, or until they're soft. Drain the tomatoes, reserving 2 tablespoons of the liquid. Combine all the ingredients except the fresh herbs in a blender, add ⅓ cup water and the reserved 2 tablespoons of drained water, and puree until smooth. Stir in the herbs.

Makes 1 cup.

Jody's Low-Cal French Dressing

So-called French dressing is actually an American invention. This dressing is also flavored with tomatoes, but the result is very different. Jody Main contributed this recipe. On some days she is my venerable garden manager, on others she caters healthy food to conscientious companies or tests products for a natural-food store. This dressing keeps in the refrigerator for about a week.

    1 cup tomato juice
    ¼ cup tomato paste
    Juice of 1 lemon
    1 teaspoon honey
    1 garlic clove, pressed
    ¼ teaspoon freshly ground black pepper
    1 teaspoon grated onion

    2 tablespoons red wine vinegar

Combine the ingredients by rotating them in a jar with a good seal, or whisk them together in a small bowl.

Makes 1½ cups.

Herbs and tomatoes *(above)* add depth to a simple salad. It's easy to grow just a few herbs in a strawberry jar. You can even fit a cluster of herbs in a flower bed near the kitchen and add a few leaves to all of your salads.

finishing touches

Salads are a wonderful way to combine all sorts of ingredients: herbs, edible flowers, cheeses, nuts, and vegetables can all be added to a salad.

Herbs

Chopped herbs of all sorts can be simply sprinkled over a salad before serving or can be added to the dressing. I prefer fresh herbs, as I find dried ones tasteless and papery. The best herbs for salads are soft fleshy ones like basil, dill, tarragon, chervil, fennel, sorrel, mint, lemon balm, parsley, cilantro, salad burnet, and chives. For salads I shy away from the tough-leafed herbs, especially strong-flavored ones like sage, oregano, and rosemary.

Herbs are best prepared just before using them because they become discolored and limp and lose some of their volatile oils once cut. To coarsely chop them, roll the leaves in a ball and with a large, sharp, chef's knife, slice down and forward, moving along the whole mass. To cut them more finely (to mince), stack the chopped herbs and change your hand position: hold the knife with one hand and gently guide it with your other hand resting on top. Bring the front of the blade down first, then the back, continuing in a rapid rocking motion. Occasionally draw the pile of cut herbs back together as you work.

Edible Flowers

Not all flowers are edible—in fact, some are poisonous—so you need to identify the species carefully. The following flowers are edible and suitable for salads: anise hyssop, borage, calendulas, chives, chrysanthemums, Japanese honeysuckle, marigolds, nasturtiums, edible peas (not sweet peas), dianthus, roses, runner beans, violas, pansies, and violets. You can also feast on the edible blossoms of broccoli, mustard, radishes, and arugula.

Edible flowers are easy to prepare. When possible, pick them in the cool of the day, wash them if needed, and examine them for critters. Put them in water if they have a stem, or lay them out on damp paper towels and put them in a plastic bag, and refrigerate. With some flowers—such as roses, calendulas, and chrysanthemums—only the petals are edible. With others—violas, violets, pea and runner blossoms—the whole flower can be eaten. If you are using only the petals of a flower, separate them just before using, as they wilt within minutes.

To use edible flowers in a salad, it is customary to sprinkle them over a dressed salad at the last moment before serving, in what's called a flower petal confetti, or to arrange them on the sides of a bowl or platter. If you pour salad dressing over them and mix them into the salad, they usually clump up.

Sprouts

Sprouts are flavorful baby plants that have just emerged from their seeds. All sorts of sprouts can be used on salads; they are filled with many nutrients, disease-fighting substances,

'Strawberries and Cream' nasturtium (*above*) is but one of a dozen varieties of dwarf nasturtiums available to gardeners. Many more varieties of edible flowers also grow well in a salad garden. They include the 'Jewel Mix' and 'Alaska Mix' nasturtiums (*right, top*), all sorts of pansies including the 'Antique Mix' and 'Blues Mix' (*right middle*), and 'Pacific Beauty' calendulas (*right, bottom*).

and lots of flavor. The most popular sprouts for salads are alfalfa, sunflower, radish, clover, lentils, and black and mung bean. New to the sprout world are broccoli sprouts, proven to be even higher in cancer-fighting chemicals than broccoli itself, and almond sprouts, which are a real culinary treat. They taste like slightly sweet almonds and have the texture of cucumbers.

Sprouting seeds is simplicity itself. All you need is a clean mason jar, a metal screen lid or a piece of cheesecloth and a rubber band, and seeds. Purchase seeds at a natural-food store. If you get them from a nursery or seed company, make sure the seeds have not been treated with a toxic fungicide. Soak the seeds in the jar overnight. Depending on the type of plant, you need different amounts of seeds to make approximately 1 cup of sprouts. For one batch of sprouts, use 1½ tablespoons alfalfa seeds, or ½ cup hulled sunflower seeds, ½ cup lentils, ½ cup black beans, ½ cup mung beans, 2 tablespoons radish seeds, 1½ tablespoons clover seeds, or 3 tablespoons broccoli seeds. (See below for information on sprouting almonds.) In the morning drain the seeds and run cool water through them a few times to rinse them well. Put the screen lid or cheesecloth over the top and set the jar on its side in a cool, fairly dark place. Rinse the seeds two or three times a day for two to four days, or until the sprouts are a quarter inch or so long. Rinse them a last time to remove any seed hulls. (Place the broccoli sprouts in light, but not sunlight, to green up

for half a day.) Refrigerate all sprouts in a sealed jar or plastic bag and use them within a few days.

Almond sprouts are grown the same way, but with a few exceptions. Purchase raw, unblanched almonds and sprout ½ cup for only two to three days, or until the white "nib" just emerges. Then refrigerate. If you allow almond sprouts to get any larger, they get very bitter. To use sprouts in a salad, sprinkle the sprouts over the salad just before serving, dress, and serve.

Fruits

While obviously a whole salad can be made with fruits, a number of fruits make stellar additions to green salads. Raspberries sprinkled over a green salad make it company fare, as does raspberry vinegar. Pears, peaches, and kiwifruit can be peeled and sliced to adorn a green salad just before serving. The texture is luscious when combined with butter lettuces and mâche. Apples and Oriental pears add a pleasant crunch and slight sweetness to salads and can be used with most greens. Remember to cover these fruits with vinegar, lemon juice, or vinaigrette just after slicing them, or they will turn brown. Navel, blood, and mandarin orange sections and the related tangerine, tangelo, and grapefruit sections add zest to greens and are especially lovely with bitter radicchios and tart sorrel. Citrus juices of all types work well in vinaigrettes. Try sour lemon and lime juice and add a little honey or apple juice to cut the tartness.

Kiwifruit, pomegranates, and crisp 'Fuyu' persimmons make a salad special as do figs and grapes, when you're entertaining.

Cheeses

Dozens of cheeses have been used to glorify salads throughout the ages. Some of the most popular ones are the creamy, assertive Roquefort, Gorgonzola, and blue; the dense, strong, and crumbly Parmigiano-Reggiano, dry Jack, and Asiago; and the sharp feta. Two mild cheeses are sometimes used as well, chèvre and mozzarella. The strong-flavored cheeses can be slivered or crumbled and then sprinkled over salad greens just before serving. The best salad combinations for strong cheeses are ones made up of assertive or crunchy greens such as spinach, mustards, arugula, escarole, radicchios, and hearts of romaine. A couple of traditional combinations to try are mozzarella slices with tomatoes and lettuce, and Roquefort cheese with pears and fall greens. In French bistros, chèvre is traditionally spread on thin toasted bread and warmed slightly to accompany a green salad. The blue cheeses and Roquefort are most famous in rich creamy dressings.

Toasted Nuts and Seeds

Nuts are a great final addition to salads—they give crunch, richness, and extra protein and are packed with vitamin E. Most nuts, including pecans, walnuts, hazelnuts, pistachios, pine nuts, and peanuts, enhance a salad. All lend their own distinctive flavor, which is heightened if you toast them and even more so if you dress the salad with a nut oil. Seeds too are great in salads; include pumpkin, squash, and sesame—either toasted or plain.

Use shelled nuts whole or chopped, salted or unsalted, glazed or flavored or plain. To roast nuts and seeds, lay them out on a cookie sheet and bake at 325°F until they perfume the air, 3 to 4 minutes, and have browned oh so slightly. Stir often by shaking the tray, and watch nuts and seeds carefully because you don't want them to burn. To roast a small amount of nuts or seeds, put a few tablespoons in a dry cast-iron skillet and toast them over

low heat for 2 or 3 minutes. Plain or roasted nuts that you won't use immediately should be stored in sealable bags in the freezer, or they will quickly turn rancid.

Glazed Walnuts

2 cups raw shelled walnut halves

4 teaspoons sugar

½ teaspoon salt

Dash of ground red pepper

Heat the oven to 350°F.

Put the walnuts in a saucepan and cover them with water. Boil them for 5 minutes and then drain them in a colander. Mix the sugar, salt, and ground red pepper in a small bowl. Toss the mixture with the nuts until they're coated. Spread the nuts on a cookie sheet. Bake for 6 to 10 minutes, or until they have colored slightly, shaking the tray occasionally so they cook evenly. Watch carefully to prevent burning.

Makes 2 cups.

Vegetables

Vegetables of all types have an affinity for salad greens. Of course, most of us use raw tomatoes, cucumbers, celery, carrots, radishes, peppers, sweet and green onions, and avocados in our salads. Still others are inspired to use pea pods, corn kernels, cauliflower florets, and julienned celeriac, daikon, Jerusalem artichokes, and kohlrabi. The fact is, almost any vegetable can be added to a salad in one form or another. When you consider cooked vegetables for a green salad, it's harder to think of ones that can't be used. Some can be placed on the greens warm, and others can be added once they've chilled. To get an idea of the range of choices, try adorning your green salad with roasted potatoes, carrots, beets, and parsnips; blanched beans, both string and shelling; baked or steamed beets or carrots; steamed broccoli, cauliflower, nopals, and chayotes; roasted or grilled fennel, bell and Anaheim peppers; or marinated tomatoes, bell peppers, artichoke hearts, and beans.

As a rule, vegetables are added toward the end of the salad-building process. They are generally julienned or cut very thin or into small bites so they don't weigh down the greens and clump at the bottom of the bowl.

Croutons

Croutons, I'm sure, started out as a way to use up stale bread, but what a creative and delicious solution. All sorts of breads can be used: whole wheat, rye, rustic Italian and French, baguettes, even corn bread if it's substantial enough. When making croutons, if the bread is not very stale, it helps to cut it into cubes and bake them at 350°F on a cookie sheet for 10 to 15 minutes to dry them out so they absorb less oil or butter. Croutons can be cut so they are square cubes, the type that is sprinkled over a salad, or they can be small slices of a baguette dressed with goat cheese and served on the side of the plate in the French manner.

Croutons add crunch and substance to a salad and, if coated with bacon drippings, herbs, garlic, Parmesan cheese, or chili powder, they can add a lot more flavor as well. Add croutons at the very last minute so they don't turn soggy. Extra croutons can be put in a freezer bag and frozen for a few months. Crisp them up in a 325°F oven for a few minutes before using.

Garlic Croutons

You can make garlic croutons by toasting cubes or slices of bread in the oven and then rubbing them with a clove of peeled raw garlic or you can use the following recipe.

2 garlic cloves, pressed

3 tablespoons extra-virgin olive oil

15 to 20 thin slices of stale French baguette

Heat the oven to 350°F.

Combine the garlic and oil in a small bowl. Place the baguette slices on a cookie sheet. Brush the top side of each slice with the garlic oil. Bake the croutons for 6 to 10 minutes, until slightly golden.

Herb Croutons

4 tablespoons extra-virgin olive oil

2 tablespoons mixed, minced fresh herbs such as rosemary, oregano, thyme, marjoram, or tarragon

4 cups (1-inch) bread cubes

Heat the oven to 350°F.

In a small bowl combine the oil and herbs. Lay out the bread cubes on a baking sheet and drizzle the herb oil over them. Toss. Bake them for 6 to 10 minutes, or until golden brown.

Basic Garden Salad

One of the great things about a salad is that you can usually take whatever is in the garden and mix it in the bowl, from early spring to late fall—even in the winter if you have a cold frame or a little greenhouse. Most times the base of your salad will be a lettuce or some other neutral green. To determine quantities, figure on one large handful of greens per person. To the greens you can add all sorts of goodies like baby beet thinnings, wild chickweed, pea shoots, cooked vegetables, meats, nuts, and croutons. The list is almost endless. The following is a jumping-off-type recipe; the point is to let your imagination and your garden dictate what goes into your glorious salads.

For the dressing:

1½ tablespoons balsamic or rice wine vinegar

1 garlic clove, minced

1 teaspoon Dijon-style mustard

3 to 4 tablespoons extra-virgin olive oil

1 teaspoon fresh dill or basil

Salt and freshly ground black pepper

For the salad:

1 small head butter lettuce

1 small head Oak Leaf lettuce

1 small Belgian endive, base removed and leaves separated

1 small head of frisée

10 arugula leaves

6 dill flowers

1 large red chard stem, cut into 2-inch pieces

To make the dressing: In a small bowl, mix the vinegar, garlic, mustard, oil, and herbs; add salt and pepper to taste; and whisk until emulsified.

To make the salad: Combine the greens in a large bowl. Pour the dressing over the greens, and toss. Garnish with dill flowers and chopped chard stem.

Serves 4.

Mesclun

Mesclun is a Provençal term for a mix of many varieties of young red and green lettuces, arugula, endives, and chervil, either grown together or grown separately and then mixed in the salad bowl. See the section on mesclun in "How to Grow a Salad Garden" (page 94). Mesclun is traditionally served with a simple vinaigrette. There are endless variations using different vinegars, lemon juice, sprinklings of fresh herbs, and all different types of croutons and seasonings.

For the dressing:

2 tablespoons red wine vinegar

Salt and pepper

6 to 7 tablespoons extra-virgin olive oil

For the salad:

4 to 6 large handfuls of mixed mesclun greens

To make the dressing: Mix the vinegar, salt, and pepper and using a whisk blend in the oil to taste.

To make the salad: Toss the dressing gently with the mesclun greens and serve.

Serves 4 to 6.

Caesar Salad

Tijuana, Mexico, was the unlikely birthplace of this famous salad. It remains one of the best treatments for crisp, fresh romaine. Worcestershire sauce, not anchovies, was part of the original recipe. They are both listed here as optional; use one or the other.

For the dressing:

5 or 6 tablespoons extra-virgin olive oil

1 garlic clove, pressed

4 tablespoons fresh lemon juice

1 teaspoon Worcestershire sauce (optional)

Dash of Tabasco sauce

4 to 6 anchovy filets, diced and mashed (optional)

For the salad:

1 large head romaine lettuce

1 egg, boiled 1 minute

½ teaspoon salt

Freshly ground black pepper

½ cup freshly grated Parmesan cheese

Garlic croutons

To make the dressing: In a large salad bowl, combine the olive oil, garlic, lemon juice, Worcestershire sauce, and Tabasco. Add the anchovy filets, if you're using them, and blend them well into the dressing.

To make the salad: Add the romaine to the dressing and toss. Crack the egg into the salad; sprinkle the salad with salt, pepper, and Parmesan cheese; and toss again until all the leaves are well coated. Add the croutons and toss one final time.

Serves 6.

Garden Bouquet Salad with Lemon-Herb Vinaigrette

Here's an elegant and exotic salad from Renee Shepherd of Renee's Garden.

For the dressing:

1 small green onion, chopped fine

1 teaspoon Dijon-style mustard

2 or 3 tablespoons lemon juice

1 tablespoon dry white wine

1 egg yolk

1 tablespoon minced fresh parsley

1 tablespoon minced chive flower petals or chopped fresh chives

¼ teaspoon salt

Pinch of freshly ground black pepper

¾ cup olive oil

For the salad:

2 small heads radicchio (or red-leaf lettuce as a second choice)

2 handfuls mâche (corn salad)

2 small heads Bibb lettuce

12 to 14 leaves (2 handfuls) young arugula (rocket) or watercress

2 or 3 fresh sorrel leaves

¾ cup fresh green and purple basil leaves

½ cup calendula petals

¼ cup borage flowers

To make the dressing: With a whisk, combine all the ingredients except the oil. Slowly whisk in the oil, beating continually until the mixture is thoroughly blended. Season to taste. Refrigerate until ready to use.

To make the salad: Wash and dry the greens. Reserve 6 to 8 leaves of radicchio or red lettuce. Tear the remaining radicchio, mâche, Bibb lettuce, arugula, and sorrel into bite-size pieces and combine them with the basil leaves in the center of the salad bowl. Line the outer edges of the bowl with the reserved radicchio or red lettuce. Sprinkle the calendula petals and borage flowers around the outside border.

Stir the dressing again and pour it over the salad after presenting it at the table.

Serves 6.

Tangy Salad with Roasted Garlic Dressing

This salad appeals to mustard- and garlic-lovers alike. The greens are primarily members of the tangy mustard family, and the richness of the roasted garlic rounds out the flavors and gives body to the dressing.

For the dressing:

    4 roasted garlic cloves (see below),
        peeled
    1 raw garlic clove, minced
    1 teaspoon mustard powder
    4 tablespoons extra-virgin olive oil
    3 tablespoons red wine vinegar
    Dash of salt and freshly ground black
        pepper

For the salad:

    1 small head romaine lettuce
    1 small head frisée
    1 small bunch watercress
    1 small handful tatsoi leaves
    1 small handful red mustard leaves
    Garnish: mustard or nasturtium flowers

To roast the garlic: Heat the oven to 350°F. Place a whole head of garlic on a baking pan and roast it for 20 or 30 minutes, or until it's soft. Cool the garlic. The pulp can now be squeezed out to use in the dressing. (Extra roasted garlic can be served as a spread for rustic bread.

To make the dressing: Into a small mixing bowl, squeeze the roasted garlic pulp. Add the raw garlic and mustard powder and work them into a smooth paste with a spoon. Gradually stir in the olive oil and vinegar. Add salt and pepper to taste. Beat the mixture with a wire whisk until the ingredients emulsify.

To make the salad: Wash and dry the greens in a salad spinner or on paper towels. Tear the leaves into bite-size pieces and arrange them in a large salad bowl. Before serving, stir the dressing again, pour it over the greens, and toss. Garnish with the mustard or nasturtium flowers.

Serves 4.

165

Spicy Valentine Salad

In some parts of the world, hot peppers are considered an aphrodisiac. What would be more appropriate for a Valentine's Day dinner for two than a hot, spicy salad combining a sprinkling of red pepper with the cool, sweet taste of tender lettuces?

For the dressing:

1 teaspoon Dijon-style mustard

2 tablespoons lemon juice

4 tablespoons extra-virgin olive oil

½ teaspoon honey

½ teaspoon hot sauce

½ teaspoon dried hot red pepper flakes

For the salad:

1 small head romaine lettuce

1 small head butter lettuce

2 tablespoons Parmesan cheese, grated

2 tablespoons snipped chives

To make the dressing: In a small bowl, combine the mustard and lemon juice with a whisk. Slowly whisk in the olive oil until it is incorporated. Add the honey, hot sauce, and red pepper flakes and combine. Refrigerate until ready to serve.

To make the salad: Wash and dry the lettuce leaves. Arrange medium-size whole leaves of romaine inside the perimeter of a large bowl. Overlap the leaves like the petals on a flower. Arrange whole butter lettuce leaves in the center, overlapping the leaves to form the center of the flower.

Before serving, drizzle the dressing over the salad. Sprinkle on the Parmesan cheese and chopped chives.

Makes 2 large servings.

Riot of Color Salad

How about a really colorful salad for a special occasion? Use your imagination and the edible flowers from your garden.

For the dressing:

1½ tablespoons white wine vinegar

3 or 4 tablespoons sunflower oil

1 tablespoon clover or wildflower honey

Salt and freshly ground pepper

For the salad:

1 large head romaine

1 large head butter lettuce

1 small head frisée

4 to 6 young leaves of yellow chard

A dozen or so edible flowers such as yellow and blue violas, purple pansies, nasturtiums, yellow calendulas, or red dianthus

To make the dressing: In a small bowl, whisk together vinegar, sunflower oil, and honey; add salt and pepper to taste; and set aside.

To make the salad: Arrange the romaine, butter, and frisée lettuces, and the yellow chard leaves on a large colorful platter. Remove the petals from some of the flowers and leave some whole. Sprinkle on the flower petals and garnish with whole blossoms. Bring the salad to the table and let diners dress their own salads.

Serves 4.

Jody's Almond Sprout Salad

Jody is my garden manager and a longtime sprout enthusiast. This is her wonderful salad.

For the dressing:

⅛ teaspoon salt

1 garlic clove, peeled and chopped

¼ cup extra-virgin olive oil

2 tablespoons balsamic vinegar

¼ teaspoon Dijon-style mustard

Freshly ground black pepper to taste

For the salad:

1 medium head leaf lettuce

1 small bunch spinach

1 small bunch baby red chard with stems, or ½ pound mixed baby greens

1 cup assorted sprouts: radish, mung, sunflower, alfalfa, or other sprouts, rinsed and drained

1 cup almond sprouts

Garnish: nasturtium flowers and leaves

To make the dressing: In a small bowl, pour the salt over the chopped garlic and crush it with a fork to make a paste. Add the oil, vinegar, mustard, and pepper. Whisk the ingredients together until the mixture is creamy.

To make the salad: Wash and spin-dry the lettuce, spinach, and chard. Tear the leaves into bite-size pieces and place them in a large salad bowl. Sprinkle the sprouts on top. Dress and toss the salad. Garnish with nasturtium flowers and leaves.

Serves 6 to 8.

Sorrel and Avocado Salad

Food maven Carole Saville and I were working on a cooking project together when we created this recipe, in which the citrus tang of sorrel is melded with lemon juice and is tamed with honey and creamy avocados.

For the dressing:

3 tablespoons fresh lemon juice, divided

⅓ cup of avocado oil, or extra-virgin olive oil in combination with walnut or hazelnut oil

1 tablespoon honey

1 teaspoon chopped fresh thyme leaves

For the salad:

6 large handfuls of mixed salad greens

½ cup baby sorrel leaves

1 avocado

½ cup sugar snap peas, strung and cut on a diagonal

Garnish: lemon slices, yellow violas, and calendulas

To make the dressing: Into a small pitcher, pour 2 tablespoons of the lemon juice; add the oil, honey, and thyme; and stir vigorously until the dressing is well mixed.

To make the salad: Wash the greens and sorrel leaves and dry them in a salad spinner. Arrange them in a large salad bowl. (Cover the bowl with plastic wrap and refrigerate it if you are not ready to assemble the salad.) Just before serving, cut the avocado into slices and dip them in the remaining 1 tablespoon lemon juice to keep them from turning brown.

Pour the dressing over the greens and toss. Arrange the avocado slices and sprinkle pea slices over the salad, garnishing with the lemon slices and flower petals.

Serves 6.

Wild, Wild Party Salad

This salad has a festive feeling and a bright minty flavor. It can include a dozen varieties of greens, even wild ones like violets or miner's lettuce, or a tamer mix of three or four lovely lettuces and baby spinach. Much depends on what's available in your garden or at the market.

For the dressing:

5 tablespoons avocado oil

5 tablespoons chardonnay

3 tablespoons white wine vinegar

1/4 teaspoon salt

1/4 teaspoon freshly ground black pepper

2 teaspoons finely chopped fresh mint

For the salad:

1 large head romaine lettuce

2 large heads leaf lettuce

1 large handful arugula (2 cups, stems discarded)

1 small bunch of young spinach

2 to 4 handfuls of greens, such as baby bok choy or chard, upland cress or watercress, violet leaves, miner's lettuce, minutina, and chrysanthemum leaves, or other seasonal greens

1/2 cup violet and violas, petals of calendula and chive blossoms, small florets of mustard or broccoli blossom

Garnish: whole calendula or viola flowers, florets of mustard or broccoli, and a few sprigs of whole greens

To make the dressing: In a small mixing bowl, combine the oil, wine, vinegar, salt and pepper, and mint. Stir the ingredients with a wire whisk. Refrigerate until ready to serve.

To make the salad: Wash the greens and dry them in a salad spinner or on paper towels. Tear the greens into bite-size pieces and place them in a very large serving bowl. Cover the bowl with plastic wrap and refrigerate until ready to serve.

Wash the edible flowers and put the stems in a glass of water or place the flowers between damp paper towels. Refrigerate until ready to serve.

To serve, remove the petals from the calendula and chive flower heads, break the mustard or broccoli flower heads into small florets, and set them aside. Stir the dressing, drizzle it over the greens, and toss lightly to coat the greens. Sprinkle the chive and calendula petals, mustard and broccoli florets, and whole viola or violet flowers over the salad. Garnish one side of the bowl with a cluster of whole calendula or viola flowers, mustard or broccoli florets, and a few whole greens.

Serves 6 to 8.

Spinach Salad with Hazelnuts and Fresh Raspberries

This recipe, from John Downey of Downey's, in Santa Barbara, makes a fine summer appetizer or, with a little grilled duck, squab, chicken, or fresh goat cheese, a wonderful lunch entrée.

For the dressing:

1 tablespoon raspberry jam

½ cup fresh raspberries

1 tablespoon Dijon-style mustard

½ cup raspberry vinegar

Lots of fresh ground black pepper

1½ cups extra-virgin olive oil, plus 1 tablespoon hazelnut oil

For the salad:

½ cup hazelnuts

2 bunches (about 2 pounds) young spinach, washed and dried

Garnish: a few whole raspberries

To make the dressing: Combine all ingredients except the oil in a bowl with a whisk, mashing the berries. Slowly whisk in the oil. Allow the dressing to sit for 30 minutes; then correct the seasoning if necessary.

To make the salad: Roast the hazelnuts in a 350°F oven for 15 minutes, or until the brown skin flakes away and the nuts are lightly browned. Let the nuts cool for 5 minutes. Rub them with a dry towel to remove the skins.

Crush the hazelnuts and toss them with the spinach and dressing. Garnish with a few whole raspberries.

Serves 6.

Spinach and Watercress Salad with Savory Mayonnaise

Robin Sanders and Bruce Naftaly at Le Gourmand contributed this cool autumn and early spring recipe as well as the suggestions for winter salad garnishes. You can add cold, moist poached chicken to this salad—it goes very well with the sage in the dressing. If you prefer a lighter flavor, substitute safflower, peanut, or corn oil for half the olive oil. In winter, use dried calendula petals as a garnish. All the ingredients except the greens must be around 70°F.

For the dressing:

2 egg yolks

3 tablespoons balsamic vinegar, divided

½ teaspoon salt

¼ teaspoon freshly ground white pepper

1 teaspoon chopped fresh sage (optional)

1 cup kalamata (or other virgin) olive oil

⅓ cup glace de viande (dark-brown reduced brown stock)

For the salad:

A generous amount of spinach and watercress leaves for each serving in a 2:1 ratio (or substitute young nasturtium or rocket leaves for the watercress)

Garnish: calendula petals

To make the dressing: In a large bowl, use an electric beater on medium-high speed or a whisk to beat the egg yolks well. Add 1 tablespoon of the vinegar, and the salt, pepper, and sage (if desired). While beating, very slowly add the oil and the remaining vinegar by droplets until half the oil is used; add the rest in a slow stream. Beat in the glace de viande. Remove the dressing to a storage or serving container using a rubber spatula. Refrigerate if you will not be using it immediately.

To make the salad: Warm the dressing to room temperature by beating it in a bowl before tossing it with the greens. Dress the greens to taste and garnish with calendula petals. You may have more dressing than you need; refrigerate the remainder.

Serves 8 or more.

Baked Beet Salad with Fall Greens and Feta Cheese

The richness of beets and the hearty flavors of fall greens and feta cheese make for a satisfying salad for a cold fall evening. When possible I use French feta as it is not so salty.

For the dressing:

1 tablespoon rice wine vinegar

½ teaspoon Dijon-style mustard

4 tablespoons extra-virgin olive oil

2 tablespoons finely chopped fresh chervil or 1 tablespoon tarragon

Salt and freshly ground black pepper

For the salad:

4 medium-size beets, either red or yellow, or a combination of the two

4 handfuls of young fall greens (mâche, spinach, lettuce, tatsoi, mustard) in bite-size pieces

¼ pound feta cheese, crumbled

To make the dressing: In a small bowl, whisk together the vinegar, mustard, and oil until they're well blended. Add the chervil and salt and pepper to taste.

To make the salad: Remove the tops of the beets and set them aside to use in another dish. Wash the roots and put them in a small casserole dish that has

a lid. Bake at 300°F for about 1½ hours, or until tender. (If you are baking different-colored beets, cook them in separate casserole dishes, or the colors will bleed.) Remove the dish from the oven, let beets cool, then peel and thinly slice them into a ½-inch thick julienne. Refrigerate until ready to use.

Put the greens in a large bowl and pour ¾ of the vinaigrette over them. Toss to coat the greens evenly. Arrange the greens on a large serving plate. Put the beets in a small bowl and pour the rest of the dressing over them and stir to coat the beets. Arrange the beets over the greens. Sprinkle feta cheese over the beets and serve.

Serves 4 to 6.

Hearty Greens with Pears, Blue Cheese, and Chives

Serve this salad as a first course or increase the quantities by 50 percent and use it as the centerpiece of a luncheon menu.

For the dressing:

¼ cup nonfat yogurt

⅓ cup crumbled blue cheese

1 teaspoon Dijon-style mustard

½ teaspoon Worcestershire sauce

2 teaspoons white wine vinegar

¼ teaspoon curry powder

3 tablespoons snipped chives

1 teaspoon honey

Salt and freshly ground black pepper

For the salad:

4 large handfuls of mixed salad greens: lettuces, spinach, mâche, endive, and radicchio

1 tablespoon lemon juice

2 ripe, medium-size Comice or Bartlett pears

8 thin triangular slices of blue cheese

Garnish: chive leaves and blossoms

To make the dressing: In a small bowl, stir gently the yogurt, blue cheese, mustard, Worcestershire sauce, vinegar, curry powder, chives, and honey to combine. Add salt and pepper to taste. Adjust the seasoning if necessary. Refrigerate until ready to serve.

To make the salad: Wash and dry the greens in a salad spinner or on paper towels. Just before serving, set out four large salad plates. Put a handful of greens on each plate. Into a small bowl, pour the lemon juice and 4 tablespoons water. Cut each pear into ⅓-to ½-inch thick slices and dip the slices into the lemon water to prevent them from browning. Arrange four to six slices of pear on top of the greens on each plate. Place two slices of blue cheese on the side of each plate. Garnish with chive leaves and blossoms. Pour the dressing in a serving bowl. Serve immediately.

Serves 4.

Wild Greens with Oranges and Almonds

This salad has a base of neutral greens. To these are added greens that have a bit of bite. If you want to add more flavors, consider adding some slightly bitter greens like endive, radicchio, or escarole.

For the dressing:

Juice of 1 orange

1 tablespoon lemon juice

3 tablespoons extra-virgin olive oil

1 tablespoon walnut oil

1 tablespoon honey

For the salad:

3 generous handfuls of neutral greens such as lettuces, mâche, minutina, or spinach

1 handful of spicy and/or bitter greens such as arugula, mizuna, mustard, sorrel, red mustard, or cress

1 navel orange, peeled and sectioned

¼ cup sliced almonds

To make the dressing: In a small bowl, whisk to combine the orange and lemon juice, olive and walnut oils, and the honey.

To make the salad: Wash the greens and dry them in a salad spinner or on paper towels. Combine the greens in a large salad bowl. Drizzle the dressing over the greens and toss. To serve, garnish the salad with the orange slices and sprinkle on the almonds.

Serves 4.

Endive Salad with Oranges and Pistachios

This salad is lovely on a buffet table or served as part of a light luncheon.

For the dressing:

1 tablespoon extra-virgin olive oil

1 tablespoon white wine vinegar

2 tablespoons freshly squeezed orange juice

¼ teaspoon salt

¼ teaspoon freshly ground black pepper

For the salad:

2 Belgian endives

1 cup young spinach leaves

2 oranges

1 cup red seedless grapes

¼ cup shelled pistachios, coarsely
  chopped

To make the dressing: Combine the
oil, vinegar, orange juice, salt, and
pepper.

To make the salad: Pull apart the
endive leaves. Wash and spin-dry
them. Arrange the leaves in a concentric circle on a serving plate. Intersperse the spinach leaves. Peel the
oranges and cut them into slices.
Arrange the oranges on the endive and
spinach leaves. Add the grapes and
sprinkle on the pistachios. Drizzle
dressing over the greens and grapes.

Serves 4.

Oriana's Cabbage Salad

This recipe could also be called Latin
Coleslaw; it was given to me by my
young neighbor, Oriana Mendy. She
says it tastes best when made using
tomatoes from a friendly neighbor.

½ medium-size green cabbage, finely
  shredded

3 or 4 ripe tomatoes, diced

1 large ripe avocado, cut into 1/2-inch
  cubes

3 or 4 green onions, finely sliced

¼ to ⅓ cup chopped fresh cilantro

Juice of 1 lime

Salt

Place the cabbage, tomatoes, avocado,
and green onions in a large bowl.
Sprinkle the cilantro, lime juice, and
salt (to taste) over the cabbage mixture
and gently stir to combine the ingredients. Serve immediately in a large bowl
or prepare individual serving plates.

Serves 4.

Rainbow Slaw

This slaw is fairly low in calories for a party dish, and it's packed with nutrition. Serve it with grilled meats or as part of a buffet.

For the dressing:

Juice of 1 lemon

⅔ cup white wine vinegar

1 teaspoon salt

¾ teaspoon celery seeds

⅓ cup vegetable oil

3 or 4 tablespoons frozen apple juice concentrate

Freshly ground black pepper

For the salad:

8 cups finely sliced green cabbage (1 large head)

1 cup thinly sliced chard leaves

2 cups finely sliced carrots

1 small sweet onion, thinly sliced

1 cup thinly sliced red chard stems

To make the dressing: In a small bowl, mix together the lemon juice, vinegar, salt, celery seeds, oil, apple juice concentrate, and pepper (to taste) and stir until the ingredients are fairly well blended.

To make the salad: Place the cabbage in the bottom of a large salad bowl. Creating a decorative pattern, arrange the chard leaves, then the carrots, then the onions, and finally the chard stems.

Pour the dressing over the slaw and serve. The salad may be refrigerated for a few hours, but the dressing separates, and the red chard stems lose some of their color if the salad sits too long.

Serves 8 to 10.

Tomato and Basil Salad

This recipe is a regular summer feature on the menu of John Downey's restaurant in Santa Barbara when local farmers bring John luscious ripe tomatoes and fragrant basil.

For the dressing:

2 tablespoons extra-virgin olive oil

4 tablespoons red wine vinegar

1 garlic clove, minced

½ cup coarsely chopped fresh basil

Salt and freshly ground black pepper

Garnish: green peppercorns (optional)

For the salad:

4 large ripe garden tomatoes, sliced

1 small sweet red onion, thinly sliced

To make the dressing: Combine the oil, vinegar, garlic, basil, and salt and pepper in a small bowl.

To make the salad: Place the tomatoes in a shallow pan. Pour the dressing over the tomatoes and let them sit for about half an hour, then remove them with a slotted spoon. Arrange the tomatoes on four serving plates. Divide the onion slices among the plates, garnish with peppercorns, and serve.

Serves 4.

Crab and Asparagus Salad with Fancy Greens and Sorrel Dressing

This is a show-off dish fit for the fanciest "do." Fresh, fresh crab; fresh, fresh asparagus; and fresh, fresh greens all deserve this special pastry presentation.

For the puff pastry shell:

6 tablespoons butter

1 teaspoon salt

1 cup flour

4 eggs

For the dressing:

1 cup mayonnaise

¼ cup yogurt

1 tablespoon Dijon-style mustard

1 garlic clove, minced or pressed

1 tablespoon grated onion

¾ cup sorrel, finely chopped

½ teaspoon salt

Freshly ground pepper

For the filling:

1 pound asparagus

1 medium-size head romaine lettuce

1 pound crabmeat (about 3 cups)

½ pound mixed young greens such as
    mâche, baby butter lettuce or
    spinach, and tatsoi

To make the pastry: Heat the oven to 400°F.

In a 2-quart saucepan, bring 1 cup water to a boil over high heat. Add the butter and salt. As soon as the butter has melted, take the pan off the heat and add the flour all at once. Using a wooden spoon, stir the mixture quickly until the flour is completely blended. Put the pan back over medium-high heat and beat the dough until it comes away from the sides of the pan and forms a loose ball. Remove the pan from the heat. Let it cool for 5 minutes. Stir in the eggs, one at a time, beating thoroughly after each addition. The dough will appear to break apart with each egg but will reform with vigorous stirring. The eggs should be completely incorporated and the dough smooth and glossy.

Spoon the dough into a buttered 9-inch springform pan and spread it evenly over the bottom and up the sides a few inches. Bake for 40 minutes. Turn off the oven. Prick the pastry with a wooden pick in at least a dozen places and leave it in the oven to dry for 10 minutes. Remove the pan from oven and let it cool completely. Remove the sides of the pan. (This pastry shell may be made up to a day ahead.) Wrap the pastry loosely in aluminum foil and store it in a warm, dry place. Before using, crisp it in a 400°F oven for 5 minutes.

To make the dressing: Blend all the ingredients in a small bowl. If the dressing is too thick, thin it with a tablespoon or so of cream or milk.

To make the salad: Wash the asparagus and cut the spears into 2-inch pieces on a diagonal. Cook the asparagus in boiling water for 4 minutes. Drain and set aside.

Wash, dry, and separate romaine lettuce leaves. Set aside six of the tender inside leaves and coarsely chop the rest. You should have about 2 cups, chopped.

Combine the asparagus, crabmeat, and chopped romaine lettuce in a bowl. Mix with 1 cup of the dressing and refrigerate for up to 1 hour. Just before serving, place the pastry shell on a very large platter and fill it with the crab mixture. Surround the pastry shell with the remaining romaine leaves and the assorted young greens. Pour the remaining dressing in a small pitcher to be used on the greens.

Serves 6.

179

Duck Breast Salad

This is truly an elegant salad and perfect for an intimate dinner party. It is best served as a first course and then followed by a seafood entrée. The duck is succulent and tender if cooked to medium rare and begins to get drier and tougher as it approaches thoroughly done.

1 teaspoon black peppercorns

2 boneless duck breasts (1 pound total), skin and fat removed

¼ teaspoon salt

1 tablespoon vegetable oil

For the greens:

1 small heart of romaine

3 cups lightly packed spinach

2 cups lightly packed mâche

1 small head frisée

For the dressing:

1 shallot, minced

1 tablespoon dry sherry

1 tablespoon red currant jelly

2 tablespoons extra-virgin olive oil

2 tablespoons balsamic or sherry vinegar

¼ teaspoon fresh thyme

Heat the oven to 450°F.

On a flat surface, break up the peppercorns into a coarse grind by rubbing them with the bottom rim of a small cast-iron skillet. Rub the broken peppercorns into the sides of both duck breasts and season the meat with salt. Heat the vegetable oil to quite hot in a heavy cast-iron skillet. Add the duck and cook one side for about 2½ minutes, or until brown. Turn the breast over and place the skillet in the oven. Roast the duck for 6 to 8 minutes, or until medium rare.

While the duck is cooking, arrange the greens on a large platter, cover, and refrigerate.

Remove the duck from the skillet and place on a cutting board to rest. Put the skillet over medium heat, add the shallots, and sauté until they're soft, about 3 minutes. Deglaze the pan with 2 tablespoons water and the sherry. Add the red currant jelly and simmer until the jelly has melted. Transfer the sauce into a bowl, add the olive oil, vinegar, and thyme. Whisk until blended.

Remove the platter of greens from the refrigerator. Slice the duck breast on a diagonal into thin slices. Slide a long spatula under one of the sliced breasts and fan the slices out over the arranged greens. Repeat the process with the other breast. Drizzle the still-warm dressing over the duck and some of the greens. Serve immediately.

Serves 4.

appendix A planting and maintenance

This section covers the basics of planning a vegetable garden, preparing the soil, starting seeds, transplanting, fertilizing, composting, using floating row covers, cold frames, rotating crops, mulching, watering and installing irrigation, and maintaining.

Planning Your Garden
Vegetables

Vegetables are versatile. You can interplant a few colorful varieties among your ornamentals—many vegetables grow well in the same conditions as annual flowers. Or you can add ribbons and accents of color to your existing vegetable garden. Or you can create an entire rainbow garden from rough sketch to harvest. In addition, most vegetables grow well in containers and large planter boxes.

The first step in planning any vegetable garden is choosing a suitable site. Most chefs recommend locating the edible garden as close to the kitchen as possible, and I heartily agree. Beyond that, the majority of vegetables need at least six hours of sun (eight is better)—except in warm, humid areas, where afternoon or some filtered shade is best—and good drainage.

Annual vegetables need fairly rich soil with lots of organic matter. Note the type of soil you have and how well it drains. Is it fertile and rich with organic matter? Is it so sandy that water drains too fast and few plants grow well? Or is there a hardpan under your garden that prevents roots from penetrating the soil or water from draining? Poor drainage is a fairly common problem in areas of heavy clay, especially in many parts of the Southwest with caliche soils—a very alkaline clay.

It's important to answer such basic questions before proceeding because annual vegetables should grow quickly and with little stress to be tender and mild. Their roots need air; if the soil stays waterlogged, roots suffocate or are prone to root rot. If you are unsure of the drainage in a particular area in your garden, dig a hole about 10 inches deep and 10 inches wide where you plan to put your garden. Fill the hole with water immediately and again the following day. If there's water in the whole eight to ten hours later, find another spot in the garden that will drain much faster. Amend the soil generously with organic matter and mound it up at least 6 to 8 inches above the ground level. Or grow your vegetables in containers. Very sandy soil that drains too fast also calls for adding copious amounts of organic matter.

Find out the garden soil pH and nutrient levels with a soil test kit purchased from a local nursery or your state's university extension service, which can also lead you to sources of soil tests and soil experts. Most vegetables grow best in soil with a pH between 6.0 to 7.0—in other words, slightly acidic. Soil below 6.0 ties up phosphorus, potassium, and calcium, making them unavailable to plants; soil with a pH much higher than 6.5 ties up iron and zinc. As a rule, rainy climates have acidic soil that needs the pH raised, usually by adding lime; arid climates have fairly neutral or alkaline soil that needs extra organic matter to lower the pH.

After deciding where you are going to plant, it's time to choose your plants. See "Designing a Rainbow Garden" for suggested vegetables and flowers. Be sure to select species and varieties that grow well in your climate. As a rule, gardeners in northern climates and high elevations do well with vegetables that tolerate cool and/or short-summer conditions. Many vegetable varieties bred for short seasons and most salad greens are great for these conditions. Gardeners in hot, humid climes have success with plants that tolerate diseases well and are especially heat tolerant.

The USDA Plant Hardiness Zone Map has grouped eleven zones according to winter temperature lows, a help in choosing perennial plants but of limited use for annual vegetables. The new *Sunset National Garden Book,* published by Sunset Books, gives much more useful climatic information; it divides the continent into forty-five growing zones. Several regional maps describe the temperature ranges and growing season in detail. The maps are an integral part of this information-packed resource. Of additional interest to the vegetable gardener is the AHS Plant Heat-Zone Map, published by the American Horticultural Society. The heat map details twelve zones that indicate the average number of days each year when a given area experiences temperatures of 86°F or higher—the temperature at which many plants, including peas and most salad

USDA Plant Hardiness Zone Map

The USDA Plant Hardiness Zone Map is most useful when you are growing perrenial plants because it indicates how cold a given area will be during an average winter, In order to use the map, locate your geographical area and consult the color code that indicates which zone you are in. When you select plants for your garden, choose ones that grow in your zone. Remember, however, that the zone indicates how cold your garden will get, but there are many factors that affect the health of your plants, namely summer high's and your area's soil type.

greens, begin to suffer physiological damage. In "The Rainbow Vegetable Encyclopedia" on page 21, I indicate which varieties have a low tolerance to high temperatures and those that grow well in hot weather.

Other design considerations include bed size, paths, and fences. A garden of a few hundred square feet or more benefits from a path or two with the soil arranged in beds. Paths through any garden should be at least 3 feet wide to provide ample room for walking and using a wheelbarrow; beds should generally be limited to 5 feet across—the average distance a person can reach into the bed to harvest or pull weeds from both sides. Protection too is often needed, so consider putting a fence or wall around the garden to give it a stronger design and to keep out rabbits, woodchucks, and the resident dog. Assuming you have chosen a nice sunny area, selected a design, and determined that your soil drains properly, you are ready to prepare the soil.

Greens

The majority of salad greens need at least six hours of sun (eight is better) except in warm humid areas when afternoon or filtered shade is best, and good drainage. There are only a few salad greens that tolerate much shade: sorrel, cress, arugula, and some of the wild greens. Salad greens need fairly rich soil with lots of added organic matter. They can be planted in rows or in a bed by themselves—as part of the classic vegetable garden, say; some of them, especially Swiss chard, orach, Japanese red mustard, mizuna, and amaranths, are beautiful and work well interplanted in a flower bed with annual flowers, most of which need the same conditions. In addition, all salad greens can be grown in containers or in large planter boxes.

Once you've decided on where you are going to plant, it's time to choose your greens. Your major consideration will be, of course, what flavors you enjoy using in the kitchen. With this in mind, look for species and varieties that will grow well in your climate. As a rule, gardeners in northern climates and high elevations need vegetables that tolerate cool and/or short summer conditions. Salad greens are great for these conditions. Gardeners in hot, humid

areas require plants that tolerate diseases well and need to consider carefully how to work around the high summer heat.

The USDA Plant Hardiness Zone map has designated eleven zones according to winter lows. These demarcations are a help when you're choosing perennial plants but of only limited use for selecting annual plants like salad greens. The map in the new *Sunset National Garden Book* gives more detailed climatic information; it divides the continent into forty-five growing zones and describes the temperature ranges and growing season in much detail. Of additional interest to the salad gardener is the Heat Map, published by the American Horticultural Society, which details twelve zones that indicate the average number of days each year when a given area experiences temperatures of 86°F—the temperature at which many plants, including most salad greens, begin to suffer physiological damage. In the "Encyclopedia of Salad Greens" you'll find information on greens that have a low tolerance to high temperatures and those that grow well in hot weather.

In addition to analyzing your climate, knowing what type of soil a particular salad green needs is equally important. Consider how well your soil drains: is the soil rich with organic matter and fertility? Poor with bad drainage? So sandy that few plants grow well? Find out too what your soil pH is; nurseries have kits to test your soil's pH, and University Extension Services can lead you to sources of soil tests

and soil experts. As a rule, rainy climates have acidic soils that need the pH raised, and arid climates have fairly neutral or alkaline soils that need extra organic matter to lower the pH. Most salad greens grow best in soil with a pH about 6.5—in other words, slightly acidic soil. Soils that are below 6 tie up phosphorus, potassium, and calcium, making these elements unavailable to plants, and soils with a pH much over 6.5 tie up iron and zinc. Further, is there hardpan under your garden that prevents roots from penetrating the soil, or water from draining? This is a fairly common problem in areas of heavy clay. You need answers to these basic questions before you proceed because to be tender and mild, salad greens need to grow fast and with little stress. Salad greens do best with good drainage. Their roots need air, and if the soil stays waterlogged for long, roots suffocate or are prone to root rot. If you are unsure of how well a particular area in your garden drains, dig a hole about 10 inches deep and 10 inches across and fill it with water. The next day fill it again—if it still has water in it eight to ten hours later, you need to find another place in the garden that will drain much faster, amend your soil with much organic matter and mound it up at least six to eight inches above the ground level, or grow your salad greens in containers.

Soil Preparation

Vegetables

To prepare the soil for a new vegetable garden, first remove large rocks and weeds. Dig out any perennial weeds, especially perennial grasses like Bermuda and quack grass. Sift the soil and closely examine each shovelfull to remove every little piece of grass root or they will regrow with a vengeance. Taking up part of a lawn requires removing the sod. For a small area, this can be done with a flat spade. Removing large sections, though, warrants renting a sod cutter. Next, when the soil is not too wet, spade over the area.

Most vegetables are heavy feeders and few soils support them without supplements of lots of organic matter and nutrients. The big-three nutrients are nitrogen (N), phosphorus (P), and potassium (K)—the elements most frequently found in fertilizers. Calcium, magnesium, and sulfur are also important plant nutrients. Plants also need a range of trace minerals for healthy growth—among them iron, zinc, boron, copper, and manganese. A soil test will indicate what your soil needs. In general, most soils benefit from at least an application of an organic nitrogen fertilizer. While it's hard to say what your soil needs without a test, the following gives a rough idea of how much organic fertilizer to apply per 100 square feet of average soil: for nitrogen, apply blood meal at 2 pounds, or fish meal at 2 $\frac{1}{4}$ pounds; for phosphorus, apply 2 pounds bonemeal; for potassium, apply kelp meal according to the package, or in acidic soils 1 $\frac{1}{2}$ pounds of wood ashes. Kelp meal also supplies most trace minerals. In subsequent years, adding so many nutrients will not be needed if composting and mulching are practiced, especially if you rotate crops and use cover crops as green manure.

After the area has been spaded, cover it with 4 or 5 inches of compost, 1 or 2 inches of well-aged manure, and any other needed fertilizers or lime. Shovel on a few more inches of compost if you live in a hot, humid climate where heat burns the compost at an accelerated rate, or if the soil is very alkaline, very sandy, or very heavy clay. Add lime at this point if the soil test indicates the garden soil is too acidic. Follow the directions on the package. Sprinkle fertilizers over the soil. Incorporate all the ingredients thoroughly by turning the soil with a spade and working the amendments into the top 8 to 12 inches. If your garden is large or the soil is very hard to work, consider using a rototiller. (When you put in a garden for the first time, a rototiller can be very helpful. However, research has shown that continued tiller use is hard on soil structure and quickly burns up valuable organic matter if used regularly.)

Finally, grade and rake the area. You are now ready to form the beds and paths. With all the added materials, the beds will be elevated above the paths—which further helps drainage. Slope the sides of the beds so that loose soil will not be easily washed or knocked onto the paths. Some gardeners add a brick or wood edging to outline the beds. Putting some sort of gravel, brick, stone, or mulch on the paths will forestall weed growth and prevent your feet from getting wet and muddy.

Before planting the garden, the last task is to provide support for vining crops like pole beans and tomatoes. There are many types of supports—from simple stakes to elaborate wire cages; whatever you choose, it's best to install them before you plant. A salad garden need not be large. If succession plantings are planned, an area 10 by 12 feet will provide sufficient salad greens for a family of four in the spring and fall, and in winter in mild climates. The area can be rectangular, square, or free-form.

Unless you are installing a small salad patch off the patio or along the lawn, you will need to plan for a path or two. Paths through any garden should be at least 3 feet across, to allow ample room to walk and use a wheelbarrow. Beds are generally limited to 5 feet across, as that is the average distance a person can reach into the bed to harvest or pull weeds from both sides. Consider putting a fence or wall around the garden to give it a stronger design and to keep out rabbits and woodchucks if need be. Assuming you have chosen a nice sunny area, selected a design, and determined that your soil drains properly, you are ready to prepare the soil.

Greens

A salad garden need not be large. If succession plantings are planned, an area 10 by 12 feet will provide sufficient salad greens for a family of four in the spring and fall, and in winter in mild climates. The area can be rectangular, square, or free-form.

Unless you are installing a small salad patch off the patio or along the lawn, you will need to plan for a path or two. Paths through any garden should be at least 3 feet across, to allow ample room to walk and use a wheelbarrow. Beds are generally limited to 5 feet across, as that is the average distance a person can reach into the bed to harvest or pull weeds from both sides. Consider putting a fence or wall around the garden to give it a stronger design and to keep out rabbits and woodchucks if need be. Assuming you have chosen a nice sunny area, selected a design, and determined that your soil drains properly, you are ready to prepare the soil.

To prepare the soil for a new vegetable garden, first remove large rocks and weeds. Dig out any perennial weeds and grasses, making sure to get out all the roots, or the plants will come back and, unfortunately, up through your new salad plants. If you are taking up part of a lawn, the sod will need to be removed. If it is a small area, this can be done with a flat spade. Removing large sections, though, warrants renting a sod cutter. Next, when the soil is not too wet, spade the area over. As salad greens, like most vegetables, are heavy feeders, you need to supplement your soil with much organic matter and an organic nitrogen fertilizer, because most soil is deficient in these materials. Very sandy soil also needs much added organic matter to help hold moisture and fertility. Most soil benefits from adding phosphorus too, as plants need a sufficient amount for good root development and disease resistance. Phosphorus doesn't move in the soil like nitrogen does, so it must be incorporated into the soil before the plants are in place to make it available to the roots. A good source of organic phosphorus is bonemeal, worked into the top 8 inches of soil before planting at the rate of 4 cups per 100 square feet.

After the area has been spaded up, cover it with 4 or 5 inches of compost and an inch or two of well-aged manure. Add a few more inches of compost if you live in a hot, humid climate where heat burns the compost at an accelerated rate, or if you have very alkaline, very sandy, or very heavy clay soil. Since most salad greens grow best in a neutral soil, add lime at this point if a soil test indicates that your soil is acidic. Follow the directions on the package. Incorporate the ingredients thoroughly by turning the soil over with a spade. If your garden is large or the soil is very hard to work, you might use a rototiller. (When you put in a garden for the first time, sometimes one is needed. However, research has shown that continued use of tillers is hard on soil structure and quickly burns up valuable organic matter if used regularly.) If you can do this soil preparation a few weeks before you plant, so much the better.

Finally, grade and rake the area. You are now ready to form the beds and paths. Because of all the added materials, the beds will now be elevated above the paths—which further helps drainage. Slope the sides of the beds so that loose soil will not be easily washed or knocked onto the paths. Some gardeners add a brick or stone edging to outline the beds. Some sort of gravel, brick, stone, or mulch is needed on the paths to prevent weeds and to prevent your feet from getting wet and muddy. Once paths are in place, lay out plants where they are to be planted. Choose short types for the front of the beds and tall ones for the back. Check to see how far the plants will spread, so they won't be crowded once they mature; when salad greens grow too close together, they become prone to rot diseases and mildew.

Starting from Seeds

Vegetables

You can grow all annual vegetables from seeds. They can be started indoors in flats or other well-drained containers, outdoors in a cold frame, or, depending on the time of year, directly in the garden. When I start annual vegetables inside, I seed them in either plastic pony packs recycled from the nursery or in Styrofoam compartmentalized containers variously called plugs or seedling trays (available from mail-order garden-supply houses). Whatever type of container you use, the soil depth should be 2 to 3 inches deep. A shallower container dries out too fast; deeper soil is usually a waste of seed-starting soil and water.

Starting seeds inside gives seedlings a

safe place away from slugs and birds. It also allows gardeners in cold or hot climates to get a jump on the season. Many vegetables can be started four to six weeks before the last expected frost date, then transplanted into the garden as soon as the soil is workable. Furthermore, some vegetables are sensitive to high temperatures. By starting fall crops inside in mid- or late summer, the seeds will germinate and the seedlings will get a good start and be ready for transplant outside in early fall when the weather has started to cool.

The cultural needs of seeds vary widely among species. Still, some basic rules apply to most seeding procedures. First, whether starting seeds in the ground or in a container, use loose, water-retentive soil that drains well. Good drainage is important because seeds can get waterlogged, and too much water can lead to "damping off," a fungal disease that kills seedlings at the soil line. Commercial starting mixes are usually excellent as they have been sterilized to remove weed seeds; however, the quality varies greatly from brand to brand. I find most commercial mixes lack enough nitrogen, so I water with a weak solution of fish emulsion when planting the seeds, and again a week or so later.

Smooth the soil surface and plant the seeds at the recommended depth. Information on seed depth is included in "The Rainbow Vegetable Encyclopedia" on page 21, as well as on the back of most seed packages. Pat the seeds gently into the soil and water carefully to make the seed bed moist but not soggy. Mark the name of the plant, the variety, and the date of seeding on a plastic or wooden label; place the label at the head of the row.

If you are starting seeds in containers, put the seedling tray in a warm, but not hot, location to help seeds germinate more quickly.

When starting seeds outside, protect the seed bed with either floating row covers or bird netting to keep out critters. If slugs and snails are a problem, encircle the area with hardwood ashes or diatomaceous earth to repel them and go out at night with a flashlight to catch any that cross the barrier.

For seeds started inside, it's imperative that they have a quality source of light immediately after they have germinated; otherwise, new seedlings will grow spindly

and pale. A greenhouse, sun porch, and south-facing window with no overhang will suffice, provided the growing spot is warm. If bright ambient light is not available, use fluorescent lights, which are available from home-supply stores and specialty mail-order houses. Hang the lights just above the plants for maximum light (no farther than 3 or 4 inches away). Adjust the lights upward as the plants get taller. An alternative: If the temperature is above 60°F, I put my seedling trays outside on a table in the sun and protect them with bird netting during the day, then bring them in at night.

When seedlings have sprouted, keep them moist. If you have seeded thickly or have crowded plants, thin some. Using small scissors, cut the extra plants off, leaving the remaining seedlings an inch or so apart.

Do not transplant seedlings until they have their second set of true leaves. The first leaves that sprout from a seed are called seed leaves; they usually look different from the later-forming true leaves. If the seedlings are tender, wait until all danger of frost is past before setting them out. In fact, don't put heat-loving tomatoes and peppers out until the weather has thoroughly warmed up and stayed that way. Young plants started indoors should be "hardened off" before they are planted in the garden—that is, they should be put outside in a sheltered place for a few days in their containers to let them get used to the differences in external temperature, humidity, and air movement. A cold frame is perfect for hardening off plants.

Greens

You can grow all salad greens from seeds. They can be started indoors in flats or other well-drained containers, outdoors in a cold frame, or, depending on the time of year, directly in the garden. When I start salad greens inside, I seed them in either plastic pony packs in their trays that I recycle from the nursery or in Styrofoam compartmentalized containers, variously called plugs or speedling trays, available from mail-order garden-supply houses. The latter are best for starting large numbers of lettuces or Oriental greens. Whatever type of container you use, the soil depth should be two to three inches deep. Seeds planted any shallower will dry out too fast, and deeper soil is usually a waste of seed-starting soil and water.

Starting seeds inside provides your seedlings with safety from slugs and birds at the outset. It also allows gardeners in cold or hot climates to get a jump on the season. Many salad greens can be started four to six weeks before the last expected frost date and then transplanted out into the garden as soon as the soil can be worked. Further, many of the greens are sensitive to high temperatures, so by starting them inside in mid- or late summer, the seeds will germinate and the seedlings get a good start and be ready to be transplanted outside in early fall, when the weather has started to cool.

While starting most greens from seeds is a fairly simple and rewarding task, the cultural needs of seeds vary widely among species. Still, some basic rules apply to most seeding procedures. First, whether starting seeds in the ground or in a container, make sure you have a loose, water-retentive soil that drains well. Good drainage is important because seeds can get waterlogged, and too much water can lead to "damping off," a fungal disease that kills seedlings at the soil line. Commercial starting mixes are usually best since they have been sterilized to remove weed seeds; however, the quality varies greatly from brand to brand, and I find most lack enough nitrogen, so I water with a weak solution of fish emulsion when I plant the seeds, and again a week or so later.

Smooth the soil surface and plant the seeds at the recommended depth. Information on seed depth is included in the "Encyclopedia of Salad Greens" as well as on the back of most seed packages. Pat down the seeds and water carefully to make the seed bed moist but not soggy. Mark the name of the plant and variety and the date of seeding on a plastic or wooden label and place it at the head of the row. When starting seeds outside, protect the seed bed with either floating row covers or bird netting to keep out birds, digging cats, and varmints. If slugs and snails are a problem, circle the area with hard wood ashes or diatomaceous earth to keep them away and go out at night with a flashlight to catch any that cross the barrier. If you're starting seeds in containers, put the seedling tray in a warm, but not hot, place to help seeds germinate more quickly.

When starting seeds inside, once they have germinated, it's imperative that they immediately be given a quality source of light; otherwise the new seedlings will be spindly and pale. A greenhouse, sunporch, greenhouse window, or south-facing window with no overhang will suffice, provided it is warm. If one is not available, use grow lights available from home-supply stores or from specialty mail-order houses. Hang the lights just above the plants for maximum light (no farther than 3 or 4 inches away, at most) and move the lights up as the plants get taller. Another option I use if I'm starting seeds and the weather is above 60°F is to put my seedling trays outside on a table in the sun and protect them with bird netting during the day, bringing them in at night.

Once seedlings are up, keep them moist and, if you have seeded thickly and have crowded plants, thin some out. It's less damaging to do so with small scissors. Cut the little plants out, leaving the remaining seedlings spaced an inch or so apart. Do not transplant your seedlings until they have their second set of true leaves (the first leaves that sprout from a seed are called seed leaves and usually look different from the later true leaves) and, if the seedlings are tender, until all danger of frost is past. In fact, don't put heat-loving amaranths and purslane out until the weather has thoroughly warmed up and is stable. Young plants started indoors or in a greenhouse should be "hardened off" before planting in the garden—that is, they should be put outside in a sheltered place for a few days in their containers to let them get used to the differences in temperature, humidity, and air movement, and brought in at night. A cold frame is perfect for hardening off plants.

Transplanting

Vegetables

I generally start annual vegetables from seeds, then transplant them outside. Occasionally I buy transplants from local nurseries. Before setting out transplants in the garden, I check to see if a mat of roots has formed at the bottom of the root ball. If so, I remove it or open it up so the roots won't continue to grow in a tangled mass. I set the plant in the ground at the same height as it was in the container, pat the plant in place gently by hand, and water each plant well to remove air bubbles. I space plants so that they won't be crowded once they've matured; when vegetables grow too close together, they're prone to rot diseases and mildew. If I'm planting on a very hot day or the transplants have been in a protected greenhouse, I shade them with a shingle placed on the sunny side of the plants. Then I install my irrigation ooze tubing and mulch with a few inches of organic material. (See "Watering and Irrigation Systems" on page 190 for more information.) I keep the transplants moist but not soggy for the first few weeks.

Greens

I generally start my salad greens from seeds and transplant them outside. Occasionally I buy transplants of chards, cabbages, and endives from the local nurseries, as I seldom need many plants. Whether you purchase transplants or start your own, when setting them out in the garden, if a mat of roots has formed at the bottom of the root ball, remove it or open it up so the roots won't continue to grow in a tangled mass. Set the plant in the ground at the same height as it was in the container and pat the plant in place gently by hand. Water each plant in well to remove air bubbles. If I'm planting on a very hot day or the greens have been in a protected greenhouse, I shade the transplant with a shingle or such, placed on the sunny side of the plant. I then install my ooze irrigation tubing (see "Watering and Irrigation Systems" on page 190 for more information) and mulch with a few inches of organic matter. I keep the transplant moist but not soggy for the first few weeks.

Floating Row Covers

Among the most valuable tools for plant protection are floating row covers made of lightweight spunbond polyester or polypropylene fabric. Unfortunately, they are not particularly attractive, so they may be of limited use in a decorative rainbow garden. Laid directly over the plants, they "float" in place and protect plants against cold weather and pests.

If used correctly, row covers are a most effective pest control for cucumber, asparagus, bean, and potato beetles; squash bugs and vine borers; cabbage worms; leafhoppers; onion maggots; aphids; and leaf miners. The most lightweight covers, usually called summer-weight or insect barriers because they have little heat buildup, are useful for insect control throughout the season in all but the hottest climates. They reduce sunlight about 10 percent, which is seldom a problem unless your garden is shady. Heavier versions, sometimes called garden covers under trade names like Reemay, and Tufbell, variously block from 15 percent to 50 percent of the sunlight and guard against pests. They also raise the temperature underneath from 2°F to 7°F, which is usually enough to protect early and late crops from frost or to add warmth for heat-loving crops in cool-summer areas.

Besides effectively protecting plants from cold weather and many pests, floating row covers have numerous other advantages:

• The stronger ones protect plants from most songbirds, though not from crafty squirrels and blue jays.

• They raise the humidity around plants, a bonus in arid climates, but a problem with some crops in humid climates.

• They protect young seedlings from sunburn in summer and in high-altitude gardens.

There are a few limitations to consider:

• These covers keep out pollinating bees and must be removed when squash, melons, and cucumbers are in production.

• They are not attractive enough to use over most flower beds and in decorative settings. In fact, they make the garden look like a sorority slumber party.

• Many of the fabrics last only a year before starting to deteriorate (I use tattered small pieces to cover containers and in the bottoms of containers to keep out slugs, etc.).

• Row covers are made from petroleum products and eventually end up in the landfill.

• In very windy areas, the tunnels and floating row covers are apt to be blown away or shredded.

• The heavyweight versions reduce sunlight considerably and are useful only to help raise temperatures when frost threatens.

Rolls of the fabric, from 5 to 10 feet wide and up to 100 feet long, can be purchased from local nurseries or ordered from garden-supply catalogs. As a rule, mail-order sources have a wider selection of materials and sizes.

Before applying your row cover, fully prepare the bed and make sure it's free of eggs, larvae, and adult pests. (For example, if instead of rotating your crops, you follow onions with onions in the same bed, you are apt to have larvae of the onion root maggot trapped under the cover with their favorite food and safe from predators!)

Then install drip irrigation if you are using it, plant your crop, and mulch (if appropriate). There are two ways to lay a row cover: either directly on the plants or stretched over wire hoops. Laying the cover directly on the plants is the easiest to install. However, laying it over hoops has the advantage of being easier to check underneath. Also, some plants are sensitive to abrasion when the wind whips the cover around, causing the plant tips to turn brown. When placing the cover directly on the plants, leave some slack so plants have room to grow. For both methods, secure the edges completely with bricks, rocks, old pieces of lumber, bent wire hangers, or U-shaped metal pins sold for this purpose.

To avoid unwanted surprises, it's critical to look under the row covers from time to time. Check soil moisture; the fibers sometimes shed rain and overhead irrigation water. Check as well for weeds; the protective fiber aids their growth too. And most importantly, check for any insect pests that may be trapped inside.

Cold Frames

Cold frames are a device for keeping plants warm in the winter. This low-tech answer to a greenhouse provides a place to protect salad greens in the winter and to propagate summer crops. Here I cover the basics, but if you're interested in extensive winter salad green production, Eliot Coleman's book *Four Season Harvest* gives detailed instructions.

A cold frame is fundamentally a shallow box with a glass or acrylic lid, called a sash, and a back wall taller than the front; it is heated only by the sun. It can be a perma-nent structure or moveable, and made of wood, metal, or cinder blocks.

Cold frames are available from specialty garden-supply houses and include directions for their installation, or you can make your own from scratch. In all cases, find a location that receives maximum sun in the fall, winter, and spring—up against the house or a sheltering wall is optimal for warmth. Cold frames located near the house are easiest to maintain. You also need an area where the soil under the cold frame drains well. The size of the sash dictates the size of the cold frame, which is then built in multiples of that size; for example, a 3 x 6 sash means a 3 x 6, or a 6 x 6, or a 12 x 6, and so forth, cold frame. Green-house acrylic windows work well, are nearly shatterproof, and give more insulation than glass. They are available from building-supply houses. Also consider how much room you need for the crops you want, the ease of maintaining the plants, and the size of your propagation flats. Generally, a cold frame is built into the soil a foot and sticks up 12 inches above the soil in front and 16 inches in the back, with the low side facing south.

Prepare the soil by adding lots of added organic matter, well-aged manure, and nutrients. Form the frame with cinder blocks, metal, or wood and make sure they are below ground level and secure so rodents can't come in under the frame and the wind will not dislodge it. Build a frame for the sash, making sure it fits exactly. Attach the lid along the back wall and provide a prop of sorts to hold the lid off the frame. To control the temperature, the lid needs to be adjustable, from a few inches to wide open.

Maintaining a Cold Frame

The optimal use for cold frames is to grow salad greens in the fall, winter, and early spring; to start transplants in the spring; and to harden off transplants started indoors. A cold frame extends the fall salad harvest by keeping the temperature higher longer. However, when days get below ten hours or so of light, the plants slow down and start to either deteriorate or go dormant, depending on the species and variety. See the "Encyclopedia of Salad Greens" for specific information. According to Shep

Ogden, as a general rule, northern gardeners start their greens about a month before the first average expected frost date. To provide greens for the winter table, your plants must be about 4 inches tall and have five or six leaves. As they stop growing—think of them as being in cold storage for the winter—you can harvest a few leaves but there will be almost no regrowth from November through February. In spring, with sunlight and warmth, the greens will grow again and give you an early harvest. In addition, you can then start more greens in the cold frame to transplant into the garden once it warms.

Day-to-day maintenance involves regulating the temperature and watering the plants when needed. To increase the temperature when the weather is cold or cloudy, lay floating row covers over the plants and then lay an insulating canvas or burlap cover, or wooden boards, over the lid. A thick layer of snow will also give insulation and should not be removed unless you need access to the frame.

Keeping the plants warm is one issue, but it's equally important to keep them cool. On a sunny fall or spring day temperatures inside will get hot. To prevent this on warm spring days, after the sun is up, prop the sash open two to three inches; as the sun goes down, close it. Hardy greens in the fall need even more ventilation, to prevent them from being forced into unwanted growth. In the winter the sash is kept closed most of the time. The plants need occasional watering, about every ten days or so, but be careful not to make the plants too soggy, or they will rot. Try to schedule waterings for mornings on sunny days.

Maintaining the Garden

The backbone of appropriate maintenance is knowledge of your soil and weather, an ability to recognize basic water- and nutrient-deficiency symptoms, and a familiarity with the plants you grow.

Annual vegetables and greens are growing machines. As a rule, they need to grow rapidly with few interruptions so they produce well and have few pest problems. Once the plants are in the ground, continually

monitoring for nutrient deficiencies, drought, and pests can head off problems. Keep the beds weeded because weeds compete for moisture and nutrients. In normal soil, most vegetables benefit from supplemental nitrogen fertilizer. Fish emulsion and fish meal, blood meal, and chicken manure all have their virtues. Sandy or problem soils may require more nutrients to provide potassium and trace minerals. If so, apply kelp meal or kelp emulsion as well as the nitrogen sources mentioned above or add a packaged, balanced, organic vegetable fertilizer. For more specific information on fertilizing, see the individual entries in "The Rainbow Vegetable Encyclopedia" on page 21.

Weeding

Weeding is necessary to make sure unwanted plants don't compete with and overpower your vegetables. A good small triangular hoe will help you weed a small garden if the weeds are young, few, and easily hoed. When the weeds get large or out of control, you'll have to dedicate your muscles to a session of hand pulling. Applying a mulch is a great way to cut down on weeds; however, if there's a big problem with slugs in your garden, the mulch gives them more places to hide. Another means of controlling weeds, especially annual weeds like crabgrass and pigweed, is a new organic preemergence herbicide made from corn gluten called Concern Weed Prevention Plus. This gluten meal inhibits the tiny feeder roots of germinating weed seeds, so they wither and die. It does not kill existing weeds. Obviously, if you use it among new seedlings or in seed beds, it kills them too, so it is only useful in areas away from very young plants.

Mulching

Mulching can save the gardener time, effort, and water. A mulch layer reduces moisture loss, prevents erosion, controls weeds, minimizes soil compaction, and moderates soil temperature. When the mulch is an organic material, it adds nutrients and organic matter to the soil as it decomposes, making heavy clay more porous, and helping sandy soil retain moisture. Mulches are often attractive additions to the garden. Applying a few inches of organic matter every spring helps keep most vegetable gardens healthy. Mulch with compost from your compost pile, pine nee-

dles, composted sawdust, straw, or one of the many agricultural byproducts like rice hulls or apple or grape pomace.

Black plastic mulch

Composting

Compost is the humus-rich result of the decomposition of organic matter such as leaves and garden trimmings. The objective of maintaining a composting system is to speed up decomposition and centralize the material so you can gather it up and spread it where it will do the most good. Compost is useful as a soil additive or a mulch. Compost's benefits include providing nutrients to plants in a slow-release, balanced fashion; helping break up clay soil; aiding sandy soil to retain moisture; and correcting pH problems. On top of that, compost is free! It can be made at home and is an excellent way to recycle our yard and kitchen "wastes."

There need be no great mystique about composting. To create the environment where decay-promoting microorganisms do all the work, just include the following four ingredients, mixed well: three or four parts "brown" material high in carbon, such as dry leaves, dry grass, or even shredded black-and-white newspaper; one part "green" material high in nitrogen, such as fresh grass clippings, fresh garden trimmings, barnyard manure, or kitchen trimmings like pea pods and carrot tops; water in moderate amounts so the mixture is moist but not soggy; and air to supply oxygen to the microorganisms. Bury the kitchen trimmings within the pile, so as not to attract flies. Cut up any large pieces of material. Exclude weeds that have gone to seed and noxious perennial weeds such as Bermuda grass because they can carry those weeds into your garden. Do not add meat, fat, diseased plants, woody branches, or cat or dog excrement.

I don't get stressed about the proper proportions of compost materials, as long as there's a fairly good mix of materials from the garden. If the decomposition is too slow, that's usually because the pile has too much brown material, is too dry, or needs air. If the pile smells, either it is too wet or contains too much green material. To speed up decomposition, I often chop or shred the materials before adding them to the pile. I may turn the pile occasionally to encourage additional oxygen throughout. During decomposition, the materials can become quite hot and steamy, which is great; however, it is not mandatory that the compost become extremely hot.

You can make compost in a simple pile, in wire or wood bins, or in rather expensive containers. The size should be about 3 feet high, wide, and tall for the most efficient decomposition and so the pile is easily workable. It can be up to 5 feet by 5 feet, but that's harder to manage. In a rainy climate it's a good idea to have a cover for the compost. I like to use three bins. I collect the compost materials in one bin; the second is a working bin; when the working bin is full, I turn its contents into the last bin for final decomposition. I sift the finished compost into empty garbage cans so the nutrients don't leach into the soil. Then the empty bin is ready to fill up again.

Crop Rotation

Crop rotation in the edible garden has been practiced for centuries for two reasons: to help prevent diseases and pests and to prevent depletion of nutrients from the soil, as some crops add nutrients and others remove them.

To rotate crops, you must know what plants are in which families as plants in the same families often are prone to the same diseases and pests and deplete the same nutrients.

The following is a short list of related vegetables:

Goosefoot family (Chenopodiaceae)—includes beets, chard, orach, spinach

Cucumber family (gourd) (Cucurbitaceae)—includes cucumbers, gourds, melons, summer squash, winter squash, pumpkins

Lily family (onion) (Liliaceae)—includes asparagus, chives, garlic, leeks, onions, Oriental chives, shallots

Mint family (Lamiaceae)—includes basil, mints, oregano, rosemary, sages, summer savory, thymes

Mustard family (cabbage) (Brassicaceae)—includes arugula, broccoli, cabbages, cauliflower, collards, cresses, kale, kohlrabi, komatsuna, mizuna, mustards, radishes, turnips

Nightshade family (Solanaceae)—includes eggplants, peppers, potatoes, tomatillos, tomatoes

Parsley family (carrot) (Apiaceae)—includes carrots, celeriac, celery, chervil, coriander (cilantro), dill, fennel, lovage, parsley, parsnips

Pea family (legumes) (Fabaceae)—includes beans, cowpeas, fava beans, lima beans, peanuts, peas, runner beans, soybeans, sugar peas

Sunflower family (composites) (Asteraceae)—includes artichokes, calendulas, celtuce, chicories, dandelions, endives, lettuces, marigolds, tarragon

The object to rotating crops is to avoid growing members of the same family in the same spot year after year. For example: cabbage, a member of the mustard family, should not be followed by radishes, a member of the same family, as both are prone to flea beetles and the flea beetle's eggs will be in the soil ready to hatch and attack the radishes. Tomatoes should not follow eggplants, as they are both prone to fusarium wilt.

Crop rotation is also practiced to help keep the soil healthy. One family, namely the pea family (legumes), that includes not only peas and beans but also clovers and alfalfa, adds nitrogen to the soil. In contrast, most members of the mustard (cabbage) family deplete the soil of nitrogen. Members of the nightshade and cucumber families are other heavy feeders. Because most vegetables deplete the soil, knowledgeable gardeners not only rotate their beds with vegetables from different families, they also include an occasional cover crop of clover or alfalfa and other soil benefactors like buckwheat and vetch to add what's called "green manure." The gardener allows these crops to grow for a few months, then turns them into or under the soil. As they decompose, they provide extra organic matter and many nutrients, help stop the pest cycle, and attract beneficial insects. Some cover crops (like rye) are grown over the winter to control soil erosion. The seeds of all sorts of cover crops are available from farm suppliers and specialty seed companies.

Watering and Irrigation Systems

Even gardeners who live in rainy climates may have to do supplemental watering at specific times during the growing season. Therefore, most gardeners need some sort of supplemental watering system and a knowledge of water management.

There is no easy formula for determining the correct amount or frequency of watering. Proper watering takes experience and observation. In addition to the specific watering needs of individual plants, watering requirements depends on soil type,

A three-bin composting system

wind conditions, and air temperature. To water properly, it's important to learn how to recognize water-stress symptoms (often a dulling of foliage color as well as the better-known symptoms of drooping leaves and wilting), how much to water (too much is as bad as too little), and how to water. Some general rules are:

1. Water deeply. Except for seed beds, most plants need infrequent, deep watering rather than frequent, light sprinkling.

2. To ensure proper absorption, apply water at a rate slow enough to soak deeply into the soil rather than run off.

3. Do not use overhead watering systems when the wind is blowing.

4. Try to water early in the morning so foliage has time to dry before nightfall, thus preventing some disease problems. In addition, less water evaporates in cooler temperatures.

5. Test your watering system occasionally to make sure it covers the area evenly.

6. Use methods and tools that conserve water. The pistol-grip nozzle on a hose will shut off the water while you move from one container or planting bed to another. Soaker hoses, made from either canvas or recycled tires, and other ooze- and drip-irrigation systems apply water slowly and more efficiently than overhead systems.

Drip, or the related ooze/trickle, irrigation systems are advisable wherever feasible; most gardens are well-suited to them. Drip systems deliver water a drop at a time through spaghetti-like emitter tubes or plastic pipe with emitters that drip water right onto the root zone of each plant. Because of the time and effort involved in installing one or two emitters per plant, these systems work best for permanent plantings such as in rose beds, with rows of daylilies and lavender say, or with trees and shrubs. Drip lines require continual maintenance to ensure the individual emitters are not clogged.

Similar systems, called ooze systems, deliver water through either holes made every 6 or 12 inches along solid flexible tubing or ooze along the entire porous hose. Neither system is as prone to clogging as are emitters. The solid type is made of plastic and is often called laser tubing. It is pres-

sure-compensated, which means the water flow is even throughout the length of the tubing. The high-quality brands have a built-in mechanism to minimize clogging and are made of tubing that will not expand in hot weather and, consequently, pop off its fittings. (Some of the inexpensive drip-irrigation kits can make you crazy!) The porous hose types, made from recycled tires, come in two sizes—a standard hose diameter of 1 inch, great for shrubs and trees planted in a row, and 1/4-inch tubing that's easy to snake around beds of small plants. Neither is pressure-compensated so the plants nearest the water source receive more water than those at the end of the line. It also means they will not work well if there is any slope. All types of drip emitter and ooze systems are installed after the plants are in the ground and are held in place with ground staples. To use any drip or ooze system, it's also necessary to install an anti-siphon valve at the water source to prevent dirty garden water from being drawn into the house's drinking water and to include a filter to prevent debris from clogging the emitters.

To set up the system, connect 1-inch distribution tubing to the water source then arrange the tubing around the garden perimeter. Connect smaller-diameter drip and ooze lines to this. As you see, installing these systems requires some thought and time. You can order these systems from either a specialty mail-order garden or irrigation source or visit your local plumbing store. I find the latter to be the best solution for all my irrigation problems. Over the years, I've found that plumbing-supply stores offer professional-quality supplies, usually for less money than the so-called inexpensive kits available in home-supply stores and some nurseries. Their professionals also may help you work out an irrigation design tailored to your garden. Whether choosing an emitter or an ooze system or buying tubing, be prepared by bringing a rough drawing of the area to be irrigated—including dimensions, location of the water source, any slopes, and, if possible, the water pressure at the water source. Let the professionals walk you through the steps and help you pick out supplies to best fit your site.

Problems aside, all forms of drip irrigation are more efficient than furrow or stan-

dard overhead watering. They deliver water to its precise destination and are well worth considering. They provide water slowly, so it doesn't run off; they also water deeply, which encourages deep rooting. Drip irrigation also eliminates many disease problems, and there are fewer weeds because so little soil surface is moist. Finally, drip-irrigation systems have the potential to waste a lot less water.

appendix B pest and disease control

The following sections cover a large number of pests and diseases. An individual gardener, however, will encounter few such problems in a lifetime of gardening. Good garden planning, good hygiene, and an awareness of major symptoms will keep problems to a minimum and give you many hours to enjoy your garden and feast on its bounty.

There are some spoilers, though, that sometimes need control. For years, controls were presented as a list of critters and diseases, followed by the newest and best chemicals to control them. Times have changed. We now know that chasing the latest chemical to fortify our arsenal is a bit like chasing our tail. That's because most pesticides, both insecticides and fungicides, kill beneficial insects as well as the pests; therefore, the more we spray, the more we are forced to spray. Nowadays, we know that successful pest control focuses on prevention, plus beefing up the natural ecosystem so beneficial insects are on pest patrol. How does that translate to pest control for the vegetable garden directly?

1. When possible, find and plant resistant varieties. For example, in cold, wet weather choose lettuce varieties resistant to downy mildew; if fungal diseases are a problem in your garden, select disease-resistant varieties of tomatoes.

2. Use mechanical means to prevent insect pests from damaging plants. For example, cover young squash and potato plants with floating row covers to protect them from squash borers and flea beetles; sprinkle wood ashes around plants to prevent cabbage root maggots and slug damage; and put cardboard collars around young tomato, pepper, cabbage, and squash seedlings to prevent cutworms from destroying them.

3. Clean up diseased foliage and dispose of it in the garbage to cut down on the cycle of infection.

4. Rotate your crops so that plants from the same family are not planted in the same place for two consecutive seasons.

5. Encourage and provide food for beneficial insects. In the vegetable garden, this translates into letting a few selected vegetables go to flower as well as growing flowering herbs and ornamentals to provide a season-long source of nectar and pollen for beneficial insects. For the salad garden it means letting some of the salad greens go to flower and growing a few salad herbs like chervil, cilantro, dill, parsley, thyme, and fennel. Adding annual flowers like marigolds, alyssum, and species zinnias, too, provides a season-long source of nectar and pollen for beneficial insects.

Beneficial Insects

In a nutshell, few insects are potential problems; most are either neutral or beneficial to the garden. Given the chance, the beneficials will do much of the insect control for you, provided that you don't use pesticides. Pesticides are apt to kill the beneficial insects as well as the problematic insects. Like predatory lions stalking zebra, predatory ladybugs (lady beetles) and lacewing larvae hunt and eat aphids that might be attracted to your lettuce, say. A miniwasp parasitoid will lay eggs on, or inside, those aphids. Spraying aphids, even with a so-called benign pesticide such as insecticidal soap or pyrethrum, will kill the ladybugs, lacewings, and that baby parasitoid wasp too.

Most insecticides are broad-spectrum, which means that they kill insects indiscriminately. In my opinion, organic gardeners who regularly use organic, broad-spectrum insecticides have missed this point. While they are technically using an "organic" pesticide, they actually may be eliminating the beneficial insects—a truly organic means of control.

Unfortunately, many gardeners are not only unaware of the benefits of the predator-prey relationship, they often are not able to recognize beneficial insects. The following sections will help you identify both the beneficial insects as well as the pest organisms. A hand lens is an invaluable, inexpensive tool that will also help you identify the insects in your garden. For a more detailed aid to identifying insects, see *Rodale's Color Handbook of Garden Insects* by Anna Carr.

Predators and Parasitoids

Insects that feed on other insects are divided into two types: the predators and the parasitoids. Predators are mobile. They stalk plants looking for such plant feeders as aphids and mites. Parasitoids, on the other hand, are insects that develop in or on the bodies, pupae, or eggs of other host insects.

Most parasitoids are minute-sized wasps or flies whose larvae (young, immature stages of the insect) eat other insects from within. Some of the wasps are so small, they can develop inside an aphid or an insect egg. In other cases, one parasitoid egg can divide into several identical cells, each developing into identical miniwasp larvae that then can kill an entire caterpillar. Though nearly invisible to most gardeners, parasitoids are the most specific and effective means of insect control.

The predator-prey relationship can be a fairly stable situation. When the natural system is working properly, pest insects can inhabit the garden along with the predators and parasitoids without a problem.

Sometimes, though, the system breaks down. For example, a number of imported pests have taken hold in this country. Unfortunately, when such organisms were brought here, their natural predators did not accompany them. Four pesky examples are the Japanese beetle, the European brown snail, the white cabbage butterfly, and the flea beetle. None of these pests has natural enemies in the United States to provide balanced, sufficient controls. Where those imported pests occur, it is sometimes necessary to use physical means or selective pesticides that kill only the problem insect.

Weather extremes sometime produce imbalances as well. For example, long stretches of hot, dry weather favor grasshoppers that invade vegetable gardens, because the diseases that keep them in check are more prevalent under moist conditions. Predator-prey relationships also become imbalanced because common gardening practices often inadvertently work in favor of the pests. For example, when gardeners spray regularly with broad-spectrum pesticides, not all the garden insects are killed. As pests generally reproduce more quickly than predators and parasitoids, regular spraying usually tips the balance in favor of those pests. Further, the average yard full of grass and shrubs usually has few plants that produce nectar for beneficial insects. Adding a few squash plants and a row of lettuces for good measure won't help; the new, luscious growth will attract aphids but not the beneficials. Knowing the importance of ecological balance as well as safe and effective insect-control practices will help create a vegetable garden that is relatively free of many pest problems.

Attracting Beneficial Insects

Another key to promoting a healthy balance in your garden is providing a diversity of plants, including plenty of nectar- and pollen-producing varieties. Nectar is the primary food of many beneficial insects—adults and some larvae. Interplanting vegetables with flowers and numerous herbs helps attract beneficials. Ornamentals—like species zinnias, marigolds, alyssum, and yarrow—provide many flowers over a long season that are shallow enough for insects to reach the nectar. Large, dense flowers like tea roses and dahlias are nearly useless as their nectar is usually out of reach. Herbs rich in nectar include fennel, dill, anise, chervil, oregano, thyme, and parsley. Allowing a few vegetables like broccoli, carrots, and kale, in particular, to go to flower helps because their tiny flowers—full of nectar and pollen—are just what many beneficial insects like.

Following are a few of the predatory and parasitoid insects helpful in the garden. Their preservation and protection should be a major goal of your pest-control strategy.

Ground beetles and their larvae are all predators. Most adult ground beetles are fairly large black beetles that scurry out from under plants or containers when you disturb them. Their favorite foods are soft-bodied larvae like Colorado potato beetle larvae and root maggots (Root maggots eat cabbage-family plants.); some ground beetles even eat snails and slugs. If supplied with an undisturbed place to live, like a compost area or groupings of perennial plantings, ground beetles will be long-lived residents of your garden.

Lacewings are one of the most effective insect predators in the home garden. They are small green or brown gossamer-winged insects that in their adult stage eat flower nectar, pollen, aphid honeydew, and sometimes aphids and mealybugs. In the larval stage, they look like tiny tan alligators. Called aphid lions, lacewing larvae are fierce predators of aphids, mites, and whiteflies—all occasional pests that suck plant sap. If you have problems with sucking insects in your garden, consider purchasing lacewing eggs or larvae by mail-order to jump-start your lacewing population. Remember to plant lots of nectar plants so the population continues from year to year.

Lady beetles (ladybugs) are the best known of the beneficial garden insects. Actually, there are about four hundred species of lady beetles in North America alone. They come in a variety of colors and markings in addition to the familiar red with black spots, but lady beetles are never green. Lady beetles and their fierce-looking alligator-shaped larvae eat copious amounts of aphids and other small insects.

Spiders are close relatives of insects. There are hundreds of species. They are some of the most effective predators of a wide range of pest insects.

Syrphid flies (also called flower flies or hover flies) look like small bees hovering over flowers, but they have only two wings. Most have yellow and black stripes. Their larvae are small green maggots that inhabit leaves and eat small sucking insects and mites.

Wasps comprise a large family of insects with transparent wings. Unfortunately, the few large wasps that sting have given the family a bad name. In fact, all wasps are either insect predators or parasitoids. The miniwasps are usually parasitoids: the adult female lays her eggs in such insects as aphids, whitefly larvae, and caterpillars; the developing wasp larvae devour their host. These miniature wasps, available for purchase from insectaries, are especially effec-

193

tive when released in greenhouses.

Pests

The following pests are sometimes problems in the vegetable garden.

Aphids are soft-bodied, small, green, black, pink, or gray insects that produce many generations in one season. They suck plant juices and exude honeydew. Sometimes, leaves under the aphids turn black from a secondary mold growing on the nutrient-rich honeydew. Aphids are primarily a problem on cabbages, broccoli, beans, lettuces, peas, and tomatoes. Aphid populations can escalate especially in the spring before beneficial insects are present in large numbers and when plants are covered by row covers or are growing in cold frames. The presence of aphids sometimes indicates that a plant is under stress. Is the cabbage getting enough water or sunlight? Check first to see if stress is a problem and then try to correct the situation. Also look for aphid mummies and other natural enemies mentioned above. Mummies are swollen, brown or metallic-looking aphids; a wasp parasitoid grows inside the mummy. They are valuable, so keep them.

Generally, to remove aphids wash the foliage with a strong blast of water; cut back the foliage if aphids persist. Fertilize and water the plant, then check on it in a few days. Repeat with the water spray a few more times. In extreme situations, spray with insecticidal soap or a neem product.

A number of **beetles** are garden pests. They include asparagus beetles, Mexican bean beetles, different species of cucumber beetles, flea beetles, and wireworms (the larvae of click beetles). All are problems throughout most of North America. Asparagus beetles look like elongated, red lady beetles with a black-and-cream-colored cross on their backs; they feed on asparagus.

Colorado potato beetles and Japanese beetles are primarily problems in the eastern United States. Mexican bean beetles look like brown lady beetles with oval black spots. As their name implies, they feed on beans. Cucumber beetles are ladybug-like green or yellow-green beetles with either black stripes or black spots. Their larvae feed on the roots of corn and other vegetables. The adults devour members of the cucumber family, corn tassels, beans, and

some salad greens. Flea beetles are minuscule, black-and-white-striped beetles hardly large enough to be seen. Flea beetle grubs feed on the roots and lower leaves of many vegetables; the adults chew on the leaves of tomatoes, potatoes, eggplants, radishes, peppers, and other plants—causing the leaves to look shot full of tiny holes. The adult click beetle is rarely seen; its young, brown, 1 1/2-inch-long, shiny larva called a wireworm works underground—damaging tubers, seeds, and roots. Colorado potato beetles are larger and rounder than lady beetles; they have red-brown heads and black-and-yellow-striped backs. Primarily a problem in the eastern United States, they skeletonize the leaves of potatoes, tomatoes, eggplants, and peppers. Japanese beetles, mostly problematic east of the Mississippi, are fairly large, metallic blue or green beetles with coppery wings. The larval stage (a grub) eats the roots of grasses; the adult chews its way through beans, asparagus plants, and many ornamentals.

The larger beetles, if not found in great numbers, can be controlled by hand-picking. Morning picking is best, when the beetles move slower. Knock them into a bowl of soapy water. Flea beetles are too small to gather by hand, so try a hand-held vacuum instead. Insecticidal soap sprayed on the undersides of the leaves is also effective on flea beetles. Wireworms can be trapped by putting cut pieces of potatoes or carrots in the soil every five feet or so and then digging the pieces up after a few days. Destroy the worms. When young, Colorado potato beetles can be controlled by applications of *Bacillus thuringiensis* var. *san diego*, a beetle Bt proven effective for flea beetles, as well.

Because many beetle species overwinter in the soil as eggs or adults, crop rotation and fall cleanup are vital. New evidence indicates that beneficial nematodes effectively control most pest beetles—if the nematodes are applied during the beetles' soil-dwelling larval stage. Azadirachtin (the active ingredient in some formulations of neem) is also affective against most immature beetles and can be a feeding deterrent for adults. Polyester row covers, securely fastened to the ground, can provide excellent control for most beetles. Obviously, row covers are of no use if the beetles are in a larval stage and ready to emerge from the soil (under the row cover!) or if the adult

beetles are already established on the plants. Row covers work best in combination with crop rotation. Row covers have limited use on plants such as cucumbers, squash, and melons that need bees to pollinate the blooms, as bees can't penetrate the fabric. Japanese beetle populations can also be reduced in several ways: by applying milky-spore, a naturally occurring, slow-working, soil-borne disease that infects the beetle in its grub stage; by introducing beneficial nematodes; by applying lime to acidic soil to discourage grubs.

For salad gardens, the one most apt to make holes in salad greens is the spotted cucumber beetle. Cucumber beetles (diabrotica beetles) are ladybug-like green or yellow-green beetles with black spots. They sometimes eat holes in sorrel, lettuces, and other succulent greens. If not present in great numbers, they can be controlled by hand picking—in the morning is best, when the beetles are slower. Toss them or knock them into a bowl or bucket of soapy water. Larger populations may need more control, however. Try a spray of insecticidal soap first; if you're not successful, use BioNeem

Caterpillars (sometimes called loopers or worms) are the immature stage of moths and butterflies. Most pose no problem in our gardens and we encourage them to visit, but a few are a unwelcome in the vegetable garden. The most notorious are the tomato hornworm, beanlooper, cutworm, and the numerous cabbage worms and loopers that chew ragged holes in leaves. Natural controls include birds, wasps, and disease. Encourage birds by providing a birdbath, shelter, and berry-producing shrubs. Tolerate wasp nests if they're not a threat; provide nectar plants for the mini-wasps. Hand-picking is very effective as well. The disease *Bacillus thuringiensis* var. *kurstaki* is available as a spray in a number of formulas; brands include Bt *kurstaki*, Dipel, and Thuricide. When applied, Bt is a bacteria that causes the fairly young caterpillar to starve to death. Bt-k Bait carries the disease; it lures budworms (caterpillars that bore into buds) from the vegetables to the bait. I seldom use Bt in any form, as it also kills all butterfly and harmless moth larvae.

Cutworms are the caterpillar stage of various moth species. Usually found in the soil, cutworms curl into a ball when disturbed. Cutworms are a particular problem when annual vegetable seedlings first appear or when young transplants are set out. They often chew off the stem at the soil line, killing the plant. Control cutworms by encircling young plants with cardboard collars or placing bottomless tin cans around the plant stem; be sure to sink collars 1 inch into the ground. *Bacillus thuringiensis* gives limited control. Trichogramma miniwasps and black ground beetles are among the cutworm's natural enemies. As those natural predators often are not in a new garden, consider introducing them.

Flea beetles are minute black beetles that jump like fleas but are not related to them. Immature beetles are legless grubs that feed on roots and the lower leaves of a number of vegetables, including cabbages and mustards. The adults chew small holes on the leaves as well. As a rule, flea beetles become noticeable because they show up in such large numbers that the leaves look shot full of tiny holes. Adult beetles overwinter in the soil and garden debris. To control flea beetles, clean up garden debris in the fall, rotate your crops, and place floating row covers over susceptible crops (most often members of the cabbage family) when they are first planted.

Leaf miners, the larvae of small black or black-and-yellow flies, tunnel through leaves, disfiguring them by leaving patches of dead tissue where they feed. They do not burrow into the root. Leaf miners are a particular problem on chard and beets—crops, which can be protected by applying floating row covers early in the season. Leaf miners also can be controlled somewhat by neem or by applying beneficial nematodes.

Mites are among the few arachnids (spiders and their kin) that pose a problem. Mites are so small they are nearly invisible without the aid of a hand lens. They become a problem when they reproduce in great numbers. An indication of serious mite damage is stippling on the leaves in the form of tiny white or yellow spots and sometimes the formation of tiny webs. The major natural predators of pest mites are

predatory mites, mite-eating thrips, and syrphid flies.

Mites are most likely to thrive on dusty leaves and in warm weather. Routinely washing foliage and misting sensitive vegetables help control mites. Mites are seldom a serious problem unless heavy-duty pesticides have been used to kill off predatory mites or plants are grown inside the house. To control mite infestation, cut back the plants and stop applying heavy-duty pesticides. The natural prey-predator balance could return. If all else fails, use the neem derivative, Green Light Fruit, Nut, and Vegetable Spray™, or dispose of the plant.

Nematodes are microscopic round worms that inhabit the soil in most of the United States, particularly the Southeast. Most nematode species live on decaying material or prey on other nematodes, insects, or bacteria. A few types are parasitic, attaching themselves to the roots of plants. Edible plants particularly susceptible to nematode damage include beans, melons, lettuce, okra, pepper, squash, tomatoes, eggplant, and some perennial herbs. The symptoms of nematode damage are stunted-looking plants and small swellings or lesions on the roots.

To control nematodes, rotate annual vegetables with less-susceptible varieties; plant contaminated beds with a blanket of marigolds for a whole season or plant marigolds among your vegetables; keep soil high in organic matter to encourage fungi and predatory nematodes that act as biological controls; if all else fails, grow edibles in sterilized soil in containers.

Snails and **slugs** are not insects, of course, but mollusks. They are especially fond of vegetable greens and seedlings. They feed at night and can go dormant for months in times of stress. In the absence of effective natural enemies (a few snail eggs are consumed by predatory beetles and earwigs), several snail-control strategies are recommended. Since snails and slugs are most active at night after rain or irrigation, that's a good opportunity to find, hand pick, and destroy them. Only repeated forays provide adequate control. A generous dusting of hardwood ashes around susceptible plants gives some control. A copper strip attached to the top perimeter of a planter box effectively repels slugs and snails; the mollusks get a shock when touching the

Rotting lettuce showing snail damage

copper. A word of warning: any overhanging leaves that can act as a bridge into the planting bed will defeat the barrier.

Whiteflies are sometimes a problem in mild-winter areas of the country, as well as in greenhouses nationwide. Lettuces, tomatoes, and cucumbers are especially susceptible. Whiteflies can be a persistent problem if plants grow against a building or fence where air circulation is limited. In the garden, Encarsia wasps and other parasitoids usually provide adequate whitefly control. Occasionally, especially in cool weather or in greenhouses, whitefly populations may cause serious plant damage—wilting, slowed growth, delayed flowering. Look under the leaves to determine whether the scalelike, immobile larvae—the young crawling stage—or the pupae are evident in large numbers. If so, wash them off with water from the hose. Repeat the washing three days in a row. In addition, try removing the adults with a hand-held vacuum early in the day when the weather is cool and the flies are less active. Insecticidal soap sprays are quite effective as well.

Wildlife Problems

Rabbits and mice can cause problems for gardeners. To keep them out, use fine-weave fencing around the vegetable garden. If gophers or moles are a problem, plant large vegetables such as peppers, tomatoes, and squash inside chicken-wire baskets in the ground. Make sure the wire sticks up a foot above the ground so the critters can't reach inside. In severe situations, you might have to line whole beds with chicken wire.

Gophers usually need to be trapped. Trapping for moles is less successful, but repellents like MoleMed sometimes help. Cats can help with all rodent problems but they seldom provide adequate control. Small, portable electric fences help keep racoons, squirrels, and woodchucks out of the garden. Small-diameter wire mesh, bent into boxes and anchored with ground staples, protects seedlings from squirrels and chipmunks.

Deer are a serious problem—they love vegetables. I've tried myriad repellents, but they gave only short-term control. In some areas deer cause such severe problems that edible plants can't be grown without tall electric or nine-foot fences and/or an aggressive dog. The exception is herbs; deer don't feed on most culinary herbs.

Songbirds, starlings, and crows can be major pests of young seedlings, particularly lettuce, corn, and peas. Cover emerging plants with bird netting firmly anchored to the ground so birds can't get under it and feast.

Pest Controls

Insecticidal soap sprays are effective against many pest insects, including caterpillars, aphids, mites, and whiteflies. They can be purchased or homemade. As a rule, I recommend purchasing insecticidal soaps, as they have been carefully formulated to give the most effective control and are less apt to burn your vegetables. If you make your own, use a mild, liquid dishwashing soap not a caustic detergent.

Neem-based pesticide and fungicide products, which are derived from the neem tree *(Azadirachta indica)*, have relatively low toxicity for mammals but are effective against a wide range of insects. Neem products are considered "organic" pesticides by some organizations but not by others. Products containing a derivative of neem—azadirachtin—are effective because azadirachtin is an insect growth regulator that negatively affects the growth of insects in their immature stages. Sprayed with neem, young leaf miners, cucumber beetles, and aphids don't reach adulthood. BioNeem and Azatin are commercial pesticides containing azadirachtin. Another neem product, Green Light Fruit, Nut, and Vegetable Spray, contains clarified

hydrophobic extract of neem oil and is affective against mites, aphids, and some fungus diseases. Neem products are still fairly new in the United States. Although at first neem was thought to be harmless to beneficial insects, recent studies show that some parasitoid beneficial insects that feed on neem-treated insects didn't survive to adulthood.

Pyrethrum, a botanical insecticide, is toxic to a wide range of insects but has relatively low toxicity for most mammals. Pyrethrum also breaks down quickly. The active ingredients are pyrethrins derived from chrysanthemum flowers. Do not confuse pyrethrum with pyrethroids, which are much more toxic synthetics that do not biodegrade as quickly. Many pyrethrums have the synergist piperonyl butoxide (PBO) added to increase the effectiveness. As there is evidence that PBO may affect the human nervous system, try to use pyrethrums without PBO. Wear gloves, goggles, and a respirator when using pyrethrum.

Diseases

Plant diseases are potentially far more damaging to vegetables than are most insects. There are two types of diseases: those caused by nutrient deficiencies and those caused by pathogens. Diseases caused by pathogens, such as root rots, are difficult to control once they begin. Therefore, most plant disease control strategies feature prevention rather than cure.

To keep diseases under control, it is very important to plant the "right plant in the right place." For instance, salad greens in poorly drained soil often develop root rot. Tomatoes planted against a wall are prone to whiteflies and fungal diseases. Check a plant's cultural needs of before placing it in your garden. Proper light, air circulation, temperature, fertilization, and moisture are important factors in disease control. Finally, whenever possible, choose disease-resistant varieties when a particular pathogen is present or when conditions are optimal for the disease. The entries for individual plants in "The Rainbow Vegetable Encyclopedia" give specific cultural and variety information. As a final note, plants infected with disease pathogens should always be discarded, never composted.

Nutritional Deficiencies

For additional basic information on plant nutrients, see the soil preparation information given in Appendix A on page 185. As with pathogens, the best way to solve nutritional problems is to prevent them. While vegetables can suffer from mineral deficiencies (most often caused by a pH below 6 or above 7.5), the most common nutritional deficiency is lack of nitrogen. Vegetables demand fairly high amounts of nitrogen to grow vigorously. Nitrogen deficiency is especially prevalent in sandy soil or soil low in organic matter. (Although clay and organic matter provide little nitrogen, they do hold on to it, however, making nitrogen available to plant roots and keeping it from leaching.)

The main symptom of nitrogen deficiency is a pale, slightly yellow cast to the foliage, especially the lower, older leaves. For quick-growing crops like baby lettuces, by the time the symptoms show, it's too late to apply a cure. You might as well pull out the plants and salvage what you can. To prevent the problem from recurring, supplement vegetable beds with a good source of organic nitrogen like blood meal, chicken manure, and fish emulsion. For most vegetables—as they are going to be growing for a long season—correct the nitrogen deficiency by applying fish emulsion according to the directions on the container; reapply in a month or so. Usually nitrogen does not stay in the soil for more than four to six weeks; it leaches into the ground water.

While I've stressed nitrogen deficiency, the real trick is to achieve a good nitrogen balance in your soil. Although plants must have nitrogen to grow, too much nitrogen causes leaf edges to die, promotes succulent new growth savored by aphids, and makes plants prone to cold damage.

Diseases Caused by Pathogens

Anthracnose is a fungal problem primarily in the eastern United States on beans, tomatoes, cucumbers, and melons. Affected plants develop spots on the leaves. Furthermore, beans develop sunken black spots on their pods and stems; melons, cucumbers, and tomatoes develop sunken spots on their fruits. Anthracnose spreads readily in wet weather and overwinters on debris in the soil. Crop rotation, good air circulation, and choosing resistant varieties are the best defenses. Neem-based Green Light Fruit, Nut, and Vegetable Spray™ gives some control.

Blights and **bacterial diseases** include a number of diseases caused by fungi and bacteria that affect vegetables, and their names hint at the damage they do—such as blights, wilts, and leaf spots. As a rule, they are more of a problem in rainy and humid areas. Given the right conditions, they can be a problem in most of North America. Early blight strikes tomatoes when plants are in full production or under stress and causes dark brown spots with rings in them on older leaves, which then turn yellow and die. Potato tubers also are prone to early blight; they become covered with corky spots. Warm, moist conditions promote the disease. Late blight causes irregular gray spots on the tops of tomato leaves and white mold on the spots on the undersides of leaves. Leaves eventually turn brown and dry looking. Fruits develop water-soaked spots that eventually turn corky. Potato tubers develop spots that eventually lead to rot. Cool nights with warm days in wet weather are ideal conditions for the disease. Halo and common blight cause spots on the leaves and pods of most types of beans and are most active in wet weather. All these blight-causing fungi and bacteria overwinter on infected plant debris. To prevent infections, avoid overhead watering, clean up plant debris in the fall, rotate crops, and purchase only certified disease-free seed potatoes. Bacterial wilt affects cucumbers, melons, and sometimes squash. Spread by cucumber beetles, bacterial wilt causes plants to wilt and eventually die. To diagnose the disease, cut a wilted stem and look for milky sap that forms a thread when the tip of a stick touches it and is drawn away. The disease overwinters in cucumber beetles; installing floating row covers over young plants are the best defenses.

Botrytis: An occasional problem with lettuces, this disease causes plants to rot off at the soil level. It occurs most commonly in damp, cold conditions such as a run of cold-and-rainy fall or winter days and in a winter cold frame. To prevent botrytis, make sure plants are not crowded and rotate your lettuce beds.

Damping off occurs when a parasitic fungus living near the soil surface attacks young plants in their early seedling stage. It causes seedlings to wilt and rot at the point where they emerge from the soil. This fungus thrives under dark, humid conditions. It often can be thwarted by growing seedlings in a bright, well-ventilated place in fast-draining soil. Whenever possible, start seedlings in sterilized soil.

Fusarium wilt is a soil-borne fungus most prevalent in the warm parts of the country. It causes an overall wilting of the plant; leaf stems droop and the lower and outer leaves turn yellow, then brown, before the plant dies. Plants most susceptible to different strains of fusarium wilt include tomatoes, potatoes, peppers, cucumber, squash, melons, peas, asparagus, and basil. Although a serious problem in some areas, fusarium wilt can only be controlled by planting resistant varieties. Crop rotation is also helpful.

Mildews are fungal diseases which under certain conditions affect some vegetables—particularly peas, spinach, lettuce, and squash. There are two types of mildews: powdery and downy. Powdery mildew appears as a white, powdery dust on a leaf surface; downy mildew makes velvety or fuzzy white, yellow, or purple patches on leaves, buds, and tender stems. The poorer the air circulation and the more humid the weather, the more apt your plants are to have downy mildew.

To control both mildews, make sure plants have plenty of sun and are not crowded by other vegetation. If you must use overhead watering, do so in the morning. In some cases, powdery mildew can be washed off the plant. Do so early in the day, so that the plant has time to dry before evening. Powdery mildew is almost always visible on squash and pea plants at the end of the season; that's not a problem as the vegetables have usually stopped producing by then.

Research at Cornell University has proven that lightweight "summer" horticultural oil combined with baking soda is effective against powdery mildew on some plants. Combine 1 tablespoon of baking soda and 2 $^{1}/_{2}$ teaspoons of summer oil with 1 gallon of water. Spray weekly. Test on a small part of the plant first. Don't use horticultural oil on very hot days or on plants that are moisture stressed. After applying the oil, wait at least a month before using any sulfur sprays on the same plant.

You can make a tea for combating powdery mildew and possibly other disease-causing fungi by wrapping a gallon of well-aged, manure-based compost in burlap then steeping the compost in a 5-gallon bucket of water for about three days in a warm place. Spray the tea on plants every three to four days, in the evening if possible, until symptoms disappear.

Downy mildew is sometimes a problem on lettuces, especially in late fall, in cold frames, and under row covers. So select resistant varieties when possible; try to keep irrigation water off the leaves; prevent plants from crowding; and dispose of all infected leaves and plants. When growing greens in a cold frame, make sure the air circulation is optimal.

Root rots and **crown rots** are caused by a number of different fungi. The classic symptom of root rot is wilting—even when a plant is well-watered. Sometimes one side of the plant will wilt; more often the whole plant wilts. Affected plants are often stunted and yellow as well. The diagnosis is complete when the dead plant is pulled up to reveal rotten, black roots. Crown rot, primarily a problem in the Northeast, is a fungus that kills plants at the crown. Root and crown rots are most often caused by poor drainage; there is no cure when they involve the whole plant. Remove and destroy the plants and correct the drainage problem.

Verticillium wilt is a soil-borne fungus that can be a problem in most of North America, especially the cooler sections. The symptom of verticillium wilt is a sudden wilting of one part of or all of the plant. If you continually lose tomatoes or eggplants, this or one of the other wilts could be the problem. There is no cure. If this fungus is in your soil, plant resistant species or varieties.

Viruses attack a number of plants. Symptoms are stunted growth and deformed or mottled leaves. The mosaic viruses destroy chlorophyll in the leaves, causing them to become yellow and blotched in a mosaic pattern. There is no cure for viral conditions, so the affected plants must be destroyed. Tomatoes, cucumbers, and beans are particularly susceptible. Viral diseases can be transmitted by aphids and leaf hoppers or by seeds. So seed savers should be extra careful to learn the symptoms in individual plant species. Use resistant varieties when they're available.

197

resources

Gardening and Cooking Supplies

Gardener's Supply Company
128 Intervale Road
Burlington, VT 05401
Extensive collection of gardening tools and supplies

Native Seeds/SEARCH
526 North 4th Avenue
Tucson, AZ 85705
Membership: 20.00
Low income/student: $12.00
Catalog: $1.00 for nonmembers
Fascinating selection of food stuffs, including red and blue cornmeals, beans, chile products

The Natural Gardening Company
217 San Anselmo Avenue
San Anselmo, CA 94960
Gardening supplies, organic fertilizers, beneficial nematodes

Nutrite Inc.
P.O. Box 160
Elmira, Ontario
Canada N3B 2Z6
Canadian source of gardening supplies

Peaceful Valley Farm Supply
P.O. Box 2209
Grass Valley, CA 95945
Gardening supplies, organic fertilizers, seeds for cover crops

Sur La Table
Catalog Division
1765 Sixth Avenue South
Seattle, WA 98134
Cooking equipment

Williams-Sonoma
Mail Order Department
P.O. Box 7456
San Francisco, CA 94120-7456
Cooking equipment and specialty foods

Wycliffe Gardens
P.O. Box 430
Kimberly, British Columbia
Canada BC V1A 2Y9
Canadian source of gardening supplies

Seeds and Plants

Abundant Life Seed Foundation
P.O. Box 772
Port Townsend, WA 98368
Non-profit organization
Membership: $30.00; Limited income: $20.00
Catalog: $2.00 donation for nonmembers
Various open-pollinated, multi-colored heirlooms

Becker's Seed Potatoes
R.R. 1
Trout Creek, Ontario
Canada P0H 2L0
Certified seed potatoes including 'All Red' and 'All Blue'

Bountiful Gardens
18001 Shafer Ranch Road
Willits, CA 95490-9626
Main Catalog: free in United States; $2.00 elsewhere
Rare seeds catalog: $2.00
Interesting selection of open-pollinated varieties; lettuces and salad greens, organic gardening supplies

W. Atlee Burpee & Co.
Warminster, PA 18974
Wide variety of types of seed

Chiltern Seeds
Bortree Stile
Ulverston
Cumbria LA12 7PB England
Wide selection of seeds including unusual and colorful vegetables

The Cook's Garden
P.O. Box 535
Londonderry, VT 05148
Great selection of colorful, tasty vegetable varieties; lettuces and salad greens also herb and flower seeds

DeGiorgi Company, Inc.
6011 North Street
Omaha, NE 68117-1634
Catalog: $2.00
Variety of vegetables, herbs, and flowers including many colorful varieties

The Digger's Club
Heronswood, 105 Latrobe Parade
Dromana 3936
Australia

Seed-exchange club and mail-order catalog with many heirloom varieties
Evergreen Y. H. Enterprises
P.O. Box 17538
Anaheim, CA 92817
Catalog: $2.00 United States; $2.50 Canada
Oriental vegetables and herbs including unusual and colorful amaranths and radishes

Fox Hollow Seeds
P.O. Box 148
McGrann, PA 16236
Catalog: $1.00
Specializes in heirloom herbs, vegetables, and flowers including hard-to-find, colorful vegetable varieties

Garden City Seeds
778 Highway 93 North
Hamilton, MT 59840
Colorful varieties rich in healthy phytonutrients; specializes in varieties for short seasons and cold climates

The Gourmet Gardener
8650 College Boulevard
Overland Park, KS 66210
Vegetables, herbs, lettuces and salad greens, edible flowers; some heirlooms, many colorful varieties

Gurney Seed & Nursery Company
110 Capital Street
Yankton, SD 57079
Wide variety of seeds and plants including purple asparagus

Harris Seeds and Nursery
P. O. Box 22960
Rochester, NY 14692
Carries many heirloom seeds

J. L. Hudson, Seedsman
Star Route 2, Box 337
La Honda, CA 94020
For catalog: P.O. Box 1058, Redwood City, CA 94064
Catalog: $1.00
Open-pollinated; heirlooms; unusual varieties

Johnny's Selected Seeds
Foss Hill Road
Albion, ME 04910-9731
Excellent selection of herb and vegetable seeds; many unusual and colorful varieties, lots of greens

Landis Valley
Heirloom Seed Project
2451 Kissel Hill Road
Lancaster, PA 17601
Catalog $4.00
Heirloom vegetable seeds and flowers

Lockhart Seeds, Inc.
P.O. Box 1361
3 North Wilson Way
Stockton, CA 95205
Mostly commercial varieties with an especially large selection of onion varieties

Native Seeds/SEARCH
526 North 4th Avenue
Tucson, AZ 85705
Membership: $20.00; Low-income/student: $12.00
Catalog: $1.00 for nonmembers
Great selection of amaranth and colorful corn. Nonprofit organization dedicated to preservation of traditional crops, seeds, and farming methods of the native peoples of the Southwestern United States and Northern Mexico. Membership includes quarterly newsletter, catalog, and 10 percent discount on items in the catalog and the retail store in Tucson.

Nichols Garden Nursery
1190 North Pacific Highway NE
Albany, OR 97321-4580
Vegetables and herbs; wide selection of interesting colorful varieties including heirlooms and European varieties

Park Seed Company
One Parkton Avenue
Greenwood, SC 29647
Wide variety of vegetables, herbs, and flowers

The Pepper Gal
P.O. Box 23006
Ft. Lauderdale, FL 33307-3006
Catalog: $2.00
Great selection of hot, sweet, and ornamental peppers

Pinetree Garden Seeds
Box 300
New Gloucester, ME 04260
Good selection of heirloom, European, and open-pollinated varieties

Plants of the Southwest
Agua Fria, Route 6, Box 11A
Santa Fe, NM 87501
Catalog: $3.50
Open-pollinated seeds of warm-season vegetables, heirlooms, grasses, and wild flowers

Redwood City Seed Company
P.O. Box 361
Redwood City, CA 94064
Catalog: $1.00 in United States, Canada, Mexico; $2.00 in other countries
Specializes in endangered cultivated plants; carries many unusual vegetable varieties, lettuces, amararth and other greens

Ronniger's Seed & Potato Co.
P.O. Box 307
Ellensburg, WA 98926
Certified organic seed potatoes and certified, disease-free seed potatoes including colorful varieties; also red scallions

Santa Barbara Heirloom Nursery
P.O. Box 4235
Santa Barbara, CA 93140-4235
Certified, organically grown, heirloom seedlings including colorful pepper, eggplant, and tomato seedlings. Offers a rainbow tomato collection of six different colored tomatoes

Seeds Blüm
HC 33 Box 2057
Boise, ID 83706
Catalog: $3.00; First Class option: $5.00
A leader in the field, offering unusual and colorful vegetable varieties and salad greens

Seeds of Change
P.O. Box 15700
Santa Fe, NM 87506-5700
Organically grown vegetable and herb seeds

Seed Savers Exchange
3076 North Winn Road
Decorah, IA 52101
Membership fee: $25.00
Low-income/Senior/Student: $20.00
Canadian: $30.00; Overseas: $40.00
Catalog for purchasing selected seeds is free to nonmembers and members.
Nonprofit organization dedicated to saving vegetable gene pool diversity. The only source for many rare and heirloom vegetable seeds. Members join an extensive network of gardeners saving and exchanging seeds.

Territorial Seed Company
P.O. Box 157
Cottage Grove, OR 97424-0061
Good selection of heirloom and other open-pollinated varieties; several colorful varieties, wilds and greens

Thompson & Morgan Inc.
P.O. Box 1308
Jackson, NJ 08527-0308
Wide variety of types of seeds

Thompson & Morgan, Ltd.
Poplar Lane
Ipswich
Suffolk 1P8 3BU
England
Wide variety of types of seeds

Tomato Growers Supply Company
P.O. Box 2237
Fort Meyers, FL 33902
Extensive selection of types and colors of tomatoes and peppers

Totally Tomatoes
P.O. Box 1626
Augusta, GA 30903
Extensive selection of types and colors of tomatoes and peppers

Vermont Bean Seed Company
Garden Lane
Fair Haven, VT 05743
Extensive selection of many types of beans as well as other vegetables

Wood Prairie Farm
49 Kinney Road
Bridgewater, ME 04735
Certified, organic seed potatoes and other organic vegetables; grains for cooking including Mandan Bride cornmeal and different colored popcorns

Shepherd's Garden Seeds
30 Irene Street
Torrington, CT 06790-6658
Many European vegetable varieties and salad greens, some of unusual colors; also herbs and flowers

R. H. Shumway's
P.O. Box 1
Graniteville, SC 29829-0001
Wide variety of seeds including many heirlooms; also bare-root purple asparagus

Southern Exposure Seed Exchange
P.O. Box 170
Earlysville, VA 22936
Catalog: $2.00
Carries many open-pollinated and heirloom varieties and a good selection of colorful vegetables; specializes in heat-tolerant varieties, lettuces and greens

Stokes Seeds, Inc.
P.O. Box 548
Buffalo, NY 14240
Wide variety of vegetables, herbs, and flowers

Non-Mail Order Source

Look for seeds by Renee's Garden in your local retail outlets. Renee's Garden offers an excellent selection of colorful, high-quality vegetable varieties. Call 1-888-880-7228 for more information.